AIN'T NOBODY
THAT CAN
SING LIKE ME

The reason I don't know, but the fact is brilliantly plain that many young Oklahomans are taking to the pen, and that not a few of them have talent. There is almost, indeed, an Oklahoma literature, or, at all events, an Oklahoma manner.

—H.L. Mencken in the *American Mercury*

COVER IMAGE: *Endless Osage County*
© Rachel C. Jackson 2009

Section Illustrations:
WHEN/WHERE: *Parking Lot Oil Slick*
by Katie Arnott Morgan
WHY/HOW: *Self Portrait* by Danielle Knight

The original, color images may be viewed online at
www.sugarmule.com/35frame.htm

WWW.MONGRELEMPIREPRESS.COM

This publisher is a proud member of

BOOK DESIGN: MONGREL EMPIRE PRESS USING iWORK PAGES

Ain't Nobody That Can Sing Like Me

New Oklahoma Writing

Edited & Introduced by

Jeanetta Calhoun Mish

CONTENTS

WHY/HOW

INTRODUCTION

JEANETTA CALHOUN MISH

Who/What? Oklahomans/Writing

This Oklahoma Writing issue of Sugar Mule is patterned after the traditional question-pairs of journalistic writing: who/what, where/when, why/how. I chose to present it this way because in the minds of most people who do not live here, Oklahoma is an unexplored land, inhabited (if at all) by unexamined cultures and unknown people.

There is no doubt that stereotypical representations of Oklahomans abound: Indians in teepees; wealthy, obnoxious oilmen; poverty-stricken Okies; singing cowboys; outlaws like the Daltons and Pretty Boy Floyd. There are still Indians around—11% of our population claimed Native heritage on the 2000 Census—and teepees are still used for special occasions, but there are also Indian casinos and Indian businessmen and Indian orchestral-music composers and Indian writers and filmmakers. Not only do Indians live in Oklahoma, but also African-Americans (many of whom had ancestors who settled here long before white people did), Vietnamese-Americans, German-Americans, Irish-Americans, East Indians, Arab-Americans, Scots-Americans, Lebanese-Americans, and hundreds of other cultural and ethnic groups. "Okie" has been resurrected as term for pride in one's heritage, especially among radical and leftist Oklahomans who work for a renaissance of the State's strong socialist past: Eugene V. Debs won 15% of the State's presidential vote in 1914 and 175 Socialists were elected to state offices that year. I'll refrain from commenting on the oilmen, since some of them are women and some are my friends and relations.

Cowboys still work on the few remaining large cattle ranches and many country music singers hail from Oklahoma. Outlaws now are not usually the Robin Hoods of yesteryear who, like Woody Guthrie's Pretty Boy Floyd, stole from the rich and gave to the poor, but are instead hard-core criminals who cook methamphetamine and small-time crooks who steal copper wiring, leaving entire regions without electricity. Oklahoma writer Jim Thompson documented the harsh violence of an earlier time in Oklahoma history, and that criminal culture is still active today. According to the Oklahoma Commission on the Status of Women, many of the people the state brands as outlaws are women: Oklahoma has the highest incarceration rate of women in the nation, many of whom are in prison as a result of defending themselves against domestic violence or because they commit crimes associated with poverty. Despite other negative indicators of the status of Oklahoma women, or perhaps because of them, there are more women contributors to this issue of Sugar Mule than there are men. Contributor Trixie Walther's raw and haunting poetry is based on her work with imprisoned women in Oklahoma. Recently, television has given us images of Oklahoma women in *Saving Grace*, and although the accents are never quite correct, the show does capture some of Oklahoma's culture, including its problems with alcoholism and abuse, the resilience of its people, and its romance with religion.

What's right about Oklahoma culture? Among other things, a genuine friendliness in most of its inhabitants, an active and growing green movement, and a rich, varied, and beautiful landscape, with its attendant flora and fauna, that is rarely recognized by outsiders. Like the people, the landscape has also been the victim of reductionist imagery: the Dustbowl, Route 66, oilfield boomtowns, Tornado Alley; the high plains. Although some of these representations are founded in fact, they do not fully represent the State. The Dustbowl was restricted to western Oklahoma, and Route 66 is only one of the state's literally thousands of paved roads (most mile-section lines are paved, or at least graveled; see Arn Henderson's "Base Line and Meridian" poem cycle), many of which carry economic refugees out of the state, or at least out of the small towns and rural areas, just as they did in the 1930s. The flat plains of the western part of the state leave most visitors completely unprepared for the steep hills, big rivers, and verdant crosstimbers of eastern part of the State. The boggy southeast holds topographical kinship with Louisiana and the wheatfields of north central Oklahoma merge with those of southern Kansas. While tornadoes are quite frequent in the spring and summer, some of the most common recurring images in Oklahoma writing are those of red dirt (*Okla-Humma*, Choctaw for red people/land) and of the constant wind. Another recurrent image is that of empty towns and abandoned homesteads: Oklahoma's boom and bust cycle has devastated many small towns. However, one Okie stereotype is true: we don't give up easy. (Yes, I know that is grammatically improper, but it's Okie proper.)

Oklahoma writers are not exceptions to this rule: we don't give up easy, either. It's difficult being a writer in Oklahoma, for many reasons. First of all, in many families, it's a suspect occupation—you're not really doing much but sitting there writing. From the outside, it looks like you're lazy. Moreover, there exists in the state a longstanding dismissal of intellectual work. Secondly, it's extremely difficult to get writing with an Oklahoma flavor published in national magazines, a problem which holds true for most regional writing, except regional writing from New York or California. Third, there is a persistent problem with Oklahoma culture: in general, Oklahomans think that if something is from Oklahoma, it can't be any good, which is why out of state authors get teaching gigs at certain state sponsored arts institutes that, as stated policy, will not even consider hiring a writer who lives in Oklahoma, unless they got famous somewhere else. It's also the reason it's almost impossible to get stories about Oklahoma writers and publishers into major state and regional newspapers. Oklahoma does have a few well-known literary magazines such as *Nimrod* and *Cimarron Review* (published by the creative writing department which offers both an MA and a Ph.D.), but neither of them regularly publish vernacular writing. *Blood and Thunder*, the national literary magazine published by the University of Oklahoma College of Medicine, publishes writings that, as its subtitle states, are "Musings on the Art of Medicine," and therefore the journal does not actively search out vernacular work. I'll refer you here to Dorothy Alexander's poem "State of the Arts in a Red State" for another perspective on the difficulties of being a writer in Oklahoma. We don't let the obstructions keep us down, though. So, in good Okie fashion, since we can't seem to get our work heard or published nationally, we've decided to do it ourselves.

The good part of being an Oklahoma writer is that we have a grassroots literary movement that has grown steadily over the past thirty or so years. It can be traced back to at least the late 1960s and early to mid-1970s, to several poets, writers, groups, and presses, including the authors and artists associated with Frank Parman's Point Rider's Press. There are currently a few literary small presses in Oklahoma including Village Books Press, Forty-six Star Press, Literati

Press, and my own Mongrel Empire Press; these four presses recently founded the Oklahoma Small Press Association to help promote Oklahoma writers, publishers, and literary events. Several of the State's colleges have literary magazines, among them *Crosstimbers* at the University of Science and Arts of Oklahoma at Chickasha, *Arcadia* at the University of Central Oklahoma, and *Cooweescoowee* at Rogers State College in Claremore. Recently, writers associated with East Central University established a blog, *Polyphony Online*.

Live poetry and sometimes prose readings abound in Oklahoma: open mics with featured readers sponsored by Individual Artists of Oklahoma in Norman, Oklahoma City, and Shawnee; an open mic with feature sponsored by the Chickasha Arts & Humanities Council; Society of Urban Poets Open Mic at Ralph Ellison Library in Oklahoma City; a monthly open mic at Agora Coffee House in Tulsa; literary readings at the University of Oklahoma, Oklahoma State University, and Cameron University, among others. Oklahoma City University, home to the Red Earth Creative Writing MFA program, and University of Central Oklahoma's Creative Writing MFA program, both host writers on a regular basis. Oklahoma has an active slam scene led by the Home for Wayward Poets which hosts sanctioned events and sends an Oklahoma City delegation to the National Poetry Slam each year. There is more: since 2005, a group known as the Woody Guthrie Poets reads as a part of the scheduled events at the Woody Guthrie Free Folk Festival in Okemah. Last, but not least, Scissortail Creative Writing Festival, spearheaded by Ken Hada (a contributor to this issue), is the heart and soul of Oklahoma writing. Every April, writers from across Oklahoma, and some who just like to visit every once in a while, gather in Ada (at East Central University) to read their work. Nationally-known writers read for fifteen minutes alongside beginning and mid-career writers who read for the same fifteen minutes. Hada's mantra is "Check your egos at the door," and the result is a homegrown celebration of creativity that easily rivals festivals I've attended in New York. Information about these and other literary events can be found at the Oklahoma Poetry Portal (okpoetryportal.com) and by subscribing to PoetryArtsOK (lists.topica.com/poetryartsok).

Writers' organizations are also popular in the State. The Oklahoma Writers Federation is extremely active, both its statewide organization and local chapters. Oklahoma Group of Experimental Writers was founded by contributor Grant Jenkins in Tulsa a couple of years ago, and innumerable creative writing and critique groups are found throughout the state. The Oklahoma Center for the Book, associated with the Oklahoma Department of Libraries, promotes Oklahoma writing, in part by awarding the Oklahoma Book Awards. There are no individual artists' grant available from state agencies, but the Oklahoma Humanities Council co-sponsors reading programs and Poetry Out Loud! in the public schools, and the Oklahoma Arts Council maintains an artists' roster which includes writers. All this goes to show that there's a lot of writing and reading going on in Oklahoma, much more than I think most folks would imagine. However, I'm sure I'll leave out someone's journal or reading series or organization or press here, and I apologize in advance; these examples are provided only to suggest the breadth of Oklahoma literary culture.

In order to have any hope at all of covering Oklahoma literary culture, I tried my best to get the Sugar Mule call for submissions out to all the corners of the state (there are 5; check a map). The only rule I listed in the call was the the writer had to be living in Oklahoma at the time of submission. This rule was instituted because most of the time that Oklahoma writers are listed (even on lists put out by state governmental agencies), the majority of the writers are long dead or have moved away. This is not to say that we have disowned Joy Harjo or Ron Padgett or B.H. Fairchild or Joyce Carol Thomas (to name a few of the living) or that we have forgotten Ralph Ellison or John Berryman or Lynn Riggs or Ai or Gogisgi Carroll Arnett (to name a few of those who have passed). Rilla Askew and LeAnne Howe, both of whom currently live parttime in their home state, and Linda Hogan, who has returned full time, were aware of the call for submissions, but chose not to contribute, because, I think, they graciously wanted to make room for new Oklahoma voices to be heard. This issue of Sugar Mule will introduce you to a small, yet, I hope, representative sample of the who—the writers—and the what—the writing—of Oklahoma.

Oklahoma Writing was envisioned as a topographical, cultural, and historical trip through Oklahoma. The poems are divided between two general headings, "When/Where" and "How/Why."

The interpenetration of place and time is a marker of Oklahoma culture, one that can probably be traced to the influence of Native American philosophies; the category When/Where contains writings that explore the boundaries between place and time or that concentrate on one dimension or the other. "How/Why" contains writings that reveal the inner landscape of motives, of repercussions, of actions and their reverberations in the psyche. This is an entirely arbitrary division meant only to help the reader negotiate the terrain —roadsigns, if you will.

What kind of writing will you find here? The poetry varies, stylistically, from the vernacular, storytelling poetics known locally as "red dirt poetry" (see Jim Spurr's poems, for example) to cutting edge contemporary mash-ups and diastics such as those by Grant Jenkins and Hugh Tribbey. The personal lyric is well-represented, but often tinged with an unmistakable Okie accent; the poems of Yvonne Carpenter and Pamela Washington come to mind. Jonathan Stalling's visual poems based on aurally equivalent translations of Chinese phrasebooks are fascinating both to the eye and the ear. Slam poets Bryan Mitschell and Dezrea D'Alessandro capture their performance poetry on paper in the selections they've shared. Jason Poudrier's soldier-poetry, arising from active duty in Iraq and permeating his daily life on a farm in Oklahoma, is certainly among the best of its genre being written anywhere in America today.

Prose offerings include the quirky, sometimes uncomfortable fiction of Jim Drummond and JL Myers' unforgettable short story, "Wrestling the Wind." There is red dirt fiction, too, with Jeanne Dunbar-Green's "Since It's You and All" serving as a perfect example of the style. Detective fiction makes an appearance in an excerpt from Susan Miller's novel-in-progress, *The Kickapoo Cane Women*, while Susan Kates' creative nonfiction essay, "The Bird Watcher," combines nature writing and an exploration of women's relationships. In Danita Berg's prose poem/essay, "Head of the House," the author muses on her relationship to her dog and the sorrow of his (temporary) absence. There is more to read, both of prose and poetry, so I suggest you get started!

Where should you begin this journey through the nature theater of Oklahoma? You can start with Dorothy Alexander's polemic "Civility in the Slow Lane" so you can learn how to go about being friendly in our neck of the woods or you can choose to take a dip in Terry Ford's lake. You can skip down to the "W's" and join L. Michael West as he walks his dogs through Ada, OK or mosey on to the middle of the alphabet to be stunned by Laura Heller's powerful dramatic monologues or to indulge in Abigail Keegan's delicious imagery or to be shocked by Layton Isaacs's perhaps satirical poem, "Regional Delicacy." Like most journeys, it doesn't matter where you begin, only that you do!

Although I cannot name all the titles and authors here in this introduction, I want everyone to know that I am proud of every piece of writing in this issue and that I am honored to have made the acquaintance of the authors. I wish to thank Marc Weber for the opportunity to edit a special edition of Oklahoma Writing for *Sugar Mule: A Literary Magazine* (www.sugarmule.com); his offer was the impetus for this project of rewriting Oklahoma into the 21st century.

In the poem entitled "The Last Song" (1975), Joy Harjo declares, "oklahoma will be the last song / i'll ever sing." She knows, as we do, that Oklahoma is compelling in ways that can only be described creatively. And, like Woody Guthrie, each one of us believes "There ain't nobody that can sing like me." Therefore, I present to you Oklahomans singing Oklahoma. And, like Okies are prone to do, we are singing loudly, with pride in our work. We hope you enjoy your visit to the literary landscape of Oklahoma and that you find at least one image, one story, that surprises you.

WHEN/WHERE

DOROTHY ALEXANDER

Whiskey

The first time I drank liquor
was from a bottle of bootleg
whiskey bought with a double
handful of nickels and dimes
five of us had saved
from our lunch money.

It took a long time
to save four dollars
at a quarter a day.
We were farm kids
always hungry.
It was hard to give up a meal,
but we needed the whiskey.
We had a point to prove
which I have now forgotten.

The boy we sent to the bootlegger's
door to buy the bottle
drank half the whiskey
on the way back to the car.
We punched him good
when we saw the near empty pint,
but he never knew it.
He had already passed out.
That's when the good times began.

Sodbusting

They came to this place where
the sky was mirrored in the land.
Swaths of prairie stretching away
to whatever begins where space ends.
They broke it with their pitiful plows
taking the guts out of the thin top loam,
skimming off the cream where the grass
had held the buffalo.

The space is still there, broken
by the towering steel grinding away
at the underside of the land, sucking out
the black oil and spewing white gas,
and by the great specters with whirling blades
harvesting the wind, looking like fearful
creatures devised by Orson Welles,
but the heart and soul are somewhere else.

Yellow House

For my grandparents, Frank & Lue Yowell,
homesteaders on the Oklahoma prairie

The two of them made a yellow house
to light the bleak prairie, to say here the sun
is always shining, here you will find food
and rest, warmth and hope, cool water to drink.
Come, come.

Where warm rooms, beef stew, cornbread
smoky bacon, steam from a boiling pot
and a rooster crowing at dawn
were all worthy of attention,

Where a child could bury her face
in the folds of an apron or breath the flavor
of dark coffee, be given a cup with heapings
of sugar and thick cream skimmed from a jar
of cow's milk, and be counted as equal.

Where strangers, near-strangers, and kin
were all welcomed as pilgrims, given bread
and warmth and blessings, hospitality
a religion one could believe in.

Where even Republicans were heard out
over their supper.

PAUL BOWERS

Jazz in a Country Town

The round, green sax player
sways in syncopation; the trumpeter
in Hawaiian shirt and khakis
slaps his thigh, dips
a knee on high notes.
The trombonist, an elementary school principal,
leaps off and on stage,
working the sound board.

I wonder if we hear *jazz*
on Main Street, Ringwood, Oklahoma?
Have the same notes sprung before
in New Orleans, Memphis, Chicago?

Or, does the slow snappy staccato
of snare fire a less urban phrase,
delivered in the dialect of Southern Baptists
and Lutherans and Mennonites:
a wheat anthem
a cattle croon
a sorghum serenade?

The band, the Jazz Daddies,
plays atop a hay trailer
crowded by watermelons
(it is a festival to the melons)
and the crowd listens and finally concedes,
yes,
life on Mars is possible,
pigs do fly,

and jazz zings here
in early September
once the sun sinks
and the air cools
and barefooted little girls in pink dance
the yellow stripe of Main street.

What We Forget

Cauliflower trees.
Unmown swells.
A van of Mexicans wearing caps.
Fat tootsie rolls of hay.
Summer green just beyond the point of freshness
and lacking all surprise of spring.
Bumps of cows in the distance
look like figures from a model train village;
they don't seem move despite able legs.
Rather we move and time
slows in our wake.

The sky, buttered with clouds,
is open enough for us to pass along
the horizon. Fence posts stitch the sides of
the highway, the road a transplant of grey skin
that grows soft along the edges
and becomes crumble and soil and grass.

There is more room between branches
along the creek beds than we imagine
or see, more to the triangles of cedar that vee
only slightly from their cones
like fingers splayed.

On the way to visit my aging parents,
two hours on the Cimarron turnpike,
I gather up details as keepsakes
to remember: a collection of movement
and object and air and sky
swept up by the broom of my attention.

I will forget most of the journey, except
for the van, with a Mexican child staring at me
through the window, standing up in his seat,
daring accident, and the way he pulled his cap
low over his eyes as if to say
I am nothing to be recalled.

TIMOTHY BRADFORD

Concrete and Plums

Cerulean demeanor hung
on broad cheek bones, black hair,
heavy brown eyes, an accent.
Police have identified a store clerk . . .
Your language like plums, ours
hard as concrete or guns.
Still, you pressed *good mornings*
and *good nights* from your tongue.

I see the hole in your chest
like a bird's nest, red blossom
. . . fatally shot Friday . . .
you absently touch. The wound
your mother avoided during Tet,
you in her belly. And the bullet, as if shot
twenty-seven years ago and carrying speed the whole
way. In your eyes, confusion of the newly dead
. . . during a robbery at a convenience store.
and animal surprise at a country
that almost killed you, then welcomed,
only to kill you.

Sister. May I call you sister? I too
Uyen Doan, 26, was working . . .
do not understand. I too feel betrayed
by this life we have made, hard
as our language, loud as the report
of a gun, quick as a bullet to the chest.

Humbly I speak to you tonight
and say *I'm sorry*
as softly as my mouth
can carry it,
as delicately as ripe plums
hang from a tree.

Zoo Poems

> *A hippo with a horn is a rhinoceros and a lion without lunch is hungry.*
>
> —*Nicholas Troff after Chevy Chase*

1. The Real Takin

Takin: range, habitat, diet—
a bore. Signs in zoos
should read like this:
*Takins are large, magical dogs
from the Himalayas. They can fly.
They can be invisible,
not extinct.*

2. At Night In Aquaticus

Even as we sleep,
the long brown body
of the electric
eel keeps
undulating
along the edges.

3. Multi-purpose

A plastic baby bath
just big enough
for my nine-
month-old son,
full of anaconda.

4. Translation

Egyptian Cobra's
Latin name
is *naja haje*
meaning, "Watch
the fuck
out."

5. A Vision

Three dolphins
in their sleek
gray skins
with
sensual flaps
and folds
swim
in the sun-speared
water
behind
the illuminated
blue window
over
my son's
head.

6. Quotidian

Azure-winged
Magpie,
common
and beautiful.

7. Bio-diversity

In one cage
one
Golden-Headed
Lion Monkey,
one Two-
Toed Sloth,
and one Three-
Banded Armadillo,
all minding
themselves,
seemingly alone.

8. A Late Lunch

The Burrowing
Owls
keep watch
over one
decorative
horse's skull
and the fresh
heads
of two
baby chickens.

9. 4:30 p.m. in February

We came
late
to the zoo
and saw
only
the elephants'
footprints,
delicate mosaics,
circles of absence
in the
sand.

Oklahoma

—after Yehuda Amichai

On these plains, what we thought was the Rapture
was only a natural gas fire burning the sky
over the highway's line. Those who were saints
slipped into the cracked red clay while my
dead life was resurrected. Oil wells
stopped forever their bowing and rearing.
Everything motionless as a horse
listening to wind.

Our yard grew too long and I burned my shoulders
cutting it with an old green sickle. Sand burrs
migrated indoors, each one a miniature crown
drawing pain, blood, out of our soles.

Here the granite whispers to the sandstone and
the sandstone to the sand and the sand
to rivers that never cease next to grass
that always grows. By the words of our treaty, we
shouldn't be here. But the land is
of us. We die to make it. Our dead,
Cherokee dead, one and
the same earth.

(In Sulphur, in a large, corrugated tin barn,
I once saw 500 horses auctioned in one night,
as well as some frightened ponies
and one cow. This land was settled
with the same buck and clatter.)

And there's a birch near the entrance
to my school, bark peeling off
and pointing in many directions
as if asking how to get home.

MIRANDA BRADLEY

Cigarettes in Heaven

In high school, I'd sit with Chicago
on the concrete bench out front, where
she'd watch the three kids from special ed.
Everyone but her called them retards.

After lunch we'd buy a Dr. Pepper
near the front office where they sat,
newborn ducklings without a mother—
her excuse to eavesdrop just one more time.

In winter we'd huddle there, on the bench,
hands cupped breath, heads leaned to their
conversation—questions that drifted from their
bench to ours: *Do people smoke cigarettes in heaven?*

We never talked about them, but
sometimes made their questions ours:
Will we be friends in heaven?

Answered with the same honest ignorance
as the special ed. kids. Promised to grow up
and be next door neighbors, raise our kids
and husbands to be best friends too.

Somehow it stopped at *grow up.*

Checking Out at Food 4-Less

the lady in front of me
wears a man's shirt,
foot propped onto the
bottom rack of a cart
filled with Tony's pizza,
room temperature juices,
and kids she can't much
afford to feed—she tells me

complains about gas too,
and how her husband doesn't
get enough overtime at
the tea and coffee factory
on 63rd and Maybranch

smoothes the oily ponytail,
apologizes for her
appearance—grey mascara
smeared into the folds beneath

her eyes scan me then
down at herself, but I
never remove mine from
her face, smile like she's
the prettiest woman I've seen
all day, nod at everything,
convince myself we've
connected as she walks out,
turns her neck halfway to
gesture *so long* with her chin

I remember sugar, hold the line
and cashier, run to aisle six,
linger until I know she's
loaded them and gone away.

NATHAN BROWN

Biblical Proportions

When God swings the fist
of weather in Oklahoma,
we pull up seats and lean
into the performance...

here on the stage that gave us
one of the great, panoramic visions
of the 20th Century when it comes
to heaven's fits of meteorological rage.

The Dust Bowl—stirred up
by an army of angel wings—
came in like a black tidal wave
of interstellar grit and dirt.

It ground its stained teeth
as it passed over and turned
small homesteads and barns
into dunes and shallow graves.

The few surviving souls
were forced to punch holes
through shingles in the roof
to get a view of the damage.

Heard tell of one old man
who said, *Ol' Noah never
had no troubles like this.
Least he had time to build a boat.*

SHARON BURRIS

Heaven's Door

Tonight the clouds are like lattice
all the way across the sky,
a patterned fence
through which an occasional
inquiring star gazes,
and then shifts
away, bored.

Tonight the clouds are like cloth
loosely woven by sisters with
midnight for skin and
a glint of planets in hidden eyes,
their hard lips touching
looms of dreams with kisses
of silver
and dark.

Tonight the moon is imprisoned
by bars of wisp and silver
and her loneliness falls
across the blackness,
caught as a brief gleam in the cell
that keeps her
from caressing her lovers below,
the restless trees and cruelly careless rivers that
fade to gray and die
without
her
touch.

Days of Birds and Touch

Late November
with singing leaves the color of dirt, and
cobalt skies veined with
jet trails.

Ranger, skunk-colored cat/hunter
boasted his hard-stalked prize,
the mangled crimson plumage
of a male cardinal.
Dammit.
Do I feast fancy feeders
only to fatten them for the cats?

No chastisement
for sharing his work.
There are many others
to seek; surely
he'll miss next time.

He didn't
take on the two stout turkeys
leisurely strutting past the
pond this morning.

Towards evening, when
the sun rode waves
of late afternoon clouds
and the breeze had adopted
the cold children of coming night,
we took the dogs for a quick
jaunt to throw out the
decorative pumpkins, their
buttocks gone
smushy, to the deer or whatever
else likes uncooked filling.

They were there.

The entire pecan bottom
dark and bustling with hundreds
of nervously flittering robins,
burnt-orange chests muted by
shadow, flying low before the
ecstatic dogs, but never far ahead
before lighting again.
Robins everywhere, dusk-colored
spring harbingers, hordes
swarming through brown, tattered
leaves
leaving.

Walking back to the house
a *shissshing* above
was a wide ribbon of blackbirds
silent but for wing whispers
tying themselves in loveknots against
wind-crossed clouds;
perfect synchronicity
stretching across the gray
as far as I could see.
You didn't share
what made my heart break
with beauty.
You'd gone back inside.

Wing-tip to wing-tip in flight,
dipping and swerving as if one
sinuous serpent, but
never touching.
Never touching.
Like us.

ALICE BYRD

Woody Sez

They put me on a thirty-two cent stamp,
they put me on a thirty-two cent stamp,
they put me a stamp, stamp, a 1998 stamp,
they put me on a thirty-two stamp.

Stick it to my nose, nose,
put it on my toes, toes,
mail it to my president with pride,
put a little note from me inside.

Mr. President I'll have you know, know,
relief lines are starting to grow, grow,
folks have no place to call their own,
they have no need for a stamp, they need a home!

Folks call me a commie for singing of troubles,
for riding the rails for free,
for telling the truth, for encouraging the youth,
for demanding liberty. For that

they put me on a thirty-two cent stamp,
they put me on a thirty-two cent stamp,
they put me a stamp, stamp, a 1998 stamp,
they put me on a thirty-two cent stamp.

YVONNE CARPENTER

Picking Rye

We pluck the invaders
out by the roots.

With sharp knives
we cut off the sheathed heads,

leaving the bodies to rot in the sun,
 and carry the seeds away in the trophy

sacks hung from our waists.
We stop the uncircumcised

barbarians from polluting
our wheat fields.

Hours from Harvest

After months of pouring
borrowed dollars
into the ground,
the wheat stands
almost ripe—kernels
hardening to crack stage,
green bleached to gold.
Within hours
we may harvest
grain enough
to repay debt but
rising on the western
horizon cloud artillery
threatening to blast wheat from stalk,
then drown the survivors.
our wheat fields.

Morning Chores with Snow

While wind built snowdrifts in the wheat fields
but could not wrest the flakes away from the yellow nests
of blue stem grass, he hurried through the new light
to find the nine heifers who had not delivered their first calves.
When they were found safe and unlabored,
he scooped silage with the tractor/loader into the rotating bin
of the feed truck, then augured it into the concrete bunks
along the lot fence. Eighty-four new cattle,
fresh from the sale barn and through the working chute,
hurried to eat the steaming, sour roughage. Then he
gathered his wrench and pipe dope to repair the hydrant
lever the cows had rubbed, shut off and let freeze.
On the way to the diner, he four-wheeled through the wheat field
and counted the stockers, looking for any
with a drooping head or slow walk.
With all the cattle on their feet and nosing the snow aside for green,
he checked the electric fence for deer-damage. Standing
beside the open truck door, he removed his Carhartt coveralls
and overshoes, then reached behind the seat for a cleaner hat.

Rescue

"I need help," he said.
 "More help than just you."
We stood at the top
of the pipe drop

looking at the calf
trapped at the bottom
of the metal-lined hole.
The calf twisted his head

to stare back. After we gathered
a rescue team, plus John Deere
with a front-end loader,
chains and a ladder,

the cowboy climbed down, his hat
disappearing below ground level.
He fastened the chain
around the calf's neck

with the hook directly under
the bovine's throat—
off-centered, the chain
would snap the calf's neck.

The tractor lifted the loader
and the attached calf rose straight up,
neck stretched between the chain
and the weight of his body.

He landed like an
eight hundred pound fish.
Unhooked and clear of the hole
the calf staggered on numb legs.

Sometimes we need help—
an entire crew with tools.
And the alternative
to brutality is death.

In a Financial Crisis

at the end of the bull market

surprise—
    a cat,
    a flash, or
    a flutter,
startled one calf.

He jumped against the metal feed bunk
and the clatter woke the herd.
Each ran because the other ran
through the five-wire fence,
down the road,
over the embankment.

We found three dead,
twelve hiding under a bridge,
sixty-five grazing in new pastures,
    all exhausted.

K.L. CHAPMAN

Summer Sunsets in Oklahoma

My grandma told me once that
summer sunsets in Oklahoma
(at this point she allowed her hands
to stop their task and air dance)
were God's apologies for blistering days,
binding souls to the thanklessness
of working like all get out
with only a smidgen of divine grace
to grease the wheel of life.

Her dancing hands paused
and she pointed to a ribbon of pink
beautifying the eye of a nosy sun
taking a final peek at a hopeful land
of growing crops watered with sweat
and pastures freckled with cow patties.
That, she husked, was the pink sweetness
of her flouncy dress worn on Easter Sunday,
before the first of many black blizzards
darkened lives and lungs so cruelly,
except her dress wasn't as showy
and this sky ribbon of glowing pink
most likely lacked the velvety softness
of that dear dress filled with homespun love
flowing from her mother's busy hands.

I nodded and spoke of our sunset
as being akin to a twilight harvest social,
celebrating the best things gathered
from sunrise on—sort of like "Patchwork,"
Aunt Ruth's column in the evening paper.

I spied a tidbit of violet wonder
that could easily be a wide-eyed toddler
rocking her newborn brother, deciding

that maybe he was better after all
than the runt puppy born to Maxie,
the golden retriever down the road,
which is what she really wanted! crying,
when Mommy first told her about Belly Baby.

Our game had become a gift lifted from time,
and Grandma took her turn again,
pointing to a curve of smiling silver
captivating the horizon with talk of bargains
snatched up at a local church sale.

But wait, I grinned, see that whisper
of peach sherbet? That's the gently urgent
"I love you," spoken by a new wife
into the ear of her young husband
who thanks her with sunrise lovemaking
so delicious they both taste the flavor
throughout their long, boiling-hot day buried
in obligations, tasks, chores, and what have you.
Grandma's shocked "Oh!" was at odds
with her eyes that twinkled, recalling
mornings filled with sun-dried sheets
tangled by the magic of passionate flesh
blending heaven and earth for a time.

We played our game until the brilliance
of stars and moon traveled through our eyes,
becoming shimmering possibilities
willing to follow us into our dreams.

As we walked inside—away from mosquito hunger
and firefly enchantment—our hearts shared
the understanding that balancing pain and joy
in this world is the best we can hope for,
because stuck between the best and the worst
is the living.

Sand Plum Goddesses

Their collective hearts and minds nod. Yes.
The sand plums are ripe for picking,
Visions of rubies melting warmly inside glass
Jars of jelly and jam coaxing sweet talk
From their men and children remembering
The richness of it coating their lips and tongues
Flooding the golden valleys of hot buttered biscuits.

They'll open their sand plum chronicles, some old some new
Depending on how long they've danced the rituals
Like goddesses, only here and now,
Living with scratches on their hands and
Red dust on shoes that step nimbly over
Drought cuts in the ground—those cracks
You can see straight to hell through.

The thickets, they turn their backs on the June heat,
Bearing fragrant white blossoms despite dry sand
And ascetic roots with little thirst for water.
In the midst of this lack, kindly forces gather
To drum up enough spirit to right the imbalance
In a burst of red and yellow fruit, glowing
Against sunshine smiling softly in an April mood.

The goddesses live in places far down the dirt road,
From the hazy dream houses of spring brides
Whose unshaped lives never held dying hopes
Bleeding out in summer wastelands,
Gratefully savored the short drink of autumn cider,
Or prayed for fire in the eye of winter. Tears…laughter
Drip from the timeless heart of their poetic survival.

So, when speaking of nights dripping
With juicy, sugared syrup that ended up
Tempting more than taste buds on a church night;

Or of family members whose untimely deaths quickly followed
Batches of sand plum jelly that never fully jelled,
Proving the Curse of the Bad Batch was alive and well;

Or of children playing through and around goddess legs,
Challenging each other to find the first clutch
Of bobwhite eggs well hidden under a sand plum thicket,

It's important to note that these narratives never ride the wind
To their death, but journey gracefully to the earth's face,
Blessing it with the magic of ritual, friendship,
And the joyful warmth of the hearth, taking root
And sprouting red and yellow fruit waiting to be picked
By the next generation of sand plum goddesses,
Eager to begin living and breathing their own stories.

CHASE DEARINGER

Second Coming

Most would say it all began the day Sammy drowned in the Cimarron River. But others, including myself, would say that it began the day his father missed the Holy Ghost and left—walking—for God knows where.

Samuel Austin was a regular around downtown Perkins—he worked at the Coop but could be seen everywhere. Me and Zebediah always used to catch him at the beauty parlor everyday after school flirting with the wives. He would sit in one of the hair-drying chairs, reading the paper and telling all the women he would be glad to leave Margie for anyone of them if there was property involved.

"We'll run you out of here someday, Samuel Austin," Miss Burgess, the salon owner, would always say. "This isn't no library." Of course me and Zeb always knew he was just biding his time so he could read the paper for free: he loved Margie more than his news. He would always steal Dr. Peppers from the Co-op for me and Zeb and drive us back to Piney River—that was the trailer park where my family and the Austins lived.

You hardly see Mr. Austin around town anymore, not since Sammy drowned. Sammy was Zeb's identical twin. They weren't the kind of identical twins that you could tell apart by some distinguishing feature, neither. They were a spitting image of each other. They were short redheads with freckles all over their faces. A little fat, too. My mother always said it was because the Austin's let them watch too much TV.

Anyway, I don't know much about what happened the day of the drowning - I wasn't there. But Zeb was there and this is how he told it:

It was that summer it rained for a straight month all over Oklahoma. Of course this ended a three year drought, so the Cimarron was up as high as anyone here could remember. Mr. Austin took Sammy and Zeb down there every week or so to horse around and swim in the water. Usually, the river's so shallow that you can stand right in the middle. One time the Austins took me and Benny Wellington down there and we played football right in the river.

So Zeb said Sammy was out in the water, swimming around, when all of a sudden he just disappeared; went right under. I won't go into any of the gruesome details like how they didn't find his body for three days and when they did he was all decomposed and rotten and bloated. Or talk about how they had to have a closed casket that Margie Austin cried on for hours. I'll just say the kid was dead and we didn't see much of Mr. Austin around town after that.

Zeb's family would all have been glad if no one talked about it ever again, but Zeb wouldn't let it go. He was eight and a half when it happened—a mature enough age to understand death, but he kept on asking his parents when Sammy Jr. was coming back. I don't know if he was just that stupid or if he didn't want his parents to let it go neither. They always responded with silence. The question tapered off and eventually after a couple years he quit asking all together. That was the same year the Pentecostals set up a tent revival out on state highway thirty-three.

Well, what happened turned out to happen during one of the hottest summers the state has ever seen. It was July—a broiling day in the morning—and I was sitting at the Austin family breakfast table, which was unfolded in the middle of their trailer's living room. The trailers in Piney River are not exactly known for their space, so I was used to it. That day was only a month ago but it still seems like something that's never happened.

It was about eight-thirty in the morning and I was over at the Austins' waiting for waffles. You can't find a better made-from-scratch waffle anywhere outside of Margie's kitchen. My mom never gives us nothing but cold cereal and a boy needs more than cold cereal to stay healthy. Me and Zeb were at the table and Margie was stooped over the waffle press. Mr. Austin wasn't out of bed yet. He'd taken to alcohol over the past few years and rarely got up before ten. Margie tried her best to hide this from us but we all knew.

Margie was in her sweat pants, of course, and her hair was pulled back and fastened at the back of the head. I was used to her dressing like that—she didn't get out of the house much once Samuel took to the booze. Someone had to keep him under control. He lost his job at the Coop over a year ago. Zeb told me they were relyin' on Margie's parents for financial support or something like that. She turned around and sat our plates in front of us.

"So Rusty, are you planning on going with us to the revival this evening?" She sat a bottle of syrup in front of me and moved to the kitchen counter to retrieve a plate of butter.

"Sure am, Miss Margie. My folks said it was okay by them if it was okay by you." My parents didn't even know where I was. The Pentecostals had this big tent revival every few years out on state highway thirty-three, next to the cemetery. I don't think there was any particular reason that they had it next to the cemetery other than the fact that Mr. Wellington—who was a deacon at the church—owned the property.

I know it was the telephone that waked old Mr. Austin because he came in fumbling with the belt on his bathrobe while Margie was still on the phone. He leaned on the kitchen counter and stared at her like he was irritated. She ignored him.

"Of course we're coming, mama. And we're bringing Rusty Jenkins from next door, too." Margie turned her back to her husband and twisted the phone cord with her finger. "I thought we might bring some flowers from my garden to put on Sammy's grave, too." She lowered her voice and started whispering something in the receiver. Mr. Austin just grunted and sat down at the table. Margie placed a plate in front of him
while she was still on the phone. He glared at me and Zeb but didn't say anything. Margie hung up the phone.

"Go on. Say your mother wants us to go to that God-damned revival." He shook the salt shaker over his waffle. He always salted his waffles.

"She expects us there, Sam." She untwisted the phone cord and sat down at the other end of the table. "And I expect we best be doing what she thinks is best for us until you find another job." Her tone sharpened as she said the word job.

"Just don't understand what good it's gonna do us to go down there just so Brother Jerry can scare the hell out of everybody. Bunch of queer-talking, superstitious types if you ask me." He chewed his food slowly. Sweat was building up on his forehead and dripping down around his red eyes. "And we're not stepping foot in that cemetery."

Margie ignored everything he said and turned to Zeb. "Why don't you go on out after you finish those waffles. Pick a few of those yellow marigolds and put them in a cup of water. We can take them out to Sammy's grave after the service this afternoon."

The field where the tent was set up smelled like wet, cut grass. Zeb sat on an upside-down trash can, clutching the marigolds in his hand while his mother searched for Mr. Austin. I could see him, plain as day, pouring some kind of dark liquor in his iced tea behind the row of port-a-potties that lined one side of the tent. From where we were, we could see almost everything: the people, all dressed up, milling around the outside of the tent, waiting for their place in the line for food, the church deacons setting up folding chairs underneath the giant, white tent and the younger kids chasing each other around between the port-a-potties. Miss Burgess was warming up the piano.

"You two staying out of trouble?" Zeb's grandfather snuck up behind him and put him in a half-nelson.

"Yes, sir," Zeb answered, smiling and holding the flowers away so they wouldn't be smashed.

"Where're your parents?" Zeb's grandmother asked as she joined her husband and ran her fingers under Zeb's nose, wiping away the snot that the headlock had procured.

"Mama's looking for daddy," Zeb said. Grandpa Olsen put Zeb back on the trashcan and examined the crowd. For a moment I thought about telling the old man that Mr. Austin was behind the port-a-potties but I didn't see the point.

"Are those flowers for Sammy's headstone?" Zeb's grandmother inquired. "Your mother always grows beautiful marigolds. It's the perfect time of the year for them, too." She stopped fussing over Zeb when Mr. Austin came up on us.

"Well, I'll be, Samuel. Glad to see you made it out this evening." The old man stretched his arm out to shake Mr. Austin's hand but Mr. Austin just stood there.

"Nothing more I want to do on July evening than come out and praise the Lord," Mr. Austin said. He took a long drink from his cup. "Figured I might get myself saved tonight." We all sat in silence and I could tell by the look on Zeb's face that he was a little embarrassed. Margie appeared and we moved to find seats.

When word came to town about Sammy, I was already at the Austins' waiting for everybody with Margie. Mr. Austin didn't call home. We got word from the sheriff, who drove out to Piney River to deliver the news himself. I figured she already knew the news because she left the trailer door open when she ran out to meet the sheriff. Well, I'm not saying she new what news, but she knew there was trouble anyway. I knew the news, too. Margie had pleaded with Mr. Austin not to take them to the river that day. Said it was too dangerous.

She didn't speak when she came inside. I asked her what the news was and she told me that we weren't gonna see Sammy no more. That was all. Tuesday Sammy was here and Wednesday Sammy was gone. Just like that. I was nine when it happened and my mother wouldn't let me bother the Austins for a couple of weeks. I saw folks come and go with what looked liked food but I never saw none of the family leave the house.

That was the first two weeks. After that we'd see Mr. Austin wandering around the trailer park, drinking and making a fuss. We didn't say anything to him or anyone in the family. Just let it be. He waked me and my whole family up one night at three in the morning, banging on the storm door and cursing at the sky. When my daddy got to the door he just staggered back and leaned against the railing around the porch. His shirt was off and there were scratches all across his chest. "Wrong house" was all he said. This went on for a week or so until I guess he learned to keep his drinking confined to his own house.

"If I speak in the tongues of angels and of men and have not love, I am nothing." Brother Jerry began to speak and Margie took the comic book out of my hand and sat on it. She had always been a church-going lady despite the fact that no one else in her family would go with her except her parents. She always made it and always meant business. She was in her forties, I think, and had gone to church her whole life. Her first love: God and the Bible. Her second love: her children.

"Clap your hands unto the Lord! Somebody give praise! Somebody lift up a voice! Lift up a voice unto the God of our salvation!" Brother Jerry was getting excited and folks at the revival started standing up and clapping their hands. Some of them even raised their hands up towards the heavens. Mr. Austin buried his head in his hands.

It wasn't as if I hadn't seen Brother Jerry come out to the Austin's trailer, trying to convince Mr. Austin to give up the drinking and come to Jesus—arguing with him and explaining that it was God's will for his son to die and he needed to be in tune with this divine will. He'd always wait a minute at the door before he left, waiting for one last sign of repentance from Mr. Austin or something, I guess. I was surprised to see that Mr. Austin actually started listening at the revival.

"The Son will return some day. The son will return." Brother Jerry cried out. Both Zeb and Mr. Austin perked up. "Behold, he is coming with clouds, and every eye will see him, even they who pierced him. And all of the tribes of earth will mourn because of him. Pray that you may be worthy to escape all these things that will come to pass and to stand before the son of man." A woman with colored scarves was running
around the outside of the congregation, dancing and waving the scarves in the air. Miss Burgess played the piano.

One brutal summer day a year ago, when Margie was in the flowerbed tending to her flowers, Mr. Austin came out of the trailer and for no apparent reason slapped his wife across the face.

"I read what you wrote in that prayer book of yours," he roared. "When're you gonna stop blaming this shit on me. It's not my fault I couldn't hold that job down. It's not my fault I've taken to this drinking. Devil must've gotten in me, something." Margie didn't say a word. Me and Zeb just watched.

"Why're you reading in my prayer book? I told you that was private," she finally said. She stood up and brushed the dirt off of her knees. "You pry don't think it was your fault that it was raining so much that summer, neither, do you?" She immediately recoiled, expecting another hand to fall on her face. It didn't. Mr. Austin just crawled into his pickup, drunk, and drove away.

Margie sat in her flowerbed and cried for half and hour.

The tent was getting real excited towards the end of the service. A bunch of the women had made their way down to the front and they were on their knees, crying and moaning and lifting their hands up. Brother Jerry was getting especially stimulating.

"The power of your spirit according to your will and your word and your name and your blood. Holy Ghost, help my brother. Help my neighbor. Help my friend. Let us come here today that they might receive the impartation of a Holy God. My Lord! My Lord! My Lord! My Lord! Alak mana haya forsee carasta! Elosa rocka ana ma hia!

My God has come to heal! My God has come to restore! My God has come to shake up the dust where you stand!" He kept going on like this and speaking in tongues for a while, and the women below him kept crying and wailing and bowing down. That's when Grandpa Olsen put his hand on Mr. Austin's back and started yelling.

"Para ashati magasi entumbey. Para ashati magasi entumbey." He was rocking back and forth with both of his hands on him. Mr. Austin just sat there looking more patient than he ever had while Brother Jerry kept on about the return of the Son and how we need to get our lives in order if he's ever going to come back.

They appeared to bring with them the Holy Ghost, at least that's what Zeb's Grandpa said, as people began filling the aisles and moved towards the front of the tent. Or maybe the Holy Ghost brought them. They filled the tent with a loud, moaning sound; tongues mixed and danced under the canvas ceiling. Inside the tent, the track lighting filled the space with an artificial angelic glow. People's faces were illuminated as they made their way to Brother Jerry.

I'd been to a revival once before, so I expected this. Everyone gets real excited and moves to the front so they can be slain with the Holy Ghost by Brother Jerry. Around the stage, where everyone crowded in to get their piece of the action, deacons laid their hands on people and prayed over them and told them what to do when they got to the stage.

None of us could believe it when Mr. Austin got up from his chair and joined the procession.

His father-in-law went with him, holding him by the hand and whispering something in his ear. I still wonder what it is he was saying to him. Mr. Austin acted real calm and kept his eyes forward while Grandpa Olsen raised his free hand to the air and shouted something out in a strange tongue. I can say he seemed thankful. Zeb crawled up in his mother's lap and she began to cry.

Those who saw Mr. Austin make the walk to the front of the tent say he had a look of determination on his face. Miss Burgess even said when he got to the front that he almost looked happy. The reflection of light from the tent ceiling beat down on his face—it was completely dark outside. Water from the baptismal behind the stage cast a steely shimmer everywhere, full of motion like the bathroom walls at the city pool. It kind of looked like a scene of heaven from the Bible.

From where I was sitting I could see him in line, waiting to pray with one of the deacons. He sure looked determined. I wondered whether they would make him confess his sins: all that drinking and hitting Margie and not caring about no one. I'm not sure what I was waiting to see, but it seemed like it was going to be important. Important like winning a championship or an election. There was a state of exaltation and it seemed for a moment like everything was going to be okay. When he got on stage, Brother Jerry rushed up to him and grabbed him by the arm.

"Do you need the Holy Ghost, brother?" The people below were moaning and crying and shouting "Yes Lord!" Mr. Austin didn't say a thing. Brother Jerry put his hand on Mr. Austin's forehead and began shouting in tongues. When he does this, he gives a little shove and person is supposed to fall to the ground a wriggle for a while before a deacon removes them from the stage and takes them to fill out a prayer card. Mr. Austin just stood there.

"You need the Holy Ghost, brother!" Brother Jerry shoved him again. Mr. Austin just kept standing there. To this day, I don't think anyone in Perkins saw it coming. Mr. Austin just stood there for a while, looking out at the crowd with a puzzled look on his face like nothing had happened. You could see him searching the crowd for something, desperately. When he didn't find it he simply walked off of the stage, out of the tent headed for the cemetery. Zebediah grabbed the marigolds from under his seat and shouted at his dad to wait. He tried to crawl over the row of chairs in front of him but his mother pulled him back. She held him there and rocked as he clutched the flowers to his chest.

Samuel Austin hasn't shown his face around Perkins since. Margie's marigolds never made it to Sammy's grave. As far as I know, they're still sitting in a vase next to Zebediah's bed. Of course they aren't pretty any more. Still, no one knows why he did it or where he ran off to. Men like Mr. Austin don't always follow the Holy Ghost, I guess.

I would never say that to Zeb, of course.

DONNITA DEWEY

Flash Memoirs of an Okie Lesbian

Country Life
We caught rain water off the house and used it for bath water. We did not have an inside bathroom and the only running water was in our kitchen. We had an outhouse up on the hill by the barn. When it was cold we used a "pot" in our bedroom. We lived on 40 acres and this was my playground. This was also a place where, as a child, I mowed grass, bailed hay, feed the horses, pigs and dogs. These were called chores. My transportation was walking or riding the lawn mover. I got a mini-bike for my birthday one year and that was my freedom. I thought everyone lived this way. One year I went to stay with some people who had a farm. I was up at 5am, helped with the dairy cows, feed the calves, feed the chickens and then it was time for breakfast. There was always something to do, from sun up to sun down. It wasn't until I was 12 years old and we moved to town that I found out that not everyone peed off their porch and everyone had a bathroom.

In a small town
Day dreaming and staring outside at a small town lost in time. No traffic, only noise coming from the kids on the play ground. It's a sunny day, no wind, but a storm is coming. A storm like this town has never seen before. I reminisce about the time spent with my girlfriend and the secrets we have. If only they knew I am gay. Everything that I have, family, friends, classmates, social status, would be gone. I hate what I have become in order to fit in with the small mindedness of this town. Should I take that chance to be myself? This is my senior year. This is supposed to be the best year of my life. Sadly, it's not. I have been outed. There will be no senior prom, no party with friends after graduation. Nothing. I will go home alone. There has got to be more to life than this. I will commit suicide if I stay in this small town.

Mom can't drive in the snow
Winters were bad in the 70's. My mom would always get stuck going up this one particular hill by our house. She drove a Chevrolet

Corvair. She would almost make it to the top, then we would slide and she would try to stop. Mom would try to back down and end up in the ditch every time. Mom tried every year to get up that hill.

East Side / West Side

The east side of town was considered the white side and the west side was considered the black side. We had a swimming pool, cemetery and stores and so did they. Growing up in the 70's I never understood this. You would always here "don't go down there at night." Being a curious kid, that was the first thing I wanted to do. After a basketball game we would go down there for a dance. This was some of the best times I had. One day I went by their swimming pool and looked to see what the big deal was. Their swimming pool looked just like ours, used the same water, and had the same amount of bathrooms. I just didn't understand. I even visited their stores; they had a lot better stuff than we did. What I didn't understand was some of our teachers were black and we were taught to show them respect, but our elders didn't.

Submarine Races

It was a cold Oklahoma night. Coming back from the movies in Shawnee, another closet lesbian and I decided to stop by the lake to watch the submarine races. (Now, if you are from the country in Oklahoma, you know what this means. If not, we went parking.) We found a spot by the dam, which was a good place to be to watch for incoming cars. In the heat of the moment, we did not realize we had company. There was a knock on the window. I wiped off the condensation to find that the officer is someone I know. I rolled down the window and he said "you two need to get back to town and go home, this is not the place for you to be at night". He was correct, people get killed or beat up for less.

Brenda

Brenda was the first "official" gay woman I knew. She was very athletic, funny and had wonderful advice. She helped me to become true to myself. Brenda knew everyone from the area. She had her share of run-ins with "small minded country folks" or "bigots" as she would call them. She took me to her farm and showed me how to use a gun. This was not for protection, but that I should know what to do just in case. Now, growing up on the farm, there are certain things you do before you turn 12. One of those things is to learn how to handle guns. We had been there a couple of hours and she brought out a double barrel shot gun. It was huge and heavy. My instructions were "get your ground and when you are ready, fire." Simple, right? When I opened my eyes, I was flat on the ground looking up and she was laughing her ass off. I haven't handled a double barrel since!!

Nurse's Liquor Store
I could not have made it through high school without help from Nurse's Liquor Store. I thought I was something, going in there and buying Boone's Farm Strawberry Hill or Country Kwencher. On occasion I would get a bottle of vodka. We would leave school for lunch, go by the liquor store, and stop by Sonic. We would get large cups of ice and mix our drinks. Usually we would drag main and meet up with friends to see where the party would be that night. Good times!!

Gay Athlete
Sports were not offered to girls in the 70's until high school. When I got to high school, I signed up for every sport they offered for girls. I found out early on I didn't really enjoy track and field. The coaches always wanted me to jump hurdles. That just didn't appeal to me. Basketball was fun, but I didn't understand why girls had to play 3 on 3, when the boys got to play full court. I stuck it out for 3 years. Tennis was exciting to me. As far as I could remember, I always wanted to play tennis. I would practice every chance I got. This was my out. Being on that court alone against an opponent was how I took out all of my frustrations of being a closet gay athlete. It was all about the win. I made it to state 3 years in a row. Getting to play at that level was awesome and a great experience. I enjoyed being out of town and in the big city. The complex where the tournament was played was right across from a gay park. It was ok in Oklahoma City for women to be seen in public with each other? This was a wonderful thing. As long as there wasn't any public display of affection!!

Ice house

New guys in town running the Ice house. I stopped by one day to pick up a six pack of Bud Light and go out by the lake after school. Drinking was my way of dealing with a small country town and being gay. Carl was one of the owners and a very nice guy I could talk to. He and I began talking and he turned me on to black mollies and cocaine. He was one of the local drug dealers in town. We spent a lot of time together. My junior year I took Carl to the prom with me. We had a wonderful time. The pressure was starting to get to me and being with a guy made it even worse. Trying to fit in with the "norm" was killing me. Carl doesn't know it, but he saved my life that year.

First gay bar

We are living in Oklahoma City now. Our new friends are taking us out to our first gay bar. It's in the basement of an old church on Classen Boulevard. Upstairs is a dance club, mostly with gay people. It's a long dark stairway, and the door opens up to the dance floor. Disco ball is going, lights flashing to Madonna's song "Holiday." A voice comes over the speakers "let's get on the floor ladies!!" Ladies?? Nothing but women dancing with women. Women kissing women. No police. No rednecks. Oh my gosh, I am in heaven.

Now in my 40's

I am now in my 40's and reflecting on attending my high school reunion. I haven't been back to Wewoka in over 20 years. I wanted to be as far away from this town and the people as I could get. My senior year of high school was not what I had planned or expected. The hatred of certain classmates that drove me out of town has been replaced with a good life, great friends, and to know that I am above it what happened in the past. They can not take anything away from me and I will not be made to feel guilty for who I am. I have been in contact with some classmates, who, to my surprise are glad that I am coming to the reunion. My girlfriend and I will be attending and can't wait to see some of these folks—the rest can go to HELL.

JIM DRUMMOND

Nolan in the Badger Café

In the Badger Café are the usuals but as usual also some unusuals. In the circular booth in the corner are some bikers—not the greasy Outlaws with Sex Pistol knockoff names whose prodigious leather-mashed asses Nolan has kicked on several occasions—but untattooed doctors and lawyers and brokers in clean black leather, men and women. Their bikes are in clean formation out at the edge of the lot. They are considerate. A bit disappointing, really. They are thanking the waitress, tipping well.

"Fry some triple twins, Nolan?" asked Dee, her mountain of hair triple-clipped into a stout pile. He nodded, "Thanks, Dee." Two eggs and two strips of crisp bacon, two tomato slices on the side, no carbs. Nolan, who was polite to a fault, looked her in the eyes when he said it. Some found it attractive, some disconcerting, according to their characters and temperaments, that Nolan looked straight into their eyes when he talked. It was a bit weird at the least—there was no squint, no postured drollness, no twinkle—no expropriation of a straight look for some agenda of being impressive.

The truth was, directness came naturally to Nolan. The politeness did not; it was a learned safeguard against Nolan's propensity to straight talk. Some interpreted the directness as special to them, a powerfully seductive singling out as if you were the Lone Bank of Love and he was about to rob it. Others viewed it as an equally seductive indifference to them, a sign of great power and self-sufficiency: Nolan, the Loan Banker of Love: if you need it, you can't have it. . . .

Nolan sat down in the booth, reached into his black leather satchel, and pulled out his own handmade 365 day Thoughts Calendar. He turned to May 5, 2003 and read this entry:

> *Pig is the most shameless animal:*
> *The pig is the most shameless animal on the face of the earth. It is the only animal that invites its friends to have sex with its mate. In America, most people consume pork. Many times after dance parties, they have swapping of wives; i.e. many say "you sleep with my wife and I will sleep with your wife." If you eat pigs then you behave like pigs. We Indians look upon America to be very*

advanced and sophisticated. Whatever they do, we follow after a few years. According to an article in Island magazine, this practice of swapping wives has become common in the affluent circles of Bombay.

—Dr. Zakir Naik, East India, President, Islamic Research Foundation

Dee appears with his eggs and bacon, sets it down. "Want my bacon?" Nolan asks. She is used to seeing him with the book, expects the unexpected. Dee is studying for a math degree at the community college in Okmulgee. Smarter than Nolan may realize, she knows he's not a mere untouchable asymptote, only a little but infinite bit out of reach of her moving curves or, he lives in negative territory on the other side of the asymptote, visible but not even close. He is older by a lot, for one, severely attractive but weird like the assassin from the future in *Terminator II.*

"No. I don't want your bacon. Don't you want it any more?"

"If I ate it and married you, according to Dr. Naik I'd start wanting us to be swingers."

"So is that some sort of sidewinder proposal of marriage, you foregoing the bacon?"

"Just hypothesizing."

"I haven't noticed our customers getting more romantic after they eat the bacon."

"I wouldn't have thought you'd see swapping spouses as necessarily romantic."

"A shill-word for *promiscuous.* Pick at your breakfast if you want but don't pick at me. I'm not on your plate."

"Been out by Masada of late?" A closed rural Aryan conclave.

"I give it a wide berth."

"What do you hear?"

"They're still not gentlemen and ladies."

"That's freedom."

"Yeah." Nolan hears the cook ring the bell, say, "Dee Ann, please." She eases away to the pass-through. She is always polite with something in reserve, dry as a July creek bed. Nolan wonders if the cook says please when he is not there. Most of the rudeness he encounters is from the oblivious. There is something about Nolan that makes tutored men remember their manners, like the sense of a live power line unseen touching a pipe or rain gutter, you can hear the hum nearly, but you have to be deconstructing your focus to notice. Nolan knows this about himself, knows old Darwin's laws are at work there.

"Where is the *fucking* tabasco?" A deep voice with a very British accent somehow rises above the light roar of the diner. As he tightens, Nolan's vanishing Observer mind remarks that somehow a British voice even at its deepest wraps around a very high note which rises up above every other sound—a countertenor pig wrapped in a bass blanket. Listen to John Cleese sometimes. The inflection does wonders with sound!

Nolan is contra-verbal now. He stares at the source of the question, like a falcon on some invisible wrist. He is hooded by an intention concentrated with attention.

The speaker is graced with a shock of huge gray hair over a black boatneck tee, massive arms forming an A with the table, palms together before his massive hairy chest with tips touching lightly in a mockery of delicacy. "I *did* ask for it minutes ago." Nolan rises, takes a 3-quarters full tabasco from the counter to the man's table, where he sits with a very petite and rather shriveled redhead.

"I am Nolan. Helping your server, she's rather busy. And what brings you to the blasted wastes of Badgerburg, Mr. C ?"

"Roger Ray. Well if you truly care, it is a Greco-Roman exhibition on your local green."

"Gay sex on the golf course, Roger?"

Roger bursts up from the booth, his legs knocking the table against the redhead.

"This place will do as well."

"Agreed," replies Nolan, suddenly seizing Roger's neck with his left arm, casually unscrewing the tabasco bottle with his right fingers, popping off the plastic dropper, prying open Roger's clinched teeth with his left fingers, and deftly depositing the entire McIlhenny contents into Roger's mouth. Roger is absolutely immobilized by something Nolan is managing to do to the front of Roger's neck with his knuckles. Nolan shuts his mouth again and somehow holds it shut with his right hand, even making Roger's jaws pretend to masticate. Roger's face is growing ever redder as he tries to sputter but cannot.

Some there suspect that Roger might be close to death. He cannot breathe. Dee begins to cry out. The cook reaches to call the police. Nolan suddenly slams him into his seat, opens his mouth, pours a whole glass of water into it, which Roger spits out all over the table and the redhead, then takes a package of saltines from a dish on the table, unwraps it, and shoves all four crackers into Roger's mouth.

"Keep eating crackers," he says. "It will gradually take out the fire." Seeing that Roger will live now, the cook moves his hand away from the phone. Nolan turns to the redhead.

"I am sorry if you were splattered or alarmed. I am certain you neither partake of nor approve of your companion's rudeness, which is what entitled him to know fully where the *fucking* tabasco was. My principle with rude people is to teach them to be careful what they ask for. It is unfortunate that you were forced to be such an intimate witness to Roger's correction." He turned to the restaurant as a whole. "Similar apologies to you all."

After paying matter-of-factly, Nolan nodded to wary Dee and the leery chef, and exited to his van. Through the diner's window he saw Roger ignoring his advice, still downing water ferociously. Definitely a new entry in the Enemy Book, he thinks. Nolan had found a thick, very old green journal book in a Hot Springs used bookstore and had bought it—no entries—for its resemblance to a magic book. He termed it his *rutter*—maritime jargon for a sort of logbook or guidebook of the ocean and its currents, harbors, pitfalls. In it he kept names, addresses, and anecdotes about people who might have reason to do him harm. A book of baddos.

He'd really meant to feel the pulse, not be the pulse, of old Badgerville. Responding to rudeness was his Achilles heel. Nolan figured he had the sympathy of the café customers, however appalled they might have been at his lethal style of retort. He was however glad this was not really his own land.

JEANNE DUNBAR-GREEN

Since It's You and All

"Anybody born north of Pauls Valley is a damn Yankee, " Big Butchie Lindsey proclaimed as he walked up under the shade tree where Mary Jean and John Jr. were sitting, Ole Shug, their sugar mule, standing behind them, swatting the occasional fly with her semi-naked broomtail. "Anybody born north of Pauls Valley is a damn Yankee," he declared again, looking around for someone to disagree with him, hopefully someone from Purcell or Wayne, Oklahoma. Other than this one baiting and misleading refrain, Big Butchie Lindsey never did say much, but he was known to think a lot, to have what some called country common sense.

So, John asked him, "Butchie, do you think we can sell this here mule to someone today? Is there much market for mules just now?"

"I reckon you could sell just about anything down here," he said, making no commitment. He had stopped to gather information, not sow it, "if'n your price is right and you can find a buyer who wants what you got."

"This here mule," John continued while cinching the saddle on Ole Shug, a tall, dark brown sugar mule with high white socks and a white dusted muzzle "would ride you nice when you're coon huntin'. She'll jump a tight five-strand barbed wire fence. You just lay a saddle blanket over the wire, and she'll jump it like a deer," he explained, looking around as if he hoped to find a fence nearby for a demonstration of Shug's deer skills. "This here mule don't spook bad around dogs and guns, and she's gentle broke, too, and since it's you and all. . ." he began.

"Well," Butchie said, winking at Mary, "I hadn't heard that you did much fence jumpin' over at your place."

Mary laughed briefly and John went on as if he hadn't heard the pun, finding his dog trader's voice and cadence, "This here mule will stand still for you all day long if that's how long it takes you to mount her," he said, demonstrating with his own feigned-clumsy mounting technique and then when atop her, swaying around and leaning back in the saddle until he could reach Shug's rump and pat it, to show that she wasn't a kicker nor difficult to handle.

By now both Butchie and Mary were giggling but trying not to show it too much. Butchie had begun to blush a bit.

"So what do you want out'a this mule?" Butchie asked. "Ain't this the same old mule I been seein' in the front pasture up to your place for years, maybe ever since you been up there?"

"Yeah, we've had her a while. That's how we been able to train her up so much," John answered.

It was always a pleasure to take Ole Shug out for a trail ride. You just ambled along. She gave you a smoother ride than any horse, and she did your thinking for you, too. On cold mornings, John fed for his wife so she wouldn't have to leave the warmth of their bed for the abrupt cold of morning. He liked to make sure the stock all got breakfast early after enduring the chill of the night. While he was feeding the stock of a cold morning, Ole Shug would find him and follow him around like a faithful hound, stopping at the feed bins with him as he made the rounds, snorting a bit to warm her muzzle, intelligent and watchful, walking along with him in perfect lock step in spite of his stop and go pace. They put Ole Shug up at night, but fences weren't necessary to hold her. She was home and didn't stray. Ole Shug, he thought, was a keeper.

"I reckon," Butchie said, "that if you were to loan me this here mule to coon hunt every once in a while, I could get you a good discount on one a those pull-along barbeque grills my brother-in-law makes. Their real nice, come mounted right on the trailer. You can cook about 50 pound of meat, five or six briskets in 'em. Man, they're nice," Butchie finished, while the smoky tang of barbeque brisket slow roasting over mesquite or pecan wood seemed to materialize and waft through the air of the Dog Trade, overwhelming even the real smell of biscuits and gravy for sale a few hundred feet away. Later in the day they would begin selling ham hock and beans with corn bread. Even later than that, if business slowed at the Dog Trade eating place but people were still milling about, they'd throw a few onions on the grill because the aroma of fried onions would always call to the customers, bringing them back around.

Big Butchie Lindsey's brother-in-law didn't do much else, but he did build nice tow-behind grills. And Butchie, they both knew, was telling the truth. The grills cooked so much meat at one time that a man could nearly make a living just pulling his grill around from place to place, following the Weekenders' activities and selling them barbequed meat. Butchie's brother-in-law just cooked for his family. The grills were as popular as anything else that could be bought in southern Oklahoma that late summer of 2009. It was a nice offer, and it would have been a fair trade.

Unfortunately, it wasn't an offer that would help them solve the problem that had brought them and Ole Sugar to the Dog Trade. The necessity for selling Ole Shug arose from a transitory financial problem, one that the pay from two weeks' work in the oilfield could easily solve. But oilfield money was uncertain money, and Mary and John didn't ever go to the casinos, though they did like to smile a little about the irony presented by the thick stream of white middle class money the casinos funneled back onto the Nations, where John and Mary believed most of it belonged anyhow.

There had been too long a lull in work for John that spring and then too many lulls once the rig had gone back to drilling. Their thin cushion of savings was spent. Likely, John would go right back to work, and likely there would be enough money to make the mortgage payments and feed the other livestock throughout the winter, but likely wasn't surely, and the hard won credit worthiness they had spent ten years striving to establish at their bank could be lost with just one missed payment. The specter of snow coating hungry animals they might be unable to feed or care for was too horrible for either of them to even consider. They had some family, of course, but Mary's father was retired and living on a fixed income, and most of the other relatives had given up trying to mine a living in far southern Oklahoma and had moved up north to either of the major cities. Selling off Shug, they thought, would be less painful than the daily stress of not being prepared for winter, and if done properly, an action they could undo later, a payday loan without the crippling interest rate.

Normally, they subsidized the winter's expenses, expected and otherwise, with earnings from the previous year's pecan crop, but the pecan crop had failed in '08. During other years when the pecans didn't make, they had just economized and gotten by because of John's income, but as bad luck often follows more bad luck, earlier in the year when the price per barrel for oil had finally again rose high enough to make it profitable to begin drilling but not profitable enough to maintain all the hands at their former rates of pay, John and his crew, as had all the other crews on the rig, had agreed amongst themselves to take a voluntary pay cut to keep the fifth hand working on the floor of the oil rig. Every hand anted up four dollars an hour, and the fifth hand, known to everyone as, "the Worm," had been allowed to keep his job. Mary was proud of her husband and the others when John relayed the story. She knew they could have kept their rates of pay and sacrificed the fifth hand's job, but they were all third or forth generation Okie roughnecks, and they thought hard and moved slowly before they did anything that would take a man's living from him. And now they had gone back to work, but not steadily and not long enough for them to dig out from the year's setbacks. As for Mary she usually gardened, worked the pecans, and kept the accounts in order for the small ranch operation, none of which was generating an income just then. Mary would tell you it wasn't much of an operation, though, just a small ranch held together mostly with baling wire and duct tape, most precious to them, nonetheless.

The Dog Trade crowds have an ebb and flow that seems to make time pass on a slightly different clock in the shady valley alongside Rock Creek where the trade is conducted early every Sunday morning. And more time than she realized had passed before Mary finally saw Amy, one of their neighbors, who seemed to be making her way toward where Ole Shug stood beside the lawn chairs, her halter slack, her eyes calm and curious. Ole Shug hadn't traveled much, but like most mules, she traveled well. For a while, Mary watched Amy amble through the jagged line of booths stuffed to overflowing with plants, dogs, piñatas, and all else any local could conceive of selling for a profit or desiring to be rid of in a trade or otherwise. Mary's vantage point made Amy's blonde head seemed to weave and bob, and then a moment later continue meandering, apparently disembodied, along the unpaved midway of the Dog Trade, caught in that ebb and flow of trading, visiting, selling, looking, eating, laughing, and buying.

When Amy's head, distinctively light blonde and curly, caught John's eye, Mary remarked to her husband, "There's neighbor Amy coming. Bohr goats are what she's really in to. You remember how nice she keeps her yard? All that yard to mow on her own, working fulltime and raising her daughters, running her whole place and still and all her yard always mowed smooth like a carpet. Even the marigolds on her porch have stalks the same length with the same number of blooms on them just to look tidy for her. She wouldn't buy a mule, I don't think, John. She's got no use for one."

"Why Mary! Everybody has a use for a mule. Look at all Ole Shug has done for us over the years," John exclaimed, watching Amy coming toward them and thinking of how a mule he didn't want to sell could be of use to one of their neighbors, so that even if they did have to sell her, they would be able to watch over her care until they could buy her back if she still wanted to come home.

Mary's father had given Ole Shug to them along with a loaner mule shortly after they were married so that they could break new ground for a garden spot. Nothing breaks ground better than a pair of mules and a plow. After the first couple of years, they returned the loaner mule since two-mule plowing is only necessary when the ground is first broken. After that, one good sugar mule can pull the plow alone, and Ole Shug did, fall and spring for the last fifteen years of their marriage. He wondered how many gardens had failed during that time. Theirs would have dried up and long since become red dust and vegetation blowing with the wind across the hills if not for Mary. She had the green thumb, more like the whole arm he sometimes thought, maybe because she had been a Green before he married her or maybe because she could not have children.

He remembered how Mary had a plan for their futures so detailed that when she told it to him, he was flattered because he knew she had given the matter long and concentrated thought. She told him how they could use the five acres his father was giving them as a wedding present as collateral for a mobile home, small but efficient, to live in at first. They would build barns and pens, and she would raise a suckling pig and maybe a calf too, each year for their meat. She would see to the garden in which she planned to raise almost all of their vegetables. She would can. She had estimated that the savings from this toil, combined with what she could make at pecans and he in the oilfield would allow them to buy 40 more acres a few years down the road, and the income from those acres, in hay, pecans, and livestock would pay for a bigger, nicer house in 10 or 12 years. He thought it was fine plan. He thought that if you added a few children to it, then it was a plan that included everything he had ever hoped to accomplish. He didn't mind that it was a dawn to dusk workday everyday she had planned. His mind's eye saw only a well-kept red brick house shaded and saluted by tall, proud pecan trees, surrounded by railroad tie fencing around the front yard, and submerged into a manicured, verdant lawn, looking like it had been trimmed with scissors and swept with a broom. It all looked like riches and abundance beyond his imaginings, and Mary looked like the wife who would pull the yoke in tandem with him to finish the work required to make it happen. Mary looked like love to him.

John Jr. and Mary Jean were married in the spring of 1992, ten years after the first bust in the oilfields and ten years before the next boom. They both carried inside them an acute awareness of the transience of economic security to be found in work off the home place along with a keen and knowledgeable respect for what a ranching life fraught with demands and disappointments wrested out of those who chose to live it. Hence Mary had taken classes in business management from the nearest college, had become a great proponent of systems theory, and had always taken a multi-strategy approach to their finances. From the outset she planned for them to diversify their income streams. They would be a couple who demonstrated the old saw that, "there is more than one way to skin a cat," a phrase they both hated for its cruelty and stupidity since, as everyone knows, cats are part of the ranch and farm home team, catching and eating the rats and mice that would otherwise eat the grain used to feed the stock, indispensable defensive team players for country living, handsome, hearty, and clean.

And they had planted and tended all the seeds for that garden and those plans. The red dirt was good to them. Mary's eye was always on the horizon. Like most gardeners, she did nothing in the present and everything with her mind on the next season or even the season after that. Southern Oklahoma was mostly kind to them and given the long growing season, was especially kind to their plans for growing food.

Amy had seen John and Mary and what looked, through the crowded booths and at such a distance, like their mule behind them, but until she was nearly upon them, she wasn't certain what or whom

she had actually seen. Amy was short-sighted. The defect made her
seem harried at all times, perhaps because she couldn't see what was
coming at her and had grown jumpy because of it. Mary also
suspected that the jumpiness might be why Amy, a handsome,
hardworking woman with a nice ranch had yet found no man to
replace the one who had left her, without warning and permanently,
to live in Texas in an RV park. There was a good deal of speculation
about his departure, but no digging and sifting of the should, would,
and could haves, including Amy's own, had turned up any solid
answers or other women. He was just a ghost, a gone man. He wasn't
even known to stop by to visit when his trucker's route brought him
along Interstate 35, within just a few miles of the home and ranch
they had both invested all of their savings to buy. Locals wondered at
him, unable to grasp what he had done or why he had done it. As far
as anyone knew, and in that part of Oklahoma anyone knew quite a
lot about everyone's business, he had just wanted to leave the
marriage so much that he was willing to leave that weighty
investment behind in lieu of a noisy, cramped RV park, left without
knowing she would stay on and work the ranch, connected to the
land and the animals in some way that he just wasn't.

"Amy," John greeted her enthusiastically, a man very much
permanently present. "Now how are those goats doing over at your
place?" he asked, preparing the lead-in for his pitch. He wanted to
get it just right for Amy because John thought that Amy's would be
an ideal home for Shug. They could see Amy's place from theirs, and,
to John, single women were intrinsically transient and likely to need
to take off at any time, which might create an opportunity to retrieve
Shug sooner rather than later.

"Hey Mary!" Amy replied, always happy to see Mary, as most
folks were, "and hello John. Not so good. They have had the scours
and aren't putting on weight like we'd like them to. I've got a new
medicine I am trying, and we changed out their feed, so I guess we
will see," Amy answered, the furrow of worry, nowadays omnipresent
on her brow, in recent years had begun only to deepen rather than
appear and retreat when something concerned her, causing her to
wear a wrinkle belonging to a much older woman.

She worked for the local veterinarian, so she always had a new
medicine she was trying out. And she had false modesty concerning

her goat herd. It was roundly considered one of the best in an area rife with Bohr goat herds. Her daughters routinely brought home Grand or Reserve Grand ribbons at all the 4-H shows. By any standard, she was a fine keeper of goats. Modesty, abandonment, and that fear of what might be coming at her that she couldn't see yet, had exhorted a considerable toll on her well-being, hence also her confidence.

Mary had seen it happen to many good women before, so early on in life she had decided not to let it happen to her. Once Mary had a plan, there would be action. Hence, she gave a lot of her time, worry, and service to God. She cultivated her faith. She liked the Buddha, kept a small statue of him in her kitchen window where she occasionally rubbed his belly—not for luck but for amusement. He looked like a reliable friend to her, rotund and witty. She had quietly and privately read some of Buddha's words and was always struck by how much those words seemed in tandem with the words from the Bible. Buddha said that, "What we think, we become," and in this she thought he agreed with the first words of The Gospel According to Saint John were it says that in the beginning was the Word and the Word was God. Further, Christ said he gave us only one new commandment, to love one another, and Mary could not see substantial difference between that one commandment and Buddha's first law commanding us to be kind. Over time, she had come to suspect that Buddha and Jesus were up in heaven, just sitting under a tree, fishing and visiting about some point of human spiritual awareness or another, just gabbing away the afternoons, lazy like and full of pure love. She once thought to ask her preacher, Finus Steelman, if he might think so too, but she knew he must. He was a smart man, a finer preacher never did preach any gospel and a good looking man, too, when he was alive.

If her thoughts about Buddha gave her any pause or aroused any of her more slender-minded friends or family to question her faith, she would always say, "I know I am a Baptist and a Christian 'cause I was married in the First Baptist Church, right in front of God and everybody, by none other than Finus Steelman. Three, and sometimes four, generations of Greens been married and buried by that preacher. I reckon he'd a noticed had I lapsed." and then a lull in conversation would always come after the invocation of Steelman's name as he was most respected and had lived a long, productive, Christian life, a life above reproach, sprinkled with insurmountable obstacles that never stopped him, and crowned with love and hope. None questioned Finus's faith.

"Have the coyotes bothered the goats much, Amy?" John asked, sliding in another helpful segue to his sales pitch.

"No. We had some trouble back before we got our little jack ass. When we just had the sheep, we nearly couldn't keep them all alive for a day at a time, but that little jack we got now goes right after the coyotes, and it helps that goats are a lot tougher than sheep," Amy said.

"I never knew as you had any goats," Mos Chigley snapped as he walked up alongside Ole Shug, his voice mean enough to make them all jump, even over the din of the Dog Trade. Mos was grumpy all the time and on principle always doubted anyone's story. Amy could have been riding a Bohr billy—and she was small enough to do it—and leading two nannies with kids behind her, and Mos still would have said the same thing. He was a man who asked his own questions and took nothing for granted. He didn't come from Oklahoma, and it drained any native of his surfeit of courtesy to tolerate Mos for more than a few minutes. Luckily, when Mos had left California with his parents back in the forties, he had landed in one of the few places where there was enough courtesy to support him. He might not have grown to old age elsewhere.

John knew the same two things about Mos that everyone else knew. Mos subsidized his small social security retirement by earning money from the Weekender population, those city dwellers from Dallas or Oklahoma City who kept vacation homes around the lakes and mountains. He made this money, and most locals found this just incredible, by telling the Weekenders how stupid he thought they were. This was mostly an unpleasant experience for the Weekenders, so Mos was a man always on the lookout for new opportunities to get to interact with them, any reason he could find to get them to ring his phone with a need that would invite him on into their lives. He vigilantly watched them to learn their habits. Then he found companion services he could provide for them. He didn't mind collecting their city money while he explained their mistakes, ignorance, and lack of insight to them either, but a man would be hard-pressed to say just which meant more to Mos, the explaining or the money. He called this occupation, "Worrying the Weekenders," and the second thing everyone knew about him was that he managed to make it pay, year after year, failed project after failed project. And if any of the Weekenders figured out his game and thought not to pay him in reward for his incompetence and flimflam, Mos quickly summons them to small claims court, another environment he thrived in, and commenced to tie up so much of their time that the sensible ones who had put a pencil to it and knew the value of their own time, just paid him off and considered the payment a tuition fee for learning that not every old man fix-it man was an honorable one. It unsettled them somewhat until they remembered that he wasn't from Oklahoma.

"This here mule can run rabbits, tree coon, she can jump a fence, and she can pull a plow should you want to use an old time plow, nothing better to get a good start on your vegetable garden. Never can get the soil broken with a tiller the way you can with a mule and a plow," John finally got to recite his pitch to a person who was listening. However, he didn't add that he'd seen Weekenders with gardens.

Unfortunately, Mos was not only listening, he was, in John's estimation, exactly not the buyer he wanted for Shug. For all his sixty-odd years there, Mos was still an outlander. He lived a few valleys over from Mary and John's place, so they couldn't keep an eye on Shug, and Mos was mean. John felt like he just couldn't know for sure that Mos wouldn't beat a mule, even a good one. John's pitch, finally given, was flat, and his eternal positivity was not audible.

"Mos," Mary asked, "how have you been? We haven't seen you since that time up to Wal-Mart's, and that must have been over a year ago."

The Wal-Mart Corporation had inadvertently provided Mos with his current great passion and pastime when it built the local superstore. When Mos wasn't working at Worrying the Weekenders, he went up to the local Wal-Mart Superstore and played Torture the Tourists. Once opened, the local Wal-Mart gave Mos a venue replete with unlimited access to innumerable people he believed were in need of his advice. No longer was he limited to interaction with only those Weekenders desperate enough to engage his questionable and often instantly developed handyman expertise. Behind his back, the locals, believing that electricians could not be trained in less than a week nor plumbers overnight, called Mos, "a Goddamned dangerous jackleg," and did not hire him to fix their homes.

"Oh, that half-assed store. I was in there this morning, and I couldn't find a thing. They move the merchandise around every night so's the next day people can't find anything and buy more than they need lookin' for what stuff's been moved overnight. It's a cryin' shame that's the way they do business," Mos answered, "and Mary, I'm tellin' you those clerks up there, they don't know were nothing is. I was lookin' for some medicine for my arthritis, you know I've got the arthritis from working on that one stupid SOB Weekender's lateral lines last spring when all that rain fell, and I must of spent two hours searching for some liniment for it. Never did find it. Bought a bottle of stuff I found on the dog aisle. . ."

"Why Mos, that's not safe," Mary said, busying herself with packing up the lawn chairs.

Butchie and Amy had long since done the Okie Shuffle, a southern soft shoe step used when one cannot tolerate being around a person but also is too polite to show it. During the Okie Shuffle, one typically recalls "things" that need doing and unobtrusively shuffles off to do them. A few more prospects had walked by John and Shug, nodding and shuffling on at the sight or sound of Mos. So, by now the shadows were starting and the Dog Trade crowd, mostly an early, early morning bunch, had thinned, and Mary thought this an opportune time to slide away from Mos's vitriol.

"You had better just dump that stuff down the drain before you poison yourself," she told him, wondering how many souls on this earth would be sadder if he did and then immediately trying to muster up some shame for thinking such a thought.

Driving home from the Dog Trade, Mary occasionally looked back at the horse trailer they towed behind the truck. At the Wild Horse Creek bridge on Ruppe Road, when they both glanced back at the trailer, John and Mary became aware of an almost imperceptible shift that calmed everything, a change as subtle but colossal as Wild Horse Creek's red bottom dirt giving up its course in response to the unrelenting power of the surging water swollen with the run off from heavy rains. The Wild Horse can change course entirely, uproot and move whole trees, and create new undertows all in a matter of hours if the rainfall is heavy enough, yet on the creek's surface little will have appeared to change. The only change an observer might note is a steady and gentle rise in the creek's level, but the river rats say that the Wild Horse's steep banks of slick red clay and sand make it hard for a man to climb out if he has slipped into the water, but what kills even quicker is the undertow created when the swift water hits the banks at a 90 degree angle at the many hairpin turns, which give the creek its name, Wild Horse. This gauntlet area is called a suck hole, and it collects debris and cycles around in a whirlpool. In the Wild Horse, people are another form of debris that gets caught and pulled down. The river rats say the Wild Horse has drowned many. Safe in the cab of the truck, the windows closed against the heat, everything had changed. Their bills were still due and overdue. Livestock still needed hay and feed. Winter was still scheduled for a little later in the year, but something was different to her, softer somehow, less hard-scrabble, more Matthew 6:28.

Mary looked at her husband, thinking his brow was furrowed in problem-solving concentration, and said, "You know, they have that livestock auction up at Pauls Valley the first Saturday of every month. I guess we could take Shug up there next weekend."

"Yeah, and they have one of those Predatory Loan Companies up there, too. Maybe we could just take out another loan," he suggested.

Mary laughed at his deliberate malapropism and said, "You're right. It's the only thing to do. I never did want to part with Ole Shug anyhow."

"You are my sugar mule, Mary. You are exactly that, sweet sugar mule," he said as he turned into the gravel driveway of their home in the ebbing light. They pulled in against what to them was just another sunset, most all so lovely that Mary had to think of them as God's triptychs, striking, moving, soaring visual symphonies, every one unlike any other, moving across the early evening sky, blaring color, blending hues, uplifting all the souls of Southern Oklahoma, at least those souls who saw them from her vantage point on the north side of the pass through the Arbuckles.

John didn't notice the symphony of sky too much, although he did smile at it for a while, standing there in its warm ambiance beside his wife, before he opened the trailer to unload Shug. His smile was constant and his step was light. He was distracted by feelings of happiness and good fortune because his wife so often saw things his way. He knew they would find some way to get through this temporary tight spot. He knew they could do anything they agreed they wanted to do because they always had.

Big Butchie Lindsey had coon hunted along just about every easy walking draw in the hills around their homes. A good walking draw, according to Butchie, was one where he could walk on the hard ground on the edge of the timber, briars, and prairie meadows while his dogs ran the draws. On a bright night, close to the full moon back in August when the dragon's breath days made only a night walk tolerable, Butchie had taken a young Red Bone hound for a walk on a leash to get him used to night walks and hunting. Occasionally, the dog would stop and sniff around, and Butchie let him because that is exactly what he wanted to train the dog to do. Butchie liked a full moon night for walking and thinking because he didn't have to use his wheat light at all. It was at one of the dog's pauses for sniffing that Butchie had glanced up toward the back of John and Mary's place. He understood by the amount of hay stored behind the barn and the number of bred heifers in the back pasture, that they didn't have enough hay put back for the winter. The heifers would begin calving soon. He walked on with the dog trying to remember ever having known John and Mary to have taken a gamble on anything. The low of the heifers faded as he walked the dog and concentrated, maybe on keeping his footing in the moonlight, or maybe on other things. He was known to think a lot.

John and Mary were a comic sight as they rounded the back of the barn, Shug following them sans lead rope, more dog than mule, to the pasture behind the barn. They were startled to see Big Butchie Lindsey's trailer, loaded full of round hay bales and parked behind their barn. He was waiting for them to come home so he could use their tractor to unload the hay.

He tells them, "I had a few extra bales this year that didn't sell right off. I thought y'all could use 'em. I didn't want to see them go to waste, so I thought, if it was alright with y'all, I'd just credit them to you and then when you sell off your steers in the spring, well then maybe you can give me back some hay.

He admired Ole Shug because sometimes he hunted the Arbuckle Mountains where a man needed a surefooted mule to get through the cedars and avoid the long walks to get around to where the dogs had a coon treed.

"And I'd like to hunt that there sugar mule some, if'n y'all don't mind, when I go to coon huntin'. I got a load 'a grain in the back of the truck that a fella I know had bought for a racehorse he had that got hit by a car an' had to be put down. I reckon you ought to feed yer mule up on that this winter 'cause if yer hunting a mule you got to feed it well."

TERRY FORD

My Life, My Lake

Just to sit and gaze upon a mammoth boulder near the water's edge was to gaze at a tapestry of rich colors—the greens, golds, and browns of mossy growth, the glinting flicker of bits of granite, and tell-tale marks of water lines from seasons past. The warmth of the midday sun in a cloudless Oklahoma sky, soft sand between my toes, and the sparkling shimmer off the water—these have been essential elements in my life since early childhood. What era of my existence has not involved an Oklahoma lake?

John Lubbock, British statesman, once commented, "Earth and sky, woods and fields, lakes and rivers, the mountain and the sea, are excellent schoolmasters, and teach some of us more than we can ever learn from books." Then there must be much to learn in Oklahoma!

Over the years I came to appreciate the expanse of Eufaula's 600 miles of shoreline, the joy of jetting around Tenkiller, the fantastic fishing at Foss, the medieval-style fortress at Lake Murray, the rich history of Roman Nose, the surge of the breeze sailing across Lake Hefner, the autumn rainbow of leaves at Greenleaf Lake, the delicate beauty of Price Falls, and the happiness of a swimmin' hole at Turner Falls, but my lake—the one in my backyard—was at Quartz Mountain State Park.

"Kids, grab your swimsuits. We're gonna go to Lugert today," my mom would announce, to squeals of glee from me and my brother. Just like the old-timers and locals, we call it "Lugert," named for the town that was covered when the lake was formed, although its official name is Lake Altus. Occasionally we would enjoy a small picnic with just our family, but more often than not, a trip to Lugert meant a big gathering of friends and cousins, involving roasted hot dogs, swimming and three-wheeling. Oh, and how long was that trip down to the water's edge across hot sand, carrying mom's excruciatingly heavy beach bag or cumbersome lawn chair? But no matter how tired my arm or how deep the sand, I always knew at the end of that trek was joy unbounded! Playing in the sand, feeling weightless floating as mom's hand gently propped up the arch of our backs, jumping off dad's shoulders as mom confirmed for the umpteenth time that she was *indeed* watching—the memories are as clear now as a spring sky.

Fast-forwarding to the summer I turned sweet sixteen, I can remember the happy banter of my three best girlfriends, the wind in our hair, the freedom of the road curving out before us, and the lustrous shine on the hood my red-orange '65 convertible Mustang. Clad in our swimsuits, we soaked up the sun as we made our first "road trip" (sans parents) through the grasslands and irrigated fields toward the ancient mountains where my lake was nestled. During college, a trip to the lake meant a welcome respite from studying, a celebration of youth, and as dusk fell, perhaps a moonlit romance might blossom to the steady rhythm of soft wavelets lapping against the shore. The evening sky ablaze with color would flash tongues of orange and pink fire across the golden water, as only an Oklahoma sunset can. It's no wonder that when we girls dreamed of white lace and the happiest day of our lives, our plans included a lakeside wedding day, cabins filled with guests, and the breathtaking natural beauty of the shimmering sunset upon the water as a backdrop to the awesomeness of the occasion.

Soon there were my own children to introduce to the lake, and "Baby's First Trip to Lugert" became a home video classic. Then we took the plunge and bought a boat of our very own, becoming "invested" in the lake—and what adventures lay ahead after filling the boat with tents, sleeping bags, charcoal, hot dogs and marshmallows?

"Did you remember the matches?"

"Don't worry. We'll stop at that little store in Granite and pick some up. I have to stop there anyway to buy minnows."

"You brought all those fishing poles? You only have two hands."

"Honey, a man's gotta do what a man's gotta do."

How could we do it all? Water skiing, tubing, knee boarding, swimming, paddle-boating, water-sliding, putt-putt, *and* fishing? But somehow it all gets packed into a fun-filled Oklahoma weekend, along with some "lazing about" in a rusty three-fold reclining lawn chair in about six inches of water, watching clouds take on imaginary shapes, or if especially industrious, perhaps reading a good book, as the scent of tropical coconut oil fills the sun-baked air.

The next lake phase came when mom and dad bought that motor home, and they would take it down to the lake several days in advance to get the best spot, closest to the water. The kids would nearly die with anticipation until we could join grandma and grandpa on the weekend. Mom would have the coals ready and the hamburger patties formed up by the time we got there, and the delicious scent of smoke from the sizzle of the burgers would be the only thing that could drag the kids out of the water. Nothing topped off a meal like the short walk to the little store at the lake for the taste of a vanilla ice-cream cone.

As summer gives way to fall, the change of seasons makes the lake a cornucopia of color. The crisp crunch of leaves under a hiking boot, the musty scent of the earth where Kiowa and Comanche tribes had wintered, and the scuttle of woodland creatures makes the lake a year-round retreat. An exhilarating horseback ride through God's country is one of our favorite fall lodge memories. I'm told the park boasts of 29 tree varieties and 140 wildflower species.

One year there was a wonderful gift from grandmother—a sojourn aboard the Quartz Mountain Flyer, an authentic train ride past the lake and beautiful granite mountain range. What a fun trip (and history lesson) for the grandchildren. Then to welcome in a new millennium, we spent a wintry eve wrapped in a colorful Indian blanket, enjoying the reflection of a crackling fire in a champagne glass. As the apple falls and the clock ticks an exit for Grandfather Time, Dick Clark can keep his Times Square—I'll take the woodsy aroma of logs on the fireplace at an Oklahoma lodge to welcome in the new year.

My family's latest phase in lake-loving is helping my brother enjoy his cabin at Ft. Cobb. Yes, he's gone *Thoreau* on us and moved to the pond. As the famous American naturalist wrote, "An early-morning walk is a blessing for the whole day." What is it about lake air that makes you feel like rising early? Actor Johnny Depp once remarked, "I'm an old-fashioned guy . . .I want to be an old man with a beer belly sitting on a porch looking at a lake or something." I hear you, Johnny. There is little better than to recline on one's own lake-view porch and anticipate the hushed buzz of hummingbirds darting through to nip from the pinks of the Mimosa branches.

Now into my fourth decade of this love affair with the lake, I wonder if there will ever be a time when the lake and its amenities will not be a part of my life. I look forward to hiking by the falling trickle of the dam, playing a round of golf past deer and rabbit, or stealing away for a cozy winter weekend well into my next four decades.

The American novelist Hamlin Garland may have said it best when he wrote, "I remember a hundred lovely lakes, and recall the fragrant breath of pine and fir and cedar and poplar trees. The trail has strung upon it, as upon a thread of silk, opalescent dawns and saffron sunsets." The lake is a thread that runs through my life, and I can't imagine my family album without snapshots of our life on an Oklahoma lake.

JOSH GAINES

Dog Days Kid

I spent my summers sticky-sap handed,
Exploring the hurricane tipsy pines
Of that brackish country,
That delta country,
Where air is sweat
And sweet is tea,
Where neck is sunset
And red is ground,
Where foot is weight
And pedal is fast
And lightning is drunk
By the "Ball" fruit jar full.

Where I, full of the accumulated
Sun-born intoxicants of my only five years
(The beach shifting walls
Of my imagination),
Followed the ants,
Just two ants
Carrying a whole prickle backed caterpillar
Back to their black-eyed queen.

Those were the only days
I ever felt at home,
Beneath stories that grew
Even faster than me.
And there—big glasses, big eyed—
I was,
Every story's hero
In stories
More embarrassing every time I heard them,
And they told them like they were new
EVERY time I visited.

"Yes sir,"
I tell the rocking chairs,
Rocking Sunday room soon-tomb souls
To the background whirr
Of grandma's mad quilting
"Never truly felt at home since,"
And one soul nods
And the folks around him,
They nod too,
Necks going from wrinkly
To wrinkly-er
And back again
Like a bayou accordion
Because they know, in their
Storm bones,
Exactly what I mean—

This close to the end
Is just like being
Kid-close to the beginning,
Again.
And here in the middle, me
Treading time like anchored jelly fish,
With a foot in the past
And a hope,
That when I begin my last beginning
I may remember,
Amid cicada days and bullfrog nights,
Feeling at home.
And that I may forget,
The stories that embarrassed me the most,
First.

JOHN GIFFORD

Fresh Paint

After lunch, me and Melvin ride our bikes up to the little stand. It's part grocery store, part fruit stand. There is fruit and beer everywhere, flies buzzing around the tomato baskets, baby chicks and bunnies in the spring. But my grandma calls it the little stand. She lives a couple of blocks away and I stay with her during the summer. Grandma sends me up here for bread or milk, but they've got the coldest pop in Mienwell, Louisiana. Forty cents a bottle.

There's this house that sits right behind the stand and we dump our bikes in the backyard, pass through a hole in the fence to get there. We don't park the bikes at the stand because Melvin says someone will steal them.

Inside, I reach down into the cooler and grab a bottle of sarsaparilla. Melvin gets cream soda. His bottle is clear and the pop is a weird kind of blue, like electricity. Makes me think something's going to happen when he opens the top. When we put the bottles on the counter to pay, the guy starts quizzing us.

"You old enough to drink that stuff?" he asks me. There's a grin on his face that reminds me of my dad when he was living with me and mom. He used to play jokes on her all the time, hide her stuff. That's when he wasn't drinking. He's been gone a long time.

"Yep," I tell him.

"What does it taste like?" he asks me.

"Huh?"

"What does sasp'rilla taste like? You're old enough to drink it you should know."

I look at Melvin. He's always giving me tips about something.

"I don't know," he says, raising his shoulders. "I'm drinking cream soda."

What do I say? I picked it because it looks different. Never tasted it before.

"Root beer," says the man. Grinning, he rings up the pop and I give him the money. "Y'all stay out of trouble, now."

We take our pop and walk out of the air conditioning, past the green tomatoes, and the red ones next to them. Some are so red they are almost purple.

Outside, the grass around the stand is covered with old junk. It's starting to turn brown and die. They call the stuff antiques, but all of it's rusted and I never see anyone look at anything. Plus, it's way too expensive. They want twenty-five dollars for this old saw blade that has a smiley face painted on it. And the blade is missing some teeth. Crazy.

Well, we stand there next to the junk and drink our pop. There's a trash barrel out back with flies buzzing all around. Smells like bacon grease and old bananas. I look at all the watermelons and cantaloupe, kick them, try to tell which ones are ripe. I'm halfway through with my pop before Melvin gives me the tip of the day.

"That's not how you hold your bottle," he says. He's always telling me things like this. "Like this. Watch." He takes a drink. "See? You keep your top lip between the bottle and your teeth. That way if anyone comes up and whacks the end of the bottle you won't break your teeth on the glass."

"Far out."

Melvin says there's always someone waiting to jump us, to steal our money, beat us up. I've never seen them. Mienwell is a cotton town and most of the people here are old and retired, or out in the fields working. Everyone's pretty nice around here. But Melvin says they're all around us and that they come out of the woodwork if they see you with your guard down. I'm not sure where he has seen people like this, maybe over in Vicksburg, or on TV. I figure I'm pretty safe to drink with the bottle next to my teeth, but if anyone comes around I'll remember his advice and slip my lip between them.

"Hey, I've got a good idea," he says. "Come on, and don't throw your bottle away."

"Why not?"

"Just trust me," he says. "You'll need it."

We leave the flies and the smell of fruit, crawl through the hole in the fence and into the backyard where our bikes are stashed. The house looks empty when we ride by. The window curtains don't move and the driveway is empty. It's like the house went to sleep. I don't know who lives here. Never seen them. But the grass is always cut.

Out on the street we ride with our bottles in hand. Judging from the direction we're going I can tell we're headed to the old cotton gin at the edge of town.

"Squirrels," says Melvin. "I know where we can find some squirrels."

"Cool," I say. I don't know what he's got planned, but I'm up for anything. Besides, I've got lots of time. Mom's working until late this evening.

***

When we get to the gin yard we ditch our bikes next to the railroad tracks. Then we follow a little dirt trail in among the dusty buildings. The buildings are all pretty old, cracked white paint, tin roofs. The grass is thick and green just about everywhere except for in between the buildings. Here, the grass is worn down and there are dirt trails where the trucks and trailers drive. Up ahead I can see the gin building, where they separate the cotton from the seeds, and right beside it is a small wooden building with a covered porch. I'm not sure, but I think this might be the office because there is an old truck parked next to it. Except for the truck, the gin yard looks empty right now. It should be because the farmers just planted in April. They don't harvest until August.

We slip into one of the warehouses and slide the big door shut.

"Leave it cracked so we have some light," says Melvin. I pull the door open enough so a nice beam of light shines in, then open it a little more in case we have to get out quick. It's pretty dark inside, and warm, and it smells like dirt and hay. There are a couple of windows on each wall, but they don't let in much light. I guess the glass is pretty dirty. When my eyes adjust to the dim light I can see there is hay in here, lots of it, and a dirt floor. There are two truck trailers parked in the middle of the building and they're both loaded with stacks of hay bales. Must be a hundred bales on each trailer.

"Hey, look what I found," says Melvin.

I walk over to the first trailer where he is crouching down by the wheels.

"More bottles."

"That's what you call a six-pack," he says.

"Six-pack of beer?"

"Budweiser. The good beer."

"Cool. What does it taste like?"

"We're not going to drink it. They're empty, anyway."

"What are we going to do with them?"

"I'll show you. Let's get up on top of this hay."

I follow Melvin onto the trailer and up the stacks of hay bales. These are the small, square bales, so they're easy to climb. I kick my feet into the space between the bales, step up to the next, grab the next one higher. The hay is pretty dusty and it causes me to sneeze a couple of times.

When we get to the top, I notice the rafters are right on top of our heads. If I raise my hands I can touch them. Then I see Melvin grabbing on to one, pulling himself up.

"Little bastards are up here. I know they are," he says.

It's exciting here in the barn, up on top of the hay. My stomach feels light and funny, and I feel sneaky, so I say it too. "Yeah, the little bastards are up here somewhere."

After a few minutes Melvin hops back down on the hay.

"They're here," he says. "We'll find them. All we have to do is throw a few bottles up into the rafters. We'll get them to come out. Then we'll light them up."

Melvin grabs one of the bottles and flings it into the black space between two of the rafter beams. It hits something and shatters.

"Okay, you fire one over that way," he says.

I pick up a bottle and throw it in the opposite direction. Same thing.

I stand and listen for a few seconds, trying to hear any sounds of squirrels rustling up in the rafters. Melvin grabs one of the beer bottles and throws it in a different direction. I sneeze again, then listen, ready to hear the bottle crash into the beams, explode. It seems like a few seconds have gone by and I'm wondering if I missed it. Then I hear the sound of the glass breaking. Lots of glass. Then I see why.

"You broke it!"

"Screw it," says Melvin. "Nobody here, anyway. Come on."

He grabs what is left of the beer bottles, climbs down the hay bales. When I get to the bottom, he hands me two of the bottles. "You go bust out those two windows over there."

"Me? Those windows?"

"Oh, don't worry about. Nobody here, anyway. That'll get the squirrels out."

I walk over to the nearest window. Just as I lift the bottle over my shoulder I hear glass breaking behind me. I fire. The glass makes a horrible racket, falls out of the window in huge, jagged pieces. For a second I get kind of nervous, peek out the window. It's quiet though. Doesn't seem to be anyone around. So I take the second bottle and run over to the last window. I'm just about to fire the beer bottle when I hear another sound.

"There they are!"

Melvin must have found the squirrels. I turn and see the light inside the warehouse getting brighter. Then I see someone pushing the sliding door open. I take off and run to the door on the other end of the building. Melvin is already there, pushing it open. The bright light hurts my eyes, and I have a hard time seeing. But I can run all right, like a deer.

"You kids come back here!" shouts the man. He's somewhere behind us, but I don't stop to look. "Hey you kids! Get back here!"

I grab my bike and take off running. Then I jump on. But when I do, my left foot misses the pedal and I slide off the seat and onto the top tube. I rack myself, hard. Melvin is ahead of me, speeding away. For a few seconds I'm all jammed up. Can't do anything. Can't move. I'm just coasting with the bike. The pain shoots up from my crotch into my stomach. My heart is speeding and my mouth feels dry. I feel pretty stupid. Racking yourself is the worst.

Finally, the bike slows enough so that I can put a foot down, stand up off the top tube and grab the pedal with my other foot. I take off, trying to catch Melvin. The pain in my crotch and stomach is wearing off. When I catch up to him, I notice he is sitting up in his seat and grinning.

"Take it easy, Mike. He was an old man. He can't catch us."

"I don't know, Melvin." I look back over my shoulder, glad to see no one behind us. "He was pretty mad."

I notice a couple of cows beside the road. They are Black Angus and one of them is poking its head through the barbed-wire fence. The cow stretches it neck, sticks out its tongue, trying to get the thick green grass in the ditch.

Then I hear the sounds of an engine revving. I turn back and see the truck from the gin yard pulling onto the road about two blocks back.

"Here he comes!" I yell. I stand on the pedals and spin them as fast as I can, throwing the handlebars side to side. My arms and legs feel cold and shaky all of a sudden, even though it's hot.

Soon we're back in town and flying past the houses on either side of the road. Then I remember the getaway place Melvin showed me a few weeks ago. I guess he remembers it too, because a few seconds later we're shooting down a side street. I look back and see the pickup turning the corner, engine clattering.

We finally make it to the getaway house, where we turn in and ride through the backyard, under a clothesline, into another backyard and out onto the next street. It's the only place on the whole block where you can get through like that. No fences.

"See you later, Mike," says Melvin.

"See ya."

I ride down the street, cut over on another and then down an alley. The man in the pickup is gone. Two minutes later I'm at my grandma's house, out of breath, drenched in sweat.

***

"Well lookie there," says Grandma. She looks up from her crocheting, sees my sweaty red face. I feel like an angels-food cake in the oven. I don't know how she can stand it with the air conditioner on the lowest setting. The smell of bacon is still strong from this morning's breakfast.

"Hey Grandma," I say, in between gulps of water. Then I open the refrigerator, pour some iced tea, because water never does the job.

"You haven't been running with that old Melvin, have you?"

"No, Grandma. Just riding bikes."

Silence while she thinks of another question.

"Well, you shouldn't run with that old Melvin. He likes to get into trouble."

Everything is "That old" no matter how young or good it is: that old boy who works up at the little stand, the one who lets his hair grow a little too long; them old Germans down the street who keep a bottle of liquor in their house; them old weeds that spring up in the driveway, even though they're covered with an inch-thick layer of gravel; that old pipe that Uncle Gus smokes, the one that stinks up the house whenever he and Aunt Mabel come to visit every August;

that old Melvin who I shouldn't run with, even though he's only a year older than me. And I'm only twelve.

Then she looks up at me. "That old boogey man will get you if you're out a running around."

***

The next day, I ride over to my mom's office. It's not really her office; it's Doctor Savage's. Mom's his secretary. Always sitting behind the typewriter punching keys like crazy. Sometimes, at night, she works down at the ER, filing and whatnot. Always telling me we need the extra money, asking me to spend the night with Grandma.

When I walk in she's got a phone jammed between her shoulder and ear, writing something on a notepad. She looks up, smiles. There's no one in the office this morning, but usually it's packed with women and girls. Some of them don't look much older than me.

I put my hands in my pockets, walk over to a bookcase that's filled with stacks of little brochures. One of them says *The Facts about STDs*. I figure it's about something Doc Savage takes care of. He's a —well, he's one of those kind of doctors.

"You're not in any trouble, are you?" asks Mom. She hangs up the phone, rips the message off the notepad and puts it in a basket.

"No, I haven't done anything." For a second I think of the old man from the gin yard. But she doesn't know about that. "I just wondered if I could go to the gameroom this afternoon and play games. Nothing else to do."

Then it hits me that I messed up. Shouldn't have said that. Usually, if I tell her there's nothing to do she starts in on all these things that I could do—pulling weeds, washing the car, cleaning my room.

"All right, as long as you're not running around with that Melvin."

"I'm not. He's fishing today."

"I see."

"You think we might be able to go fishing sometime?"

"We'll see when the time comes. Here, you'll need some money for the arcade." She gives me five dollars. I can spend all night in the gameroom with that. Have money left over in the morning. "Sweetie, I'm going to work late tonight in the ER. Can you spend the night with Grandma?"

"Yeah, I guess so."

"I promise we'll do something this weekend," she says. "Okay?"

"Yeah. Thanks, Mom."

"Stay out of trouble."

I leave Mom's office and on the way over to the gameroom I see someone familiar coming down the street. He's riding a bike and from the way he rides I can tell that it's Melvin. Melvin's not the most graceful guy on a bike; instead, he uses his muscles and pushes and powers the bike where he wants it to go. Watching him riding up the street, he reminds me of a monkey on a football. I heard somebody say that once. I think it was Melvin's old man.

"I thought you were fishing?" I shout.

"I was." He rides up next to me, hits the brakes, skids. "Fish weren't biting today. Plus, dad ran out of beer."

"Oh," I say. I've heard that before, too.

"Where you going?"

"The gameroom. You want to go?"

"I guess. I was going to ride up to the store and get a pop. You wanna ride up there, then swing back by the gameroom?"

"Yeah, I guess so."

So we ride over to the little stand, ditch our bikes in the backyard, hop through the hole in the fence and walk into the fruit stand, then into the air conditioning of the grocery store. The same guy from yesterday is behind the counter, watching a little black-and-white TV. It's really tiny and it reminds me of the CB in Melvin's dad's truck. I go with cream soda today because I don't feel like a lecture. Melvin gets the same and we both grab a Snickers.

"What do you say, guys?" asks the man. "Staying out of trouble this summer?"

"Yeah, we're trying," says Melvin.

We pay and walk outside, between the metal roof and green outdoor carpet, where there's so much fruit and vegetables I feel like we're in somebody's blender being made into a shake. I notice the tomatoes in the baskets have a lot of flies on them today.

When we get to the trash can behind the stand, Melvin gives me today's tip.

"Okay, take a bite of Snickers," he says. He's chewing with his mouth open (something my grandma tells me not to do) and is already halfway through his candy bar. "Okay, you got the Snickers in your mouth?"

I nod, crush the peanuts with my teeth.

"Now take a drink."

I lift the bottle and take a swallow. What's the big deal? I wonder.

"Isn't that cool?" he asks. "The foam? You feel the foam in your mouth?"

I nod yes and swallow.

"Now that foam will help you out if you ever get punched in the stomach," says Melvin. He points at my stomach, rolling his mouth like a cow rolls its cud. "Say somebody comes up and sucker punches you right in the gut. Feels like you swallowed a brick. Well, you eat a Snickers and drink a pop and get that foam in your mouth. Your stomach will feel way better."

"No kidding?"

"I ain't kidding."

By now I'm ready to get going to the gameroom. I have a lot of money to spend and games to play. But Melvin starts kicking around the watermelons and says he's got an idea.

"Hut, hut," he says. He grabs a melon like a center just hiked it to him, hands it off to me. "Through the line! Blast through the line! We need yardage!" He points at the hole in the fence.

I don't know what he's up to now, so I just stand there.

"What line?" I say.

He picks up a melon and takes off running down the trail, stiff-arming invisible opponents, then he dives through the hole in the fence. A couple of seconds later, he comes back through without the melon. I'm pretty sure it busted when he fell.

"Come on, let's get some more," he says, reaching for another watermelon.

I remember the gin yard from yesterday and I start to get nervous. I look around the place, but all I see is a bunch of old rusted junk, some boxes with lettuce that has turned brown. I grab a melon and duck my head through the fence.

When I get to the other side Melvin has them lined up next to the fence like green bombs. He's really busy, moving back and forth carrying watermelons. After a few minutes we've got ten, stacked up like firewood.

"All right," he says. "Keep a lookout. You see anybody coming you whistle like a quail."

"What are we going to do?"

Then he grabs one of the melons and takes off for this little shed on the other side of the yard. Just now I notice that its doors are open. Inside, I can see a bunch of old lawnmowers and gas cans. I guess someone does live in this house. But where are they?

Melvin gets to the shed. Then he grabs the melon with both hands, raises it over his head, lobs it inside. GUNK comes the sound as the melon hits one of the mower's engines, splits open, fruit spilling all over the place. Melvin's already running back, a grin on his face.

"Come on," he says.

I look over at the house, study the windows. Since we're not being watched, I grab a melon and join in. It's a heavy one and I put it up on my right shoulder, wrap my hands around its dusty skin. My stomach has that upside-down feeling again. My heart is starting to really thump and it's kind of exciting. If my mom saw me, I don't know what she'd do. But I'd be in serious trouble.

When I get to the shed, I can see the busted melon, the red slush and little seeds all over the mowers. Someone's going to be crazy-mad when they find this, I think. My heart is beating so fast that it's getting hard to breathe. But it's exciting. I raise the melon over my head and with both hands push it down onto the mowers. It explodes. Pieces of watermelon are everywhere.

I run back to the melons, grab another and take off to the shed. Then the yelling starts.

"Hey! Stop that right now!"

I drop my melon. Someone has walked into the backyard. It's an old man.

Melvin is closer to the shed than I am. He still has a melon in his hands. My stomach feels like it's trying to crawl up to my throat and my mouth feels dry again. I start walking toward the bikes. The old man stops, looks into the shed, them back to Melvin. He's wearing faded overalls, a blue cap and big glasses. He must be a hundred, I think. Then he points his crooked finger at Melvin, spits brown juice into the grass.

"You boys is messing up!" he yells. He takes a step forward, still pointing his finger at Melvin. "What in the hell do you call this?"

I move over to my bike, pick it up off the grass. Then I see Melvin. Instead of dropping the melon and running over to grab his bike, he raises it over his head with both hands.

"Put that melon down!" says the old man. "I'm going to skin you!

Melvin throws the melon down. It splats open on the grass.

"You little shit! Come back here!" he says. I get on the bike and tear out of the man's backyard. "Goddammit! I'll skin you kids! Get back here!" I don't look behind me, but I'm pretty sure he's running after us now. I hope Melvin gets away.

I forget about the gameroom and head straight for Grandma's house. Get there in about thirty seconds. Melvin's nowhere to be seen.

I hide my bike behind some honeysuckle bushes and jump inside the house, peek out the door. Looks like we gave the old man the slip.

"Well, where you been?" says Grandma. I jump, my heart up in my throat, pounding the breath out of me. She sounds as surprised as me.

"Uh, I was just riding around…" I tell her. It's the only thing I can think of. She stops sweeping the floor, leans on the broom and points.

"You been a running with that old Melvin, ain't you?"

"No," comes my response. It's automatic; I can't help it. But then again, I'm not supposed to lie. "Well…"

"Now don't you story to me," she says. "You know you're not supposed to be a running with that boy. He'll get you into trouble again. What did you do?"

I tell her the story, part of it, almost, but leave myself out.

"I didn't have any part of it. I mean, he started it, Grandma. I was drinking my pop and then I saw him throwing watermelons into that shed."

"And you didn't take part?"

"No. Well…"

"Well, we're going to find out and I'm going to call his momma." She's pointing toward the driveway. When I look out the door I see an old pickup pulling in real slow, gravel crunching under the tires. It takes about an hour, it seems like, but finally this old man gets out.

My heart drops into my stomach. He pulls a bandanna from his overalls, wipes his face as he walks up to the door. Grandma lets him in.

***

"It was him and that other boy," says the old man. But instead of acting mad, he kind of laughs, like maybe he understands why two boys come along and blast his lawnmowers with watermelons. "I tell you Miss Ferguson, for the life of me I couldn't figure out what was a going on. I kept a hearing these funny noises. Here in a little bit there would be another noise, then another. I walked back there and seen these two boys a carrying those melons over to the shed, you know. I realized then what was a going on."

I still can't believe he's not mad. At least he's not acting that way.

"Well his momma's a going to hear about this," says Grandma, looking at me. "She sure is. And I'm going to tell that old Melvin's momma what he's been a doing."

Grandma tells Mom, all right. She tries to call Melvin's parents, too, but their phone is disconnected, so she walks up to their house and tells them in person. Doesn't matter, though. I have to go up to the old man's house and clean off his mowers, and the shed, all by myself. After it dries, that stuff is pretty hard to get off the lawnmowers. Seeds stick to the metal, sticky as molasses. The old man doesn't seem too mad; he just keeps telling me I ought to put my energy into something more productive. Says when he was my age he didn't have time to play around. Says he was always picking cotton, milking cows, plowing gardens, shoeing his mules. Says he only got to go to town twice a year and that was to buy new shoes for school. Says he only went to the eighth grade; his dad kept him at home after that to work on the farm.

I get pretty tired of listening to his stories. But he isn't too mad, or doesn't seem like it, anyway. I'm pretty happy about that.

I clean everything up and think I'm all done, but he pulls out a pocketknife, opens it up and bends down by one of the mowers. Then he scrapes out some more seeds and watermelon flesh from the flywheel. When I see this, my stomach sinks. More work.

"Looks like you missed some spots," he says.

It takes me two hours to go through all these mowers, scraping out the seeds and watermelon from the little cracks and holes in the engines. By the time I finish, my hands are sticky, my knees and neck sore from bending down for so long. He asks me if I'm going to throw watermelons on his mowers again and I tell him no. Then he shakes my hand.

Mom makes me offer to mow the old man's yard, but he says he doesn't need me to do that.

***

I get grounded for two weeks - no bike. Mom locks it in the garage; she says I can have it back when I prove that I'm responsible. But that's no big deal. It's happened before: after I clipped all the roses off Mr. Jennings' bushes, and that time I didn't go to my dentist appointment, but said I did. Both of those times Mom made me do some sort of job around the house - pick weeds, wash the baseboards. Well, this time she makes me paint grandma's house. All by myself. And it's a big one.

***

Monday rolls around and Mom drops me off at Grandma's about the time the sun comes up. Grandma cooks a big breakfast, just like always, then I take the money Mom gave me and head off to Mason's Supply to buy the paint.

"How much do you need?" asks the man in the store. "How many gallons?"

"I don't know. I'm just painting the house. It's a big one."

He thinks for a minute.

"Well, how about we start you off with two gallons?" he says. "You can come back and get more if that's not enough."

"I guess."

I pay for the paint and the brushes, and he gives me some sticks to stir the stuff. Tells me it's oil-based and to keep it away from my mouth. I already know all that.

I get started by 8:30, but the painting will have to wait. First I have to scrape off the old stuff with a putty knife. About halfway through the first board I remember that scraping is the worst part of painting. It's like two jobs in one and the first one is the hardest.

It takes me all morning to get through just one side of the house. After lunch I start on the back side and I barely finish with it when Mom picks me up to take me home.

Next day all I do is scrape. I get the little white flakes all over my arms and neck. I'm hot, sweaty and flecked with these itchy little flakes. They're scattered all over the grass around the garage, too. More work for later, I guess. I don't think I'll ever finish.

But I do. It takes me all day. I have to replace a couple of rotten boards along the bottom, but I finally get through it all.

So Wednesday morning I start painting. By 11:00 it's so hot I have to stop and take a break. The thermometer on the side of the garage says 98 degrees. We'll probably hit 104 today, I think. Maybe more.

Just before lunch Melvin rides up on his bike.

"You painting this all by yourself?" he asks. He's eating a cupcake, icing on his lips. The knees of his jeans are covered in dirt, as usual, but he looks a little different today. I can't decide just why.

"Yeah, got grounded for two weeks. I can't hang out for a while," I tell him. I look over at the windows, make sure Grandma's not watching. "I'll get in trouble if I don't keep working."

"Man, that sucks."

"What are you doing?"

"Hanging out. I'm going to go up to the gameroom later. Today's my birthday," he says. "Old man gave me twenty bucks."

"No kidding?"

"I ain't kidding," he says. He pulls the bill out of his pocket to show me. Then I notice the dark spot under his left eye. It's a little swollen, the shape of a carrot; looks like a bee got him. "How much they paying you to do this?"

"Nothing."

"That ain't good," he says. "You always want to get the money part fixed up front. That way they can't come back on you and say 'Hey, you ain't getting nothing.' Shouldn't work for free."

I take that as the tip of the day.

"Well, I guess I don't have no choice," I tell him. He finishes the cupcake, drops the wrapper on the ground. "Hey, pick that up or I'll be the one getting in trouble. And don't let my grandma catch you hanging around. She'll get mad."

"I'm out of here anyway," he says, picking up the wrapper. Then he gets back on his bike. "Hey, whatever happened with that old man?"

"Had to go up there and clean everything up. Got grounded. You know," I tell him. I wait for him to fess up, tell me what happened after Grandma told his parents, but he doesn't. I don't bring up his eye. "Well, what happened to you?"

"Nothing. Old man just said stay away from there for a while."

"Yeah, I guess I won't be around there for a while, either. No bike."

"Well, I'll see ya," he says, riding off.

"See ya, Melvin."

I watch him ride off. When he gets into the street, he drops the cupcake wrapper and disappears. I stop what I'm doing, walk down to the street and pick up the litter, place it into the trash can.

MARY B. GRAY

Closure
                for Grandma

Here she stands

grounded.

The stars' shine lost.

Death becomes her
Death is her

them,

           me.

In this moment death has become more than the lost of breath.
here is the death of dreams and visions
      she'll never see me in that white dress
      never watch me cook her thanksgiving
      never know how lost I've felt.

now, Eternity is faceless dressed in fading memories in vibrant love
      in red and yellow hues

dressed in
her milk white poncho, in her loose curls, in her deep brown eyes

in tears,
      Eternity is dressed.

The last breath has cascaded,
                  has fallen

renewing bitterness and salt

pain escapes her consuming itself in me, pain escapes her.

KEN HADA

Leveling

We untangle lawn chairs
get comfortable in the company
of strangers, beer
bracelets on our wrists.

We sip and hear the band on stage
toes begin to tap, shoulders
dipping, we bounce.
Someone gets up to dance,

his blue work cap turned backwards
so as to not bump her pretty nose.
We all watch grinning
kind of like cousins in the barn.

During set changes we speak
without introductions, munch brisket
and potato salad and I can't help
but think how cool real Oklahoma is

or how real, cool Oklahoma is
mixing folks, leveling hierarchies
we thought we needed, a common
blues heartsong. We testify.

We are irreducible witness
insatiable in our longing to be familiar.
I see our scars, our lack
of fashion, the two-dollar sandals

and false gold jewelry,
there is nothing here to pretend.
Black and white dance together:
Mexicans with green

or yellow and orange shirts
Indians wearing turquoise
yuppies fitting in, OU tee shirts
black bras, white shorts, straw hats

cheap sunglasses, sweating flesh
feeling the riffs, feeling songs
we all know like church.
Better than church, everybody grooves

everybody feels, children tug
at skirts, bounce alongside dad
and grandpa whose cigar smoke mingles
with over-priced beer and onion breath.

Gentle dark comes, a train passes
through Bricktown, other folks
going other places while we
celebrate this confessing time.

Train

for LeAnne Howe
after Miko Kings

At 12:26 am, a train softly rumbles
a few blocks from my bed
where I would be sleeping were it not
for a baseball story keeping me up

thinking about Ada, circa 1900, a town
maneuvering toward statehood where
for more than a century now, Iron Horses
have trotted that same path blowing horns

of progress, sometimes too loud to hear
Choctaw ghosts telling of Miko Kings
and our counter-clockwise rotations,

but tonight, soft enough to imagine
old days when baseball meant everything
that money could not buy.

CAROL HAMILTON

Overlooked

Handsome blue condominiums
set down among cottonwoods,
beside the gulley catching rains
as they flash through
our seared and windswept geography.
I used to run there to hear
the plains gossip, watch
the green and silver leaves twinkle
above as they laughed all around me.
Only now have I missed that place,
wonder where it went and when.
Did floods drive out those
azure-skinned homes with their
high and arched windows that
made me imagine sunlight pooling
on polished oak floors,
golden settings for Oriental rugs?
How can I have been so careless,
to lose a whole neighborhood,
compact in its treed and small valley?
We work so at trees here, tend
to lose them while the cottonwood
and blackjack oak volunteer
to shelter us. We scorn them.
We cut them down while the ice
and the wind and the blasting heat
cut down our hopeful plantings.
We try to leaf up our raked-clean
land all the while the sweep of light
from dawn to dusk has little
here to make it linger. Such a
quick-fingered magician we live with,
and before I am sure I even saw it,
suddenly it is gone.

TRACY HAUGHT

Finding Refuge

She skips child-like
Under a nebulous glow of pink sun
Exhilarated
She lets her arms
Lift with the wind
As she spins and collapses
In the pale hissing grass
Violet leaves rusted brown
Lift and settle like laughter
Around her

Music plays without keys
Or reed
Dream-fed it swirls
Winding up through the trees
The sycamores swaying with
The mesquites
Earth's overflow of rhythm
Bending and blowing
Nestling warm around her
In the cool of evening
Like a merger of senses
Nature's rapture

Forgetting How to Dance

Nadine's been living at the nursing home for over two years
But the welcome sign still hangs on her door.
A generic printout welcoming her to Lawton, Oklahoma's,
"Exclusive Retirement Community."
It is not by choice that she lives in room 18.
Nadine wants her house back.
She wants her husband back.
She wants the only life she knew, back.

I have to introduce myself every time I visit her.
I have to explain that I'm not her niece,
But a woman who just wants to spend time with her.
She doesn't remember things,
Like the year she was born,
Or where she put her medicine.
But she remembers to tell me
Every time I come to see her
That her parents divorced when she was only three,
Her father taking off with her mother's best friend.

And she remembers that she was so poor as a child
That her mother had to put newspapers on the walls
And windows of their little shack to keep out the cold.
And that she loved to dance more than anything else,
Before her husband told her to stop.
Nadine smiles mischievously, child-like, as she tells me
How she loved to wear pants but had to sneak to wear
Them when her husband wasn't around.

I know that when I see Nadine she will cry,
That she will tell me how she doesn't want to be here.
That she will smile to apologize for her lack of memory.
I know Nadine has given up on this life.
This isn't the life she signed on for when she
Married her husband at fourteen.
Now, at 81, she's two-years-alone.

But I imagine in this place two years feels much longer.
I try to tell her that there are wonderful years ahead of her,
That there's still time to dance,
But she waves this away as she turns dutifully
Toward her late husband's portrait.

Nadine may have forgotten how to dance
But she gives great hugs,
And Nadine, obviously vying
To be my favorite, now calls me Sugar.

ARN HENDERSON

Base Line & Meridian

at the juncture of two invisible lines

       witnessed

     through the glass of measurement

      marking

cardinal directions I traverse the grid of

    Base Line East & West

      and

    Indian Meridian North & South

TOWNSHIP 2 NORTH RANGE 3 WEST

    at first light
the quarreling crows demanding
      recognition of their meridian
    dancing
    gathering bits of straw
for the nesting of their featherless

     mailman
     meterman
    crossing at the intersection of purpose

     in the commonplace of because
    a red push-cart on the corner tended
by an unadorned
    white-aproned
      man

wrapping tamales
     in newspaper

whispering to a spotted dog at his feet

          si, mi chucho precioso
                    tu eres un perro bueno
          muy bonito, mi muneco peludo
          te quiero mucho
          viva! mi mejor amigo, eres un amor

wagging tail to the meter of voice
          sacudiendo la calle

TOWNSHIP 6 NORTH RANGE 2 WEST

mobile homes baking

     in the sun
          blistered and peeling

     bouquet of worn down tires
          looped
          in gully grass
     decorated
               with rusting tin cans

the celebration
of the yeoman plowman
                    at days end
          dropping the traces
               mounting gloves
                    on the ears of his mule
                         and slinging his hat
          at the fading sun

TOWNSHIP 3 NORTH RANGE 7 EAST

rounding the curve emerging from roadside bluestem

  at the edge

      wooden leaning cross

  decorated with a garland of bleached plastic flowers

TOWNSHIP 5 NORTH RANGE 6 EAST

white on blood red

      dusting of snow on Japanese maples

  in a garden of April

  St. Francis the mute smiling at dancing squirrels

     tracks of bird

 three toes in meandering line

     winding to the creek

     in silence of snow

TOWNSHIP 4 NORTH RANGE 7 WEST

riding west to the falling
   full moon of September birds
    worm searching the fields
      crows picking at the nameless
on the hardtop

      jumping
          picking
               calling the sunrise

with a plume
          of red dust following
     as the only witness
              for the plowman
    deep
    in a trance of turned-over sod
              with row after row
      of hope

listening
             to the music at dusk
    the harp of pine trees
fingering
        clouds
             in the wind whistling

TOWNSHIP 10 NORTH RANGE 3 WEST

    Wandering the grid
at the fringe of shadows
    Looking for the Jesus in common labor shoes
    Looking for the Jesus who sweats in the streets
aimlessly wandering
        sucking at the bottle of loneliness Wandering the grid
at the fringe of shadows
    Looking for the Jesus in common labor shoes
    Looking for the Jesus who sweats in the streets
aimlessly wandering
        sucking at the bottle of loneliness
    Sliding
        Drifting
            Falling into the dreams
of bicycle and dog

and the awakening:
Lined up at the Jesus House

TOWNSHIP 11 NORTH RANGE 2 WEST

Leaning   abutments
decorated with opaque dreams of
ornamental graffiti tagged
for the sleepers
man woman child

IN MY NOSE
layers of smoke and spillage choking
Quickening
the pace of stale darkness
eclipsed by the rising fumes

IN MY MOUTH
unspeakable words
the tongue
has forgotten
Falling   from the mouth in the foam
of a sucking stone
IN MY HEART
riding into the veiled mist of memory
with the whisper of
Breathing earth of promise
el paraiso de la tierra verde y el cielo azul
the quilted blue of radiance
and intensity of green
IN MY HANDS
only by the reins
slack or taut
Guiding
the impulse of the moment
to caress
the fear from your flank

IN MY FEET
          heels to ribs
   Navigating
          beneath the varnish of crumbling visions
   Leaking
             from the passage above
       shards
               of broken mirrors
  Grinding   under the hoof
  Riding   through the portal to tomorrow
  Vomiting   muted and scuffed syllables
  Rusting   in my throat

TOWNSHIP 1 NORTH RANGE 9 EAST

Star 6 Motel at the juncture of nowhere
stink of perfumed disinfectants
   puny little room
      not even big enough
      to swing a cat

In my dream:

   feasting at the shadowmouth
   of her loins
      hands caressing my shoulders
   give me your nipples
      to carry in my pocket

      hands caressing my shoulders
   give me your nipples
      to carry in my pocket

LAYTON ISAACS

Reverse Birth: I-44 West to OKC

The highway bows into a uterus of concrete and light.
As I pass through its curves and into city,
I'm coming home.

I look to the side of the highway.
Metal ladders stretch to the sky.
Their red lights signal
another—outpost—on—planet—earth.

I spin the radio dial
and ring myself like a play phone,
Is there anybody out there?
Will I find what I'm looking for?

The red dots blink in sleepy majesty
and after tears of remembering
I understand this:
you must look for the radio towers in the darkness.

RACHEL CONSTANCE JACKSON

How It Should Be

I am not sure why I ever started to think of the place as empty. My parents certainly never thought of it this way. In fact, my Dad even sort of takes offense at the notion of it. I guess it always seemed lonesome to me because, without the benefit of the memories my parents had of it, without the knowledge of what the town and countryside around it had been, Shidler could have only been what it actually appeared to be. Gone, for the most part.

To the west of my grandfolks' house, where my cousin Lori lives part-time now, there was nothing but a long stretch of horizon. The only lines between the house and that soft curving horizon were a couple of barbed wire fences. The land between the swayed wooden back porch and the sunset was also dotted with pump jacks (some still pumping and some not) and trash fires. Here and there were a few herds of quiet livestock. Further yet, beyond that horizon, the prairie went on, unaware of itself. In the mid-80's this marvelous, blank vastness was intimidating to most people, who were by now mostly urban, and especially to kids like me. I grew up in the suburbs of Oklahoma City. I was accustomed to seeing space filled up with buildings and advertisements, cars and roadways, lights and more lights. I was used to a constant background of sound.

When I was small, around eight or so, my granddad, around 82 or so, used to sit on a faded metal lawn chair on his porch and I'd sit with him in the other one. I'd bounce around a little bit, and flick the flaking green paint off the chair with my thumb, but we'd spend a long time just sitting in silence mostly, listening to the pumping jacks, and watching the orange sun inch downward through red twilight into the violet shades of the evening sky. Grandad usually had a toothpick with him, picking and sucking between his teeth at a slow pace until they were clean from the last meal. Eventually he'd remark with a subtle pride and a certain comfort that it was "put near" 30 miles to the horizon from where we sat with each other, gazing at the nothingness between us and "over yonder." As I got older, growing up right in the middle of mass culture, I couldn't help but wonder why anyone would have wanted to stay there—why he liked it. But when I was small and sitting contented with my grandad, nothing else was necessary. His liking the place made me like it.

But Grandpa Vann was born in 1900, and I was born when he was 74. I came along after the oil companies, who came in a mad rush of money-hungry panic, took what they could, merged and grew bigger, and then eventually abandoned the place for greater profit elsewhere. I was born after the families that had depended on the oil economy packed up and moved away in pursuit of another source of income. I was born after the drive-in and the cafes, the dress shops and farm supply businesses, the barbershops and the dance halls - that depended on those families—closed up and disappeared. All that was left when I was a child, in the town and around it, was in fact mostly empty space. Or at least it seemed that way to me, having been born in a city to parents who had long left the rural town they grew up in.

As a small child, I didn't mind the emptiness so much. I don't remember even really noticing it as strange until about the age of 12 or so—when everything tends to get strange for most kids. Then I began to wonder why the old buildings were abandoned. I wondered what had been in the old buildings to begin with. I wondered about the empty four-story hotel at the north end of the main street through town. Why had there ever been a need for one? I wondered why the roof of the train depot was left to rot. And why had the train stopped coming? Even more curious - why had the train ever come through the town at all? It just didn't add up to me, given what I saw as the evidence around the place. I was still too young to understand the way some things come only to pass—that the train, the folks on the train, the train depot and hotel, and the train tracks themselves had only been passing through. The country, however, still remained.

Then in 1985 when my big brother went off to school at O.S.U., and O.U. won the national championship, I came to understand that in the minds of most people "aggies," which I took to mean "countryfolks," were a subject suitable for punchlines. They were backward and stupid and maybe even dirty. Their ways were the ways of the past, just like that old town - good for nothing anymore but laughing at. By this time I was smart enough to make a few connections, and I started to feel sort of ashamed I guess, and then sort of angry. My whole family was made up "aggies," of one kind or another. Even though in my heart I was willing to defend them to the end and I did so on a regular basis, it didn't change the fact that people clearly had opinions about who was better and who was worse. I didn't have to look far to see the sophistication that the world said my folks lacked, and I could see that we lacked it. It must have been around then that I really began to see my parents' hometown as a dying thing. Then it became hard to look at without feeling sort of sad, and sort of mad.

The emptiness of the Shidler townscape and landscape became uncomfortable, like restlessness and grief. In the years while I was a teenager, we lost my grandparents. And all the while the urban life and culture imported from the coasts seemed to grow and thrive and thump around me, as though the loss of towns like Shidler, Oklahoma, was a good and necessary thing. It was an odd sort of Darwinian triumph, like bedlam football. All the little towns like my parents' hometown were the losers in the competition. Cities swallowed up the town's children and grandchildren, their vision and talent, their traditions and values, their hearts and loyalties, their whole histories, until kids like me - who were only a generation removed from the community of their parents and grandparents - were complete strangers to it all. Even as my parents took my brothers and I for regular visits, what was commonplace to them as children was a bizarre sort of mystery to us—ancient and rudimentary just like the world said it was. The natural thing for me to do, maybe the only thing a child could do, was to disregard it all and cleave to this suburban surrogate I was told to embrace. I guess it was a given that I would try. And I guess it was a given that I wouldn't entirely take to it.

Now when I look at the world, it seems emptier to me sometimes than Shidler ever did, and when I look at Shidler, I see a story as rich as any other there is to tell.

***

The people there are simple because the land is simple. The colors and the shape of it is subtle, like the people's hearts. It's not a beauty that jumps at you. It's the beauty of sagging barbed wire, overgrown blackberry patches, rusted-out trash barrels, and corrugated tin—rough and purposeful. In fact being accustomed to more obvious beauty spoils you for it. You can't be too timid or too demanding when you look at the Osage Hills rolling northward into Kansas. You have to feel secure in the middle of nowhere.

There is more space up there than most folks are used to. There are no mountains to nestle in. There's no ocean to lull and lap at you. And there's not much in the way of architecture. Here, people truly confront themselves and learn what they are made of, because here there is no pretense. The emptiness of the prairie makes for the feeling of a silent sanctuary, where nothing is exactly what calls to you - and yet there is a presence still.

Nothing calls you to move deeper into a patch of black jacks and post oaks where everything looks like it scratches. There's nothing grand or shiny here, and nothing that's particularly obvious to point to or raise a shout about. It's much more sublime than that, just a hair this side of subliminal. If you can see it, it's satisfying because it's so secretive—a strange combination of graceful and sneaky. There is no glorious scenery, only hide-out creek banks made of red clay bedrock, old as the Osage, eroded into prehistoric puzzle pieces by the passage of time. The creek beds and oak trees are the only raggedness in these hills and prairies. Otherwise, swaying tallgrass covers the land, bending quietly in brushstroke patterns, like a buffalo's coat in the wind. Once you get past the startling simpleness of it, you start to find a strange assurance in the bare truth of it. A challenging peace permeates these prairies, like that moment after looking long and hard for the face of God, right before the veil lifts.

The people of Shidler put on no false airs. When you look at them, you know you are looking at something solid. Even if you don't like what you see, you know you can trust it to be what it seems. And they carry themselves with a good deal of dignity and calm. There is no frenzy in them, because to them nothing much is worth frenzying over. They are the kind of folks that are kind and loyal even when they are tired and mean.

Shidler was an oil town in 1941, as stubborn as they come. The community had a sense of itself—an identity that appeared in the men coming off the oilfields in the middle of the night, and in the loudmouthed women keeping the grill warm for them in the café. Everyone understood that the only way folks make it in this world is together, and that each person has a place. Situated like it was in the middle of the broad horizon of northern Oklahoma, the people kept everything local. Their happiness and freedom was in their own hands, and they worked to keep it there.

That's why Susuko Yamamoto made it her home. Having come from Japan, she knew the feeling of being obligated to the ruling power in exchange for freedom. At the age of 16, Emperor Mutsuhito had asked her to be a spy in exchange for her passage to the United States in 1903, but when she got settled in and lived a little, she knew she couldn't do it. Ms. Yamamoto saw no reason to do it, and endanger this place that gave her so much more than obligation. She could have anything she wanted here with an honest effort, and she could do for herself without debt to others. She enjoyed this liberty.

Ms. Yamamoto opened the Tokyo Café in Shidler, ran it well and raised her children there. She made a pot of rice in the café kitchen every morning for her family, and generally they were the only ones who ate it except for the occasional order of chop suey from a curious townsperson. Mostly Susuko cooked American fare, and people enjoyed it as they sat and talked with each other about the day's news.

On the back of the café was a wooden porch—the kind that decorated small town main street alleyways of Oklahoma, before they were given to rot. And many pinochle games were won and lost there, as the Yamamoto's children and other children looked on. Ichiro, the eldest of her children, was at home there. Late nights when business was slow between oilfield shifts, or after his boxing matches in the local golden glove tournaments, he would rest there on the steps and listen to the pump jacks out in the field beating like life itself, and smell the brushfires and trash fires, and the food on the stove fires in the café kitchen. That made him mindful of his very own blood, and he knew that he was made of these things. Everyone at the Shidler high school always called him "Ikie." That was his nickname - and he took it with him when he entered the 442nd Infantry Battalion—the all Asian-American battalion - in WW II. They said he went "for broke" with the rest of the boys, fighting fascism in Europe.

Across Main Street in Shidler, the barbershop stayed open late too. Mr. Vol Parker kept the four chair stalls clean and ready for the oilfield hands in need of a shave after a long haul in the fields. He enjoyed their stories and their pride in their work. He appreciated their company and their business, and he treated them like friends and talked with them like fellow countrymen. They were a lively crowd in the barbershop in the black of night. Opinions and stories flew like the hair to the floor, and everyone felt the better for it.

Early evening, in January 1942, Mr. Parker and Lawrence Diehl sat in the Tokyo Café drinking coffee and exchanging ideas. The sky was filling with the first orange speckles of a red winter sunset. The United States was newly at war. Ms. Yamamoto came to their table for a fill-up, and returned the coffee pot to the electric plate on the counter. She returned to the men's table once more with her hands in her front apron pockets. She was holding onto some sort of official letter from a government agency. The men began to understand before she even said she was worried. Susuko and Ichiro had been detained in Dallas when they were there on a café supply run on the day after Pearl Harbor was bombed. She didn't have to say much more after reminding them of that. The letter, which she handed to Mr. Diehl without a word, said her family was to be interned at the Dodge City camp.

Everything went on as normal for a few weeks. The kids played "Americans-and- Germans" instead of "cops-and-robbers" or "cowboys-and-indians." Mr. Parker told them not to play Americans-and-Japanese. It didn't make much sense to him because he knew what the real enemy was. He could respect the United States for fighting for freedom, but he didn't respect fascists for fighting for control. He understood sometimes folks have to act when push comes to shove. What he didn't take a shine to was shoving.

Eventually one mid-morning, a townsman stuck his head in the barbershop and let Vol Parker know there was a couple of military men up at the café. Lawrence Diehl was there in the barbershop too, of course. He watched Vol grab his pistol from his stall drawer, hitch up his pants, and put the gun in his belt. The two of them walked outside and locked up the shop.

Main Street was alive with commerce. When Vol and Lawrence walked into the café, it was full. Only it was considerable quiet. Not a soul in the place was speaking a word, or even stirring their coffee. The Yamamotos and the military men were obviously back in the kitchen trying to be polite about the situation. Mr. Parker and Mr. Diehl continued that direction.

Once through the kitchen doorway, they stopped shoulder-to-shoulder without being especially threatening. Mr. Parker gave Susuko a sturdy nod and a kind of "Good Morning," and then asked the visitors a question.

"What's your business here, soldiers?"

One of the soldiers assured him, no doubt respectfully, "Government business, Sir. We're here to make sure these folks are preparing for the internment process."

With no hesitation, Mr. Parker added, "The government's got no business here. These people are members of this community. I can vouch for them, and so will Mr. Diehl here."

Mr. Diehl rocked back on his heels and brought his chin down toward his chest, but held his eyes steady on the soldiers. The hollows of his temples pulsed in and out as he clinched and unclenched his jaws.

"We're not here to collect opinion on the matter, Sir."
The soldier made the effort to be firm, but he came off sounding smart.

Mr. Parker was quiet for a beat, and said, "Well I don't imagine you did, but it's not my opinion, Officer. Opinion is what you have when you don't see the facts. The fact is you won't take these people anywhere—not now nor never—and everybody in this café feels the same way."

Mr. Diehl stood to the side and opened passage for the soldiers through to the kitchen doorway, and leaned himself in toward the boys in uniform.

"You heard the man," he said.

The soldier spoke up to say, "We're not authorized to use force, but we'll be back."

Mr. Diehl couldn't contain himself any longer as the officers walked out of the kitchen and into the dining room of the Tokyo Café. Everyone heard him, even up and down the alleyway, as he shouted, "And I don't give a good Goddamn if Mussolini shows up with you, that Son-of-a-Bitch!"—the implication being that the officers were acting just like him - "You're not taking anybody anywhere!"

As the young men exited, the noise of the establishment resumed as though the whole entire town was pleased with itself. Mr. Parker and Mr. Diehl left the café through the back porch and into the alleyway. They were shook up, and needed the air and the privacy.

Once he had his wits about him, Mr. Parker sent Mr. Diehl back to the barbershop while he headed to the telephone office a few doors down. He walked in and asked the operator to connect him to the office of J.W. Elmer Thomas, United States Senator. And he took a seat in one of the booths. Once on the phone, he reminded the Senator's secretary that he had campaigned tirelessly for Senator Thomas because he believed in the man. He told her that if the Senator wasn't available immediately it was a shame, but that he was to call the Shidler Telephone Office as soon as he returned. Mr. Parker made it clear he would be waiting there until the Senator called.

Two hours later the phone rang and the Senator was on the line. Mr. Parker was ready with an earful. By this time the whole town had come by to see him. He told the Senator that if there was trouble in Shidler, the people of Shidler would take care of it, and he didn't approve of the federal government intruding. He told him that furthermore there was no trouble in Shidler, and there would be no trouble in Shidler. And Senator Thomas naturally agreed with how his constituents saw the matter. For several weeks the town waited, but the Officers never returned.

Ms. Yamamoto and her family remained in Shidler until 1949, when she sold the café to Agnes Jackson, my Dad's mother. Susuko moved to Oklahoma City so she could be near Ichiro, who planned to stay there and find a good job in industry after he returned from the service.

My Dad was 16 years old when his mom opened the Shidler Café. And to him, though the building may fall into ruin and the whole town around it, the prairie open up and swallow it whole, the tallgrass grow over it like it was never there at all, it will never, ever be empty.

ROCKFORD JOHNSON

Out of the Waters

Past midnight in the full moon darkness
from a home high on a cliff,
a semi-trailer truck leapt from the side
of the hill, its bone white, fence like body
straight-lined behind the hollow cab,
then dropped downward in perfect
vertical form through the silvered night,
pierced the calm moonlit shimmer
of the lake like an Olympic diver,
and expired into the deep. Time passed.

Out of the blackjack-covered rise
above the lake sprung the pale white
specter of a school bus, each window opaque
like the glazed eyes of a corpse.
It seemed to hang in the air then fall
in an awkward tumble and, with a silent slap
of the water, floated, tipped, and slid away.

Morning sun sparkled the surface where
a herd of cattle swam toward the bank eating
from the water. Apples! Apples were falling
onto the ruddy waves and cows, big bellied cows,
like ducks congregating for free bread,
were coming for the prize.

Straddled on the bony ridge of their backs,
like happy actors on a parade float,
school children, smiling and waving, children
cheering at the mamas with baskets of apples!

ABIGAIL KEEGAN

Bestiary

In the soup of Earth's kitchen
sea water stirred with sky
until organic spices, cooked with lightening
pulled down from the hearts of stars,
tasted like energy in the first dish of life.

Earth, the mother, shifted moods often
enough to cradle new lives into being.
Sponge and protozoa soaked up the mildness
of her temperate climate in the early days
of her huge water filled sac.
Scorpions and spiders, land scouts
climbing on earth's surface,
sipped in the delicious discovery of air.
Dinosaurs and crocodiles loved splashing
and bathing in rains and swampy mudworks,
snakes waited for her to cool before
they crawled upon her belly.

We too waited for weather
to become glacially cold, then,
the first human hand touched her,
determined, we would thrive on threat.

To all these cells, and hearts, and lungs
 these openings and closings in the work of being,
earth gives and we will her delight.

KELLEY LOGAN

Transubstantiation

In the heart of Indian country,
A black and white steer,
One of a truckload sent to the slaughterhouse,
Rebels, breaking from the herd, leaping and kicking free from the chute,
Cantering down the road.

The local evening news broadcasts the slow speed chase
As the steer now walks, now sprints away from the police—
A herd of dark blue figures, arms held in semi-circles of mock embrace.
The last picture is of the distracted steer
Going house to house in a subdivision, looking into the windows,
The flickering blue light from suburban TVs
Bathing his marveling face.

Weeks after processing,
The renegade soul of this steer
Raves on in the dark heart of his meat,
Waiting in the clinical cool of suburban supermarkets.

Soon across America, a herd of grey men and women
Feel a slow burning question well up in their hearts; they
Rise from their sloppy joes and hamburger casseroles and walk out
Into the night to glaze at the spectacle
Of the heart dark sky,
And walk down the shadowed streets of a blue flickering world, new again.

VERA LONG

Oklahoma Pioneer Mothers

The women, most of them wives and mothers, who made the Land Run in Oklahoma endured extreme hardships, looked death in the face as they mended harness, cotton-sacks, socks, work clothes and broken hearts. The Oklahoma Pioneer Mother's tasks were many and endless, yet she hummed and sang and taught the young ones to find joy in life and freedom in a new kind of world.

She raised turkeys, chickens and children. She milked a cow, churned butter, cooked three meals a day, baked cakes, cookies and pies, canned fruits and vegetables and made jelly and candy.

She built fires in the fireplace, wood-stove, under the wash-kettle and fired inspiration into her tired and discouraged family. She kept a diary, wrote to far-off kin, saved the letters to re-read time and again. She read to her children by lamplight, read the bible and taught them scriptures to memorize for Sunday School.

She kept a quilt in a frame, raised to the ceiling and let down during bad spells of weather. She ironed on a quilt draped over the table, with a flat iron. She designed and sewed dresses, bonnets and men's shirts. She patched the patches on well-worn ever-day clothes, and learned to half-sole shoes. Along side of her family, she walked to church, (they let the horses rest on Sunday,) She helped neighbors through sickness and death and with gray broadcloth and bats of cotton, she lined homemade caskets.

For community affairs, she killed, dressed and fried chickens, baked yeast-bread rolls, made crocks of tea and pots of coffee to serve with home-baked cakes and pies. She kept an orchard to furnish the family with pears, apples, peaches and cherries. In her garden she raised Irish potatoes, sweet potatoes, okra, cucumbers, turnips, greens, peas, beans and melons while fighting off mice, bugs, flies, skunks, 'possums, coyotes, fox and other predators.

The Oklahoma Pioneer Mothers were not storybook characters, but real live women, only a few generations ago, in a life and death battle for survival and for their way of life. Their names can be found in our own Family Tree Books.

J.C. MAHAN

Where are the Indians?

"Where are the Indians?"
That's her question
She asks it ever chance she gets.
Sometimes not waiting for an opening
But ambushes you with it anyway.
I think she is asking it for herself
Having been crystallized into her psyche
In an all informing moment
Of realization of the characterization
Of her Native American heritage
At the young age of six or seven
When her father told her
"Hush your mouth about those Navajos.
Don't you know your mother's Indian?"

"Where are the Indians?"
Asking from the firm foundation
Of her accomplished academic accolades,
Holding the authoritative position of Chair
Historian, disciplined fact finder,
Accurate record pursuer, text book producer.
She likes to shock her Anglo contemporaries
Who are only accustomed in dealing with issues
From a distance, far distanced as possible,
Ages ago, centuries removed, earlier decades,
Before civilization, before the removal started, before emancipation,
Well before the Civil Rights confrontations,
At least as far distanced as Southside of the tracks,
Not at my kid's school,
Certainly not in my neighborhood,
And hopefully, praise God, not in my church.
"Why don't those Indians just get over it?
Let it go. I mean it's the past,
After all, you can't change history.
What are we supposed to do?

Give them back the country?
What would they do with it anyway?"
She laughs at their uncomfortable countenance
And their inability to relate to the problem
With their quick rush to shove it back
Under the carpet of history for another clean sweep.

"Where are the Indians?" asking herself,
Delving back into historic tombs
Opening ancient records and wounds
Once thought healed at least by some,
The non-Indians and maybe naïve little girls
Growing up away from their Native relatives
Outside of their tribal culture.
Now, she looks to history and the facts
To speak out and say something of importance
Reaching a paradigm shift in our present democracy
Through some profound discovery
That would, if not right all the wrongs,
Recover enough of what was lost
To reestablish the people as "The People".
She's spent a lifetime of study,
Proving herself, upholding her mother,
Vindicating the righteousness of her family,
And scraping, shaping, sculpturing something
Out of the void of the past
Pulling it into this world, yet
It's not here, not yet, not completely,
At the cost of all her labor, life, marriage,
And maybe children, and maybe other relationships
(the kind you want to last forever).

"Where are the Indians?" she ask me
Smiling that knowing smile that says
Nobody can really answer that,
Nobody really knows a solution for sure.
And I nod back knowingly
Aware she doesn't want to hear

What I have to say, because I know
Where the Indians are, I know.
Some are doing okay, they've assimilated
Into this "American" culture becoming like me,
My salesman, my stylist, the guy installing my water well,
The banker, the baker, the candlestick maker.
They're all Indian Chiefs and Princesses
Who are doing what they can
The best for their families
For their children's future.
Then, there are the others:
The homeless, impoverished, alcoholic
Drug ridden, derelicts down panhandling on Reno Street,
Hanging around the Bus Station in OKC.
There's also the poor illiterate living on the reservations
Or in the squat Indian houses lined up
Along the highways, like 33, 54 or Route 66.
Some live in shacks stuck out in the country
Not willing or able to take advantage
Of all the governments programs and schools
That could change their lives and their futures.
And listen, I'm not saying there are not reasons
For the way things are, I'm just saying
This is the way things are
And they don't have to be this way.
But what can you do? What can change?

Last, there are those American Indians
Who have climbed the highest ladders
Of success and academic achievements
To the top of the towers of knowledge
Who cling to their heritage
And rail at the injustice and disparages
And wail at the loss and debauchery
And who ask "Where are the Indians?
Why are the Indians left this way?"
They have visions like the artists and the politicians
Who as the great Chief Black Hawk before them,

Longed to lead their people somewhere
But where is there left to go?

"Where are the Indians?"
She asks herself again
Signaling the end of this conversation.
So, I say good night and go my own way.

Rural Oklahoma

Out here the towns are small and shrinking farther apart
But the cemeteries are big and growing well organized,
White fenced to hold in their occupants and
to mark their importance.
There are even directional signs alongside highways and byways
So that they can't be missed by the casual passer-by
Or by the seeking souls who search them out.
The residents don't want to lose the towns or the cemeteries
And don't realize they are becoming one with the little head stones
And marble monuments to the past,
birthing rural communities in reverse,
Old neighbors in new neighborhoods laid out in formation,
Moving to the streets of gold.

TERI MCGRATH

A Waffle House Tale

Maria has two tattoos on her neck,
one beneath each ear,
where some women wear their perfume.
They are the names of her children,
faded and blue, like old bruises:
Rosario and Juan.
But she calls them by names
of the places they've gone to.

"Oklahoma," she says,
her strong fingers pressing
the spot where you'd search for a pulse.
Then, looking down to the left,
She lifts the black curtain of hair from her neck.
She says, "Las Vegas. Last I heard."
And she lets the curtain fall again.

There is another name—Nina—
in clean black script
on the purple veined page of her wrist.
This one, she covers
and holds to her breast,
near a tiny silver crucifix.
"My youngest," she says,
"My baby."

SUSAN MILLER

The Kickapoo Cane Women
(Passage in which the body is discovered)

That fall, soon after classes started, was when I became a detective. It wasn't any fun. It was a hot day in September, and we were all moving slow around Lizard's old house on the allotment. She was in the air conditioned room getting ready for the card game that night. Lizard did a lot of "getting ready," an activity that seemed to involve lying back in a La-Z-Boy rocking recliner and thinking about things. We were all there. Maynee Charlie was with Lizard in the cool room. The two Sonnies were moving around outside: Sonnie Kincaid playing with the big puppies under the porch and Sonnie Thunder repairing the sweat lodge in the woods above the house with Milton Going Along. Jennie Skink had just gotten back from town with groceries and still had that air of someone in transition from white people's world into Indian. Millie Thunder was on the phone in the front room haggling with someone about some business. Martha Axe was cooking. Martha's husband Bob Bone had been with Lizard but had just left the cool room and was getting into his truck when the old Ford Falcon came into sight moving up the long dirt driveway toward the house. I was on the porch reading *My Antonia* for a class.

The Falcon pulled into the yard and parked in the turnaround. The regular places were already taken. Soon, both sides of the driveway would start filling up as the players arrived for the game.

Three women got out of the car, and we could see that they wore the long, tiered, calico skirts and overblouses traditional to women of some of the tribes nearby—Kickapoos, Pottawatomies, Shawnees, Sacs and Foxes . . . Only the Kickapoo women wore them daily, however. The others wore them just for ceremonial or other formal occasions. So Kickapoos were in the yard, and my attention focused in with a little rush.

They approached the porch: a very old woman moving with difficulty; a middle-aged woman, who might have seemed old in another context; and a young woman, who must have been the mother of the small children who stayed in the back seat of the Falcon. It was a dark red old car, and it sat there in the sun heating up inside like an oven. Even with the windows down, it would have been unbearable in there unless you were used to hardship and didn't imagine anything else.

The middle woman—green skirt, yellow blouse—asked for my mother, so I went inside to find someone with authority. I found Maynee and brought her to the porch. The women wanted permission to cut river cane by the creek below the house, and Maynee told them to go ahead. We all watched as they drove on down the branch of the driveway that leads toward the creek. They must have been here before to have known to take that road. Then we all went back to what we were doing. We knew they wanted the cane to build their houses, real wickiups just like their ancestors had used up around the Great Lakes before their diaspora ahead of the whites' invasion.

An hour or so later, back they came up the creek road with a load of cane strapped to the top of the old car. I expected them to nod and keep going, so I was perplexed when they stopped and the very old woman got out of the back seat and hobbled toward the house—pale blue overblouse, long red skirt flapping in the wind that had just come up. She winced with each step now, so I jumped up and met her in the yard. "Is the old woman here?" she asked. She meant Lizard. Nobody gets to see Lizard except in special circumstances. I knew that was why this Kickapoo relic had come herself on the long, painful trek from the car toward the house. This old gal *was* a special circumstance.

By the time Lizard made her entrance onto the porch, the old Kickapoo woman had completed the trek. They faced each other, relics, each an event unto herself, the rest of us staring and expecting. "There's a girl down there," the old woman croaked. "You'd better do something." The cosmos stopped. I forgot to breathe. Then the old gal turned back to the car, and Lizard yelled for Bob Bone.

BRYAN MITSCHELL

Status

Oldeview Drive separates woodlands from the only supermarket parking lot around here that automates off its lights after-hours. It's the darkest part of the city when you need it to be. The dedicated three-way traffic light entrance resembles a stoic trio of life-long friends, their unblinking green and red eyes swaying from cables in the breeze as they solemnly motion agreement with each other on things unsaid.

My hatchback is my tabernacle; an only sign of life amidst interspersed shopping-cart repositories with their cold steel frames silhouetted by star field like a boneyard of wigwams. Windows are down for tolling an approaching autumn shower, which will be traveling to the Northeast just as many of its milk-hearted ancestors before it. Like everything else, they roam on through Oklahoma and nothing ever stays. We are a forum of stories in progress. A state still young enough to be a status. It is a home tangled in a flowing and listless knot, continually weaving its loose-ends out in every direction; infinitely unfolding itself like a Buddhist dream.

My memories convene and talk shyly amongst themselves here, when customers go home and businessmen lock doors. They don't vanish into heartland mystery like the migratory skies, or hide in the Rockies birthing rumble and whisper. They just chill in the wings of a wheeled temple where I pray to nascent careers and daylit girlfriends, soft air-dried linen rascals.

But when the rain finally comes, my three glow-eyed friends start jouncing in the air, stabbing red and green rays accusingly into the nearby ruffling trees as if startled by a lurking presence in the woods. It is my future. In an explosion of tree leaves, it lunges forth, a giant puma the color of thunder, it charges and swallows my sanctum vessel whole. The flurried leaves flutter down and settle onto Oldeview as the wet calm sets back in. They pantomime the death of a panicking gas chamber, each in turn lulled to a convulsive passivity, and this is how my anamneses protest my quietus.

As my life inches through an ebony abdomen, I bundle up my beautiful loneliness in spare fast-food napkins and parking tickets. I stow it sleepily in the glove compartment, not knowing if it will survive. A network of fractures slowly starts to sprawl through the windshield. One by one the indicator lights on the dashboard flicker out and I smile wondering where I am to wake up next, because no story ends in Oklahoma.

PHILLIP CARROLL MORGAN

Aerial View

rivers are
shining snakes
trying to hide
in bottomland woods

**Today's History Lesson: The Great Casino Treaty of 2012
*(The Treaty of Riverwind)***

The Social Security Salvation Act
of 2011 was an act of Congress
requiring all Indian gaming operators
to vacate their casinos

so that
the federal government could use
gambling profits to refinance Social Security
preventing failure of the system
(and a catastrophic sell-off of RV's).

Under inspired interpretations of NAFTA,
Mexican government officials agreed
to allot vast plots of wilderness
(for a tiny cut of casino revenues)

in northern Mexico where Indians
could reestablish their casino business
and live
as long as the grass grows green
and the waters flow.

Cucumber Salad

Though looking tumble down now,
Grandma and Grandpa's modest farmhouse
always stood
on the upslope of a knoll
perhaps six or eight feet in elevation
above the plowed fields
of the Walnut Creek bottom,
perhaps six or eight feet
above the flood plain.
Grandpa Rob farmed about 1500 acres
of his extended family's allotment land.

I don't know who owns that field now.
No one has lived in the four-room house for decades.
It's out of sight in a narrow
rugged band of trees and hillocks
about ¾ of a mile from the nearest house
or traveled road.

Imagine a mile-long plowed field
shaped like a Y,
its two branches
composed of red sandy bottomland
with a woodsy ridge wedged
in between the branches,
like a giant bird's nest.

The old house, sitting right in the crotch of the Y,
atop the nest,
overlooks the point where the two long fields
merge into one long field,
much like the Walnut and Dragonfly Creeks,
outlining the Y,
become one creek
at a vanishing point on the distant
horizon of the field, at the foot of the Y.

About a mile from my house,
I occasionally walk to Grandma and Grandpa's house,
usually in the spring and fall,
when the weather calls me out to walk
when the vegetation and bugs
are not so aggressive.

I just piddle there—looking at the trees
they planted a hundred years ago,
smell the honeysuckle,
enjoy the sunlight through
gaping holes in the roof, and touch the soft gray
wood, long since weathered of any pigment.
I feel the life of this place. I listen to the silence
and hear stories. I remember there.

I saw on my commute three days ago
a new owner, a new husband of the land,
sitting straight up
on his large D-8 Cat bulldozer
and I feared the old house
might soon be gone.
I kept on driving,
with that dreadful, sinking feeling.

After work, I braced myself
and pointed my pickup
down the overgrown section line road,
closed since the fifties,
but still passable like a pasture road.

Relieved.
The house still stands,
not defiant,
but just far enough out of sight
of any traveled road
to either never make it onto,
or to be finally crossed off of,

a busy dozing husband's list of chores.

Husband is a good word
to describe Grandpa Rob's relationship
with this land—
a deep commitment on Rob's part
and a tacit commitment from the land.
More commitment than love.

That's why Rob unexpectedly
disappeared on the train,
from time to time—to Kansas City
or St. Louis or Chicago or points in between,
where he could view his alternatives
and remember that farming,
that all this, was commitment, voluntary.

My Chickasaw grandmother, Alice,
understood his needs. He had travelled extensively
before they married, and she always knew
he would work things out and return to her
and this land.

Alice always loved the farm place
with a couple of miles of Walnut Creek
within sight of her front porch
rocking chair
where she sat reading a book
in between snapping pole beans,
culling grapes, sorting plums,
washing potatoes, shucking corn,
singing songs
that echoed up from the creek bottom
after Rob finished his plowing
and stood in the slanting sunlight,
sponge bathing at the well.

I'm glad the house didn't get dozed
so I could visit Grandma and Pa
one more time. I'm glad
to stand beside Rob at the well
this warm summer evening, sponging
the red sand from my forearms
and salty sweat from my brow,
looking forward
to sliced vine ripened tomatoes,
the crunch of crispy cucumber,
the sweet of onion,
and the tang of vinegar.

Funeral

That day in Idaho
we buried Squeak and Kendra's baby
near their cabin in Paradise Valley,
the Boundary County Sheriff stopped
at the gate to their land.
There were no elders
in our bohemian tribe
so Tom and Don walked out
while those gathered
in late morning watched
the small horizon figures by the squad car.

We were hippies and a lawyer,
soldiers, an Okie guitar player,
medical researchers, carpenters,
nurses, poodle groomers, a French horn player,
a journalist, mechanics, fishers,
painters, poets and teenagers
fled to the edge of America
after the horrors of Vietnam,
relearning civics, social studies, religion.

They came back to Kendra saying
the lawmen wanted to see the death certificate
from the Washington coroner which said: SIDS,
sudden infant death syndrome, camping at Priest Lake.

The funeral had no structure. Squeak and Kendra
were not depressed but grieved and alive. We talked
friendly reverent and resilient relaxed
I volunteered to dig the grave, Squeak showed me where
on a sylvan knoll on the ground, the spot,
under the firs and pines
where the boy was conceived.

Six feet deep in sandy loam
it was not tiring
while two friends talked to me

Bob the third generation carpenter
came with the small simple well built coffin.
We talked time suspended until
somehow we knew when it was time.

"Where's the boy," I asked.
In the seat of the pickup, Squeak nodded.
Bob opened the miniature casket. I went to the truck,
opened the door and privately viewed the bundle on the seat.
Unrolled the blanket and looked at the stiff infant body.
My body clenched involuntarily,
clutching its identity with me,
but only respect showed on my face.

I re-swaddled the child, cradled him in my arms
closed the truck door
walked gently placing him in his coffin.
Some standing some sitting, round faces watched quietly.
Bob fastened the lid and two men lifted the box.
All feet fell softly as we carried
and lowered him into the grave on the mound.

If words were spoken they remain in that earth.
Don't remember if we sang, but we all shared food
around a large fire as the red sun eclipsed the west
thirty five autumns ago.
If there were tears they remain in that soil.
Do remember that we were one life,
one island in the sea.

JOHN GRAVES MORRIS

New Stories: Elegy for the Armadillos

The gay bar, for years its unsigned
entrance up the stairs at the back
of a faded, unlit building, has died.
The restauranteur, boisterous and oily—
you've seen ads for his barbeque pit,
a round, pink face overwhelming the camera
as he shouts the virtues of his sauce—-
bought the building, remodeled it to expand
his seating and is now at the center
of his own galaxy, king of the block,
pillar of the Chamber of Commerce crowd.

Imagine the vacuum, the terrible quiet
at night, that used to be filled with men
both short and tall, eyes raccooned
with mascara and false lashes, faces
aflame with magenta and jade, low-cut
taffeta and voile and sateen ballooned
with prosthetic breasts, some smouldering
with "Tainted Love," some shrinking into
"Sukiyaki," some striding around the room
as they belt "If I Could Turn Back Time."
In between performances, the best DJ in town
had full floors writhing to his thumping bass.
Surely a lament deserves to be sung.

The wet, cool springs of this state
blaze suddenly into parched summer,
a history of charity and transgression,
generosity and violence, sorrow and sanctimony.
For all the good it would do,
one might as well write an elegy for
the scarlet entrails of armadillos smeared
across lanes of the interstate in the spring,
the heaps of most others straddling the shoulder,

tiny paws held up above gray scales,
not blood-flecked and defiant as Bishop had it,
but Chaplinesque in their abjection,
and almost like the old joke's chicken,
comic losers in their desperation to cross
the road and seek mates on the other side. . .

When the barbeque man burst in
while a drag queen boiled around the floor
doing her best Beyonce, lights swirling,
he strode in shorts and Hawaiian shirt
up to the bar, behind which the owl-eyed owner,
a straight man, stolidly poured Daiquiris.
Foot on the bar railing, the new landlord
shouted his desire to keep the place open.
Tiptoeing behind him, a tall man, giggling,
his shirt swirling open, bent to caress
the new landlord's bulging calf muscle.
Grinning into a whirling, draining face,
running his eyes up and down, the tall man
simpered, "Just slap me when I get out of line."
On the spot, Barbeque Man doubled the rent.

BEN MYERS

The Circus Comes to Lincoln County

In a sequined leotard
and opaque tights
a girl stands in front of the sons
and daughters of Baptist farmers.
She has twelve white pigeons
on a revolving wheel,
flapping their wings to rotate,
and the crowd applauds
lightly, the sound of cattle
thudding slowly through the grass.

There is one ring,
a cyclops eye of reddish-brown
earth, that sees, over the course
of an hour,
one lion, two tigers, a clown,
five acrobats, and a man
in an ape suit,

but the act we love is a juggler
named Angel,
a small and dandelion kind of kid,
who spins five rings above his head
like a universe of phantom Saturns.

When we leave, not only the children
are looking back
over shoulders into the shadowed
tent where Angel
is lighting his cigarette.

B. ADDIS. NAYLOR

The Wedding Detour

The wedding was to begin after supper, about seven thirty that night, some ten miles to the south in the auditorium of the Kiel consolidated school. As the pianist, Doc felt it only fitting and proper that he should be early for the wedding, and he had every good intention of doing just that. His formal clothes were packed in a battered, brown Samsonite standing by the front door, and he was washing down a slice of chocolate cake with a glass of cold buttermilk when the phone rang. Had the call not come at that exact time, the day would have turned out differently. But come it did and he picked up the receiver on the second ring.

"Doc, it's me, Millard. Millard Helton. I got me a problem."

Doc groaned inwardly, "Not Mallard Helton," he thought and glanced at his watch. Millard was renowned locally for his inability to get to the point of any story, and Doc knew he had to get control of the conversation if he was going to make it to the wedding on time. Millard's name, his mental meandering plus a side to side waddling gait had led early in life to the nickname that had shadowed him from grade school on. "Walks like a duck," the children on the rural school bus had chanted. Millard had laughed with his tormentors, enjoyed the attention and accepted the moniker. But he preferred Millard. Now, the good-natured bachelor farmer was a fixture in the rural neighborhood, but no call from Mallard Helton could come at a really good time, and time was tight today, what with the wedding and all.

"What's the problem, Millard?"

"One of my heifers is down and havin' trouble with 'er calf. Can you come out?"

Doc glanced at his watch. The wedding was twelve miles southeast of town and the Helton place was in the opposite direction. If she'd just started her labor, maybe he could wait until after the wedding. "How long's she been in labor, Millard?"

"Oh, six, maybe eight hours, I guess. Might be longer, I guess. Saw her this morning when I fed. Missed her this afternoon, and it took me an hour to find her. Sure would hate to lose that calf."

And so it was that Doc pulled on his working boots, pushed a brown Stetson back on his head, threw the Samsonite into the back of the formerly white '54 Ford pickup parked in the yard, and headed out for the Helton place. The pickup's tires were spinning and dirt and gravel were flying as he turned north onto the highway. As the only vet in town, he was used to being called at all hours, and he wasn't really upset. That was just the way he drove when he had some place to go and was in a hurry to get there. And Doc was usually in a hurry.

The Helton place was five north, three east and a half-mile back north again on the west side of the road, just past the Deep Creek Bridge. After he returned from the war to end all wars in 1918, Millard's father bought a Sears & Roebuck house kit for $191 and built the one-story, three-room frame house on land his father had homesteaded. Not much about the house had changed since then.

Millard stood on the front porch, watching a thin wisp of red dust rise above the horizon and chuckled as it approached the house from the south. He methodically sliced a generous portion of tobacco from a plug of Day's Work, placed it between his cheek and gum and began to chew the cud slowly. He placed the remaining plug of tobacco in the bib of his striped overalls, carefully folded the knife and returned it to his pocket; then pulled the bill of his Farmer's Union Co-Op cap lower to shield his eyes from the late afternoon sun.

As the dust devil drew near, Millard leaned out over the edge of the porch, spit a hearty stream of brown juice on the dry grass, and then stepped down from the porch just as Doc turned into the drive. As he waddled toward the pickup, a couple of blue heelers ran circles around the pickup barking half-heartedly as though they thought it was expected of them.

"Shut up, dad-burn it!" he yelled at the dogs as Doc rolled his window down.

"Well, where is she Millard? Let's get after it. We're a-burnin' daylight."

Millard motioned for Doc to follow as he waddled across the yard, unlatched a wooden gate next to the barn and held it open while Doc drove the pickup through. He closed the gate, then squeezed his generous bulk onto the seat on the passenger's side and motioned to a path in the grass. "Heifer's down in a draw by the creek," and leaned out the window to spit.

Sure enough, about a half-mile back in the pasture they found her. A bald-face, dark red heifer, she was lying in knee high grass behind a plum thicket, back a little way from the creek, in the shade of a horse apple tree. Doc pulled the pickup out of her sight and parked it on the edge of the bluff above the creek.

"Don't slam that door. I want to see what we're lookin' at," Doc advised. "And I don't want to have to chase her all over the pasture to do it. So be quiet and don't spook 'er."

Doc eased down the slope and edged around the side of the plum thicket, with Millard following on his heels. As soon as she saw the men, the heifer raised her head and tried to stand, but she didn't make it. Her rear legs just wouldn't cooperate and she lay back in the grass and watched with a wild-eyed stare.

"She's all tuckered out. I may have to pull the calf, but I need to see what the problem is first. Get my black bag and that come-along out of the back of pickup?" Doc directed and backpedaled until he was behind the thicket and out of the heifer's sight.

"And get that lariat rope there in the bed in case I have to snub 'er down."

Moving just a little faster than his usual pace, Millard returned from his errand, set the bag, the rope and the come-along down on the ground and looked at Doc expectantly. "Whatcha want me to do now?" he panted.

Doc thought for minute. "Now listen, Millard. I don't want to spook her. If she manages to get up, I may have to rope 'er and I don't like to do that on foot. So here's what we'll do."

"You stand over there where she can see you, but not too close. She knows you, and if she's got her eye on you, she won't be worryin' about anything else. I'm gonna slip up from behind where she won't see me."

"What'll I do if she tries to get up again?"

"Just back off some more and talk real low. If I can, I'll get this stretcher on the calf. Then when I put on some tension and she feels the pull, I think she'll stay put."

Doc removed a tool belt from the bag, buckled it around his waist. He slipped two short lengths of soft chain into a leather pocket, tucked a towel under the belt, then picked up the come-along and disappeared from view behind the dense foliage of the wild plum thicket.

"You watch out, Doc!" Millard called out. "She's wild as a jack rabbit and likely to kick your head right off."

"Low, Mallard, low! Damn it, I said talk low, not yell to high heaven" came from the far side of the thicket.

The heifer was occupied with her own efforts and kept her eyes fixed on Millard. Doc hooked one end of the stretcher around the trunk of the horse apple tree, snapped the other end onto his belt, hung his hat on a tree limb, dropped to his knees and began to inch his way on his belly through the grass toward the south end of the heifer, dragging the stretcher behind him.

"This is a real minefield," he thought, as he cautiously navigated his way around and between piles of cow patties, particularly trying to avoid the fresh green ones.

In just a little bit, Doc was close enough to see what he needed to see. One of the calf's feet was visible, but that was all. He crawled closer, grasped the foot and began to pull gently but steadily. The heifer seemed to sense the pulling sensation and began to quiet down some, but continued grunting softly with each contraction. Doc formed a loop in the soft obstetric chain, slipped the loop around the protruding calf's foot, just above the hoof and below the fetlock, hooked the other end of the chain to the come-along and slowly cranked the ratchet just enough to create some tension on the foot, but not too much.

"Now, if she'll just hold still for a couple of minutes," Doc thought to himself, and began to speak soothingly to the heifer.

"Soo bossy, soo," Doc repeated over and over again as he rolled up his sleeves and checked her out. He could tell right off that the problem wasn't the calf's size. It was just in the wrong position to deliver. Instead of leading with its nose, the calf's lower jaw was touching its chest. So, Doc pushed the calf just far enough up to create enough room for him to get his hand under the jaw and he pulled upward until the nose appeared on the outside next to the chained foot. Quickly he found the other leg, and drew it into view as well. The calf wasn't overly large, and ordinarily, that would have been all that was necessary for the heifer to deliver her calf, but she was too exhausted to push any more and help was needed. He attached a second chain to the newly found foot, and called to Millard.

"If you want to see this, come on over here."

Millard straightened up, edged away from the heifer's view and retreated behind the plum thicket, shortly appearing behind Doc.

"Is it still alive?" Half squatting, hands on his knees, Millard anxiously rubbed his hands on the pants legs of his overalls and leaned over Doc's shoulder to get a better view. In spite of the shade from the plum bushes, beads of sweat covered his face. The red heifer just lay there, wide-eyed, her breath coming in shallow grunts.

"You don't look so good, Millard. What happened? Swallow your chew?" Doc grinned. "Maybe you'd better sit down."

Doc gave ratchet lever a slow pull and the calf's head appeared. He gave the stretcher another pull, then grasped the calf's legs and tugged on one leg and then the other, as though walking the calf through the birth canal and into the world. Another crank or two on the come-along and the chest appeared, followed by the belly, rear legs and tail, in that order. The calf took a couple of shallow breaths and moved its head. Doc cleared the calf's nose and mouth of mucus, unhooked the chains and he and Millard retreated to the base of the rise, below the pickup to see what would happen.

Well, the heifer began to low for her calf. She struggled to get her rear legs under her, then managed to get up on all fours and began licking and nudging the calf. The calf responded with a little bawl itself and struggled to stand. Unsteady at first, it tottered for a few steps then found a teat and started to suck.

"Well, I'll swan," Millard sighed, "a little heifer."

Doc was a mess. Glancing at his watch, he saw he had only about forty-five minutes until the wedding was to begin. The single dressing room at the school would be packed by the time he arrived, and as the pianist he needed to be ready to play. He could see he was going to have to get dressed before he left Millard's place, so he knelt down on some grass beside the creek and washed up as best he could.

When they got back to the house, Doc sent Millard to the house for something cold to drink, and then placed the Samsonite on the tailgate of the pickup. He flipped open the locks, raised the lid of the suitcase, then took off his shirt and started to change. He removed an old black evening gown from the open suitcase and pulled it over his head. The gown had ruffles around the top and bottom, and was held up by little black straps, leaving his broad, hairy shoulders bare. There was plenty of padding sewn in just the right places to add some curves, and the dress came with a pair of black ear bobs to match, which he clipped on. Next from the bag came an auburn wig with a sturdy permanent wave, followed by white gloves with the fingers cut out so he could still play the piano. Stepping to the outside rear view mirror he added some rouge and red lipstick, and then stuffed his shirt into the empty suitcase.

Millard, who had returned a few moments earlier, stood transfixed, with a cold RC Cola in each hand. He stared slack-jawed as Doc rolled his pant legs up to the knees.

"Well, that oughta do it. What do you think?" Doc asked with hand on hip and a lilt in his voice.

"What in the Sam-Hill is goin' on here?" Millard stuttered.

Millard's expression, Doc said later, made the drive to deliver the calf well worth the trip, and after he quit laughing, he explained.

"Well, it's like this. The Roundup Club is tryin' to raise money for some new buckin' chutes down at the rodeo arena. They're puttin' on these skits when they get a chance, and if they sell enough tickets, we'll have some new chutes.

"Jest what kinda skit you talkin' 'bout?"

"It's a spoof on weddings. We call it a Womanless Wedding, 'cause everyone in the skit's a man, and a roper or a rider, to boot. You think I look funny? You ought to see Stubby Ludwig."

"What in damnation 'er you supposed to be?" asked Millard.

"Why, I'm the piano player. And probably the only roper-piano player in the county," Doc chuckled as he took a bottle of RC from Millard's outstretched hand and popped the cap on the side of the tailgate. "You oughta buy a ticket and come."

As he opened the door of the pickup, Doc glanced at the house, at the privy between the house and the barn, and then at Millard. "It'll only cost you a dollar, and from the looks of things around here, I think it'd do you some good to get out once in awhile. In fact, I think you'd make a fine bridesmaid."

"Bridesmaid? Like hell! I'll tell you one damn thing," Millard said. "They'll never get me in a rig like that!"

Doc took a big swig of RC and said, "Well, you could at least turn loose of a buck now and then. You never can tell. You might even have a good time."

"Tell the truth Doc, I do think you're kinda cute, so you be careful, now" Millard guffawed and punctuated his compliment with a particularly heavy stream of brown juice and a wide tobacco chewer's grin...brown saliva oozed from at the corners of his mouth, framing an array of yellowing teeth, flecked with dark remnants of his Day's Work plug.

Tossing his hat in the front seat and hiking the dress up to his waist, Doc crawled into the pickup. "You see this boot? One more crack like that Mallard Helton, and you know where I'll put it," he warned. "And, you'll need more than that come-along to get it out."

With that he turned the key in the Ford, pulled the gearshift into first, and made those tires spin as he retraced his way toward town.

Doc came to a full stop at the four-way red light in town, and flipped on the radio in the pickup to 930 on the dial. The Four Freshmen crooned "a white sport coat and a pink carnation, I'm all dressed up for the dance" as he crossed the intersection and headed south on the road to the consolidated school with just about twenty minutes to spare. He would have made it on time too, if the left rear tire hadn't blown just as he crossed the Salt Creek Bridge five and a half miles south of town.

Well, that was just about the last straw, and before getting the jack out, he gave the flat a good hard kick with the toe of his boot. He pulled off the white gloves first, lit a Lucky Strike, stuck it in the corner of his mouth and then got to work. He'd just finished tightening the last lug nut and replacing the jack, when a dark blue Cadillac pulled onto the shoulder and stopped a ways back from the pickup. The driver, a stranger, got out, surveyed the scene and asked, "Could you use some help ma'am?"

Well, the "ma'am" didn't register. In the past hour and a half Doc had delivered a calf, changed into his formal clothes, driven nearly twenty miles, had a blowout, changed a flat tire, and now was about to be late for the wedding. He was in a hurry and needed to put that tire in the pickup and get back on the road. He stopped for a second, dropped the cigarette on the pavement, ground it out with the heel of his boot and looked right at the stranger.

"Nope, I think I've just about got 'er whipped."

When a fellow is in a hurry and wants to keep his dress clean, he'll do just what Doc did then, if he's stout enough. He reached down, picked up the flat tire, rim and all, and one- armed it up and over the side of the pickup, where it landed with a thud. With that he hiked his dress back up, got in the pickup, cranked up the engine and tore off in his usual way, leaving the Good Samaritan standing right there on the road beside his Caddy.

As Doc told it later, when he glanced in the rear view mirror, what he saw was that fellow standing at the side of the road next to the Cadillac, watching as the pickup drove away. He looked again, and saw his own reflection in the mirror; the wig, the ear bobs and smeared lipstick. He started to laugh, and for as long as he could see, neither the car nor the driver budged one bit. They just got smaller and smaller and finally disappeared.

And there you have it. That's the way it happened after the call came, or at least that's the way it was told to me. Doc was a little late for the wedding, but no one seemed to mind when he told why later on. That was the same night that Keck Logan's balloon bosom exploded when his groomsman accidentally stuck him with a straight pin on the way down the aisle. And Cletus Polk, who had drawn the shortest of the short straws and had to be the bride, had some more bad luck when he tripped and fell down the steps in front of the altar. Well, it wasn't as much a trip as it was a push. The fall broke his collarbone and he had to go to the hospital emergency room in the wedding dress. But that's another story, entirely.

JUDITH TATE O'BRIEN

Camp-Women's Feet

In summer in the hour or so between drying supper
dishes and chasing fireflies, us oil-patch kids lay
under a porch in the cool dirt, poked roly-poly bugs

with sticks, printed *Bobby Joe loves Lula* and waited
for Lula to erase the accusation with a wild swipe
of forearm. We listened for floor creaks above us

as some kid's mama walked from her smoky kitchen
to a chair just over our heads. She'd carry a jar of tea
for herself and a talkative neighbor. Sprawled on our

bellies on ground that hadn't been sun-scorched, we
nearly dozed to the middle-C monotony of their voices.
Occasionally, as if by prearrangement, all six mamas

would meet on one porch, say Aunt Beulah Mae's.
At such times, I liked to scramble from underneath,
stand eye-level to the porch, and connect our mamas'

voices to our mamas' feet. *Old Man Barnes is gonna
drill a new well over by Seminole*: (that would belong
to a pair of bare feet); *I'll be damned if I'll move back*

there vowed carpet slippers; and so it went—two sets
of bare feet, a pair of leatherette slippers, a pair of men's
shoes and my mother's nearly wordless black pumps.

Cave Artists

Geneticists say the 3 billion of us now living descended from
just a few of you and thus everyone is kin. I think of you,

great grandmother, grinding stone to get just the right color
and tone for the deer-like animal you painted on the rock

walls of cave museums, art that still leaves us gaping
in awe. The whole world was your home in those ancestral

days—every place, any cave. Today hundreds of thousands
of your progeny live no place. I see some of them—cousins

I presume—sleeping in the shallow caves of downtown doorways
trying to keep warm under yesterday's newspapers or

in deeper caves beneath bridges where they're rocked to sleep
by semis driven by all-night truckers. Sometimes, great grandmother,

they seek caves formed by overpasses where they paint
despair with spray cans: *up yours*, and *fuck you*. Graffiti art.

PATRICK OCAMPO

Family Reunion

We have a full house tonight. The rooms
Are filled with illumination and laughter,
my siblings and cousins are dwelling
in the summer satisfaction
of their constructed lives,
sharing stories like pennies,
celebrating the everyday achievement
of memory.

On a couch in the corner, my old aunt sits,
almost alone, her weathered eyes focused
on faded snapshots she can barely see.
"I was there," she tells me slowly,
"and I saw how brutally it was done. And later,
at the funeral, his family refused to clean him up,
because they wanted them to see, they
wanted the Filipinos to see what they did to him.
He was a good man…he was a very good man."
She pauses, reaching inside herself with tired hands.
"There was a song…I don't remember all the words,
But we sang it in the street…"
her low cracking voice begins to sing,
but she loses the words
in the cracked and crumbled
pieces of her memory.
It's a song I know, so I pick up the tune,
my younger voice filling in the words for her.
Nobody else is listening.

She is speaking in fragments now, short words
disconnected memories, scraps of scrolls
from the Holy Land. I want to preserve her,
gather up the faded pieces of parchment
and have her tired hands
show me where to fit the pieces

into the tapestry of her life.
We sit together,
isolated in shadows,
dwelling silently
on the empty spaces
we will never fill.

JASON POUDRIER

Red Fields

My feet sink
into the soil
of my father-in-law's
Oklahoma land,
reminding me of times
before I met his daughter.

When I drove along
in a tank convoy
towards Baghdad
at the same
pace as a tractor
over an unplowed field,
we dug foxholes
in the sand
with every stop we made.
My driver and I would have
fifteen minutes to dig
two foxholes,
with e-tools
better designed for
digging 1'x1' cat-holes.

When the sand was soft
like the overworked
edges of the short-rows
of my father-in-law's fields,
it was a blessing.
We'd dig our holes deep,
safe, to plant ourselves into
if we came under fire,
so we could rise out
when the lead rain ended.

When the sand was as hard
as the unworked
ground hiding under
the buffalo grass,
our e-tools would chink
at the surface with every hit;
our holes would be shallow,
and we'd push the sand up around
the perimeter, making
a false reservoir of safety,
knowing bullets would penetrate
the powdered walls if we were ambushed,
and our bodies would lie
half-exposed in shallow graves,
in pools coloring the sand
Oklahoma clay.

When his daughter was only
a pin-up girl in my mind,
the sandstorms would erase
the foxholes after we left;
now I drive my father-in-law's tractor
and set the plow into the soil
to cultivate his land.

Baghdad International

The ninety-four left
of 3-13 Field Artillery,
Red Dragon Battalion,
drove over
bumps by night,
bodies by day;
then in the afternoons, they bagged
the scrunched, scorched remains
from yesterday's artillery fires,
clearing their claim
of the Baghdad airport.

Then they guarded their plot
with .50 cals, M-249s, 16s, and 203s,
weapons unable to distinguish
between civilians and suicide bombers,
and futile against the harpy-sized,
flesh-eating flies that would invade
night and day, every day.

Nineteen miles and two days
south of Baghdad,
four Dragons went to Heaven,
at least we presume;
their Bibles were recovered.
They traveled by means of burning
in a Humvee lit up
by an Air Force bomb.

Three others were medivacted out,
detached from the ninety-four
as our limbs were detached from our bodies,
saved from witnessing the airport
by means of shrapnel, bullets, and a Blackhawk;
we flew south as the unit continued
on the road home.

One soldier on a stretcher beside me,
his legs had apparently sinned
or traveled upward prematurely
because they didn't accompany us
any longer, nor did what looks my other buddy had.
His face now looks as if it were rained on
by burning shrapnel, which it was.
The ninety-four rose
from Baghdad by means of a 747.
They returned to what once was home.
At least the only other man
to go through Hell and arise
went straight to Heaven after.

They entered another damnation
full of divorce decrees, drugs,
and broken bank accounts;
some brought the death back with them,
just as we all brought back our badge,
and their families got to go through it too.

Few returned to a moment's awkward embrace
of a family knowingly never understanding.
But each of the ninety-four still had each other
until car accidents, drug overdoses,
and return deployments began to pick them off
like a sniper, one by one.

Fort Sill's New Housing Division

> *Military bases name buildings, roads, training areas,*
> *and everything else after highly decorated soldiers,*
> *retired soldiers, soldiers killed in action, or people the*
> *military killed or captured. Geronimo Road can also be*
> *found on Fort Sill.*

I find Robbins Road.

    His freckles sink down,
        the color of his lips runs off
            into his white, opaque skin
                that sags down
                    like a sheet
                        placed over his face.
    Subtle red and blue lines,
        like broken glass
            that stays intact,
                show through.
                    A dark worm of red stretches out
                      from his lips down
                        to the gurney at his back.

I see him finishing
    right after me around the track,
    his gray PT shirt clinging to his heaving chest,
    his freckles shimmering under sweat.
    His crimson lips form a smile.
    I smile back and nod,
    knowing he didn't make time
    for max points,
    but with no heart
    to tell him he didn't.
    He trains me on push-ups
    and sit-ups during the week;
    on the weekend,
    if his wife permits,
    I train him on the run.

I turn left onto Oaks Road.

    He stands guard half out of the top
       of an armored Humvee.
          A bomb hits and he is almost severed
        at the waist. The medics cut
          off his blood-saturated DCUs,
            place his intestines back in,
              and bundle him with bandages.
   But the bleeding doesn't stop.
     He makes it onto the Blackhawk
     but never gets off.

I see him in my peripheral
   standing at attention.
   I curse his creased,
   dark green BDUs
   that make my month-old
   set look wrinkled and faded,
   his kiwi boots that outshine mine,
   which I spent hours on
   the night before.
   The platoon sergeant praises him
   and then steps over to me.
   After cursing Oaks, I ask him,
   and he shares his military secrets with me,
   like he shared his life secrets with his fiancé.

I turn right onto Rhen Road.

   He can't be found at first.
      He took the impact of the bomb.
         They piece him back together,
            no gauze or tape necessary,
         place all that can be found
            of him into one bag with
               his dog tags for identification
                  and send him home
                     to his wife and daughters.

I see him in his dress blues
      at the Saint Barbara's Ball;
      I admire his many rows of ribbons,
      his tight high-and-tight,
      the shine of the brass U.S. and cross cannons
      on his lapel. He is the complete package
      of military bearing, the NCO on the
      Army commercials.
      I watch him smile
      toward his wife
      and her return.
      I don't approach him
      with the smudge on my brass U.S.

I keep searching for my road.

   Shrapnel pierces my back,
      weaving through organs and bones,
         only serrating muscle,
            leaving me perforated, but intact.
   My blood strains out of my body,
      but with several field bandages
         my blood coagulates.
            My lungs keep filling with air.

My PT shirt clings to my chest
   after I pump out the max
   pushups and sit-ups
   while I await the run.

   I press my BDUs with an iron
   and can of spray starch an extra time
   just before formation.
   After heating my kiwi with a lighter,
   I pour it lightly over
   the toes of my boots,
   then begin to shine.

   I remove the smudge
   off my brass
   and call my girlfriend
   to apologize
   for the fight
   we had the night before.

DAVID P. PRICE

Caught in a Rainstorm

as the silver bolts
struck south,
Ramon, his tiny boy,
legs in a grocery cart,
pounded the store glass window
with keys;
then the rain came down
pounding the pavement
in buttercups.
I was wishing for my own set
squatting on the sidewalk
out of the rain
near the tortured turquoise truck,
my tiny bag beside me.

But all there was was the sweeping rain
gushing the streets
blinding the blind
flooding the already flooded fairground fields
across from the all-night grocery store
where the less shop for more
way into the wee hours.
We waited it out,
the rainstorm,
but it never let up.
the rain kept coming on down.

Across the River

he lives across the river,
that boy of mine.

from the weeded plains,
he lives now across the river
among dotted hills
where, i'm told, late at night
deer run through the streets,
and a church bell rings
everyday at six o'clock.

at night as the clock chimes the hour,
i ponder what rights and wrongs I've done;
but i find some peace at last

knowing that he sleeps
while deer browse among the leaves
under shining city lights.

GREG RODGERS

Revenger of Blood

> *By tradition, rather than by the Tribal Law, a Choctaw Indian who had forfeited his right to live by the violation of Tribal law was sentenced to be shot, which was the manner of execution among the Choctaws. The condemned men were privileged to select the person whom he desired to fire the fatal shot. A convicted person always sought the most expert marksman so that his death would be swift and sure.*
> —*Mrs. Mary Darneal*
> *Indian Pioneer History Project for Oklahoma*
> *October 25-26, 1937.*

CHUH-KOWWW

A single rifle shot pierced the quiet green-gold landscape a few miles northeast of Panama, Choctaw Nation. The hot August sun of 1882 punished all those gathered to witness this final rendering of justice. Thin-leafed shade trees surrounding the tribal courthouse, sycamores and one skinny oak, hosted the onlookers, fifty-strong and clinging together in small family clusters.

For over the last fifteen years and twice as many executions, Skullyville County Sheriff Jim Darneal, a half-blood Choctaw, had not missed once. A single shot and another convicted man lay dead. His marksmanship was both—a gift and curse.

While family and friends of the dead gathered for a final glimpse of the body, Darneal removed his hat and mopped his brow. He looked older than his forty-seven years. Dark eyes reflected blue sky as he lifted his face toward the Maker. Streaks of white touched his temples; black despair gripped his heart. By legal decree of the Mushulatubbe District Courts, he had just killed another man. It was his sworn duty to do so if asked, and while there was honor in the old ways, there was also pain - and a price to pay.

The following weeks did little to ease the hurt, but duty kept him strong in the knowing. Three Sundays later, Jim sat in the small Presbyterian church looking sidewards at his wife Caroline, his grown son Stephen, and his son's new bride, Mary. He was lost in the loving memories of years gone by. Caroline gently squeezed his forearm turning his attention away from her and back toward the pulpit. The sermon was starting, and she wanted him paying attention.

Jim heard the preacher begin, "A time to be born, and a time to die; a time to plant, and a time to pluck up that which is planted; A time to kill, and a time to heal; a time to break down, and a time to build up; A time to weep, and a time to laugh; a time to mourn, and a time to dance…"

A time to kill. The words hit hard. Again, he looked toward his family sitting on the pine bench beside him. This was a time to heal. If there was any salvation left to be found, it would come through them.

Outside, an older, brown-skinned man waited on the church steps, his horse tethered nearby. He stood as the door swung open following the service, stepping aside as the people exited. When he spotted Jim and Caroline, he removed his hat and approached. He nodded first to Caroline, then turned to Jim.

"Mornin' Sheriff," he said, kicking his boot dust on the warped wooden stairs leading to the church door.

"Mornin' Elias. What brings ya here?"

"There's been a shooting. Levi James got ta drinkin' and had it in for old Isaac Folsom. He shot him down last night," said Elias. "They're holding Levi at the courthouse for now. Thursday they gonna decide what to do with him."

Jim's shoulders slumped.

After helping Caroline down the steps, he turned back to Elias. "Okay," he said, "tell 'em I'll be there."

Come the day of reckoning, Mushulatubbe District Judge Loring S. Walker sentenced Levi James to die for his crime. By custom of the law, Levi was released to the custody of Sheriff Darneal till the following spring. He would then be returned to the court's custody and shot until dead.

The year he became sheriff, Jim built a one-room log barracks behind his home, for housing prisoners. The room had no windows and could hold up to eight men at a time. The front door was made of two-inch thick oak planks and was secured by a large chain and a sturdy padlock. Escape was possible, but unlikely.

Traditional law had once allowed for a Choctaw who had killed another, whether accidentally or with purpose, to stay at their homes until the execution date. Time was given to settle accounts and make provisions for the welfare of their families. Even then few tried to escape. Whether bound by honor or the fear of retribution upon family members, they appeared on their own recognizance come execution day.

But times were changing. The influx of American law diluted tradition. The need for stricter security demanded adaptation—leaving Levi James to spend most of his remaining days in the dark, cramped room behind Sheriff Darneal's house.

For the next eight months Levi worked the surrounding fields and showed himself to be amiable, harmless, and trustworthy. For Sheriff Darneal tradition was deeply ingrained and hard to forget. He sometimes allowed trusted, married prisoners to return to their homes for one night a month. In time, Levi James was allowed these same privileges, leaving for his home early one morning and always returning by the next.

With nine days left until his execution, Levi left for a final visit home. Jim watched him ride away, wondering if had just made a mistake in judgement.

The next morning, a gentle breeze flowed down from the hills, rolling soft and fluid with the sweet aroma of bursting dogwood buds. New leaves fluttered as if just now waking. A downy wind hugged the tall grass and wafted through an open window, caressing Jim's weathered cheek as he stood looking, waiting.

"What if he don't come back?" asked Caroline.

"If he ain't back by tomorrow mornin' then I gotta go get him," Jim said.

"His poor family must feel so shamed."

"Things change, Caroline. Some men are less inclined these days to be moved by shame. Or honor."

"Well, just don't go off half-asleep, just because he's been behavin'. He's still a killer." In the lingering silence, Caroline stepped to him and touched him lightly on the shoulder. "Jim, you hear me?"

"I'm always careful," came his soft reply.

Well before sunrise of the following day, Sheriff Darneal was packed and ready. Levi had not returned. He mounted his dapple mare and left behind the warmth and comfort of his wife and home. The chilled morning fog blended with the breathy mist of horse and rider.

He arrived at the rutted road leading up to Levi's home around noon. Hugging the trail till a cluster of buildings came into view, he veered off the path and entered a thicket of new-growth maples. White smoke rose from the rock chimney of Levi's clapboard house.

Jim dismounted and tied his horse to a tree. Using the maples as cover, he edged closer to the buildings. He positioned himself behind a broke-down wagon, a hundred feet from the house.

With his rifle in place, Sheriff Darneal hollered, "Levi. You can't stay, and you know it. Now come on out."

No answer. A woodpecker's clack-clacking in the distance marked the passing time. Sheriff Darneal checked his firing pin, making sure it was cleared. Searching for added cover, he moved ahead.

Without warning, the front door opened. Jim raised his rifle. Levi stepped to the porch with his wife and then to the hard-packed dirt below. His oldest boy came out to stand with his mother.

"Go get my horse, son. It's time for me to go."

The boy returned shortly with the horse Levi had borrowed. It was already saddled. Levi took the reins and walked toward the main road. Sheriff Darneal followed behind. As they came to the sheriff's mare, the two men mounted. As Jim turned his horse toward home, Levi stopped.

"I was comin' back Sheriff. I swear it. I just wanted a little more time with Emmie and my boys. You got family. In a matter of days I'll be gone to mine. You understand, don't ya?"

"You killed a man, Levi, and the judge says you gotta pay for it. It ain't got nothin' to do with my feelings about it. *Kil-ia*. Let's go."

Neither spoke as they rode south. Silence clung to the humid air as small beads of sweat trickled down the back of their necks. Both men looked forward, at the dusty road ahead and the dismal days to come. Only seven days remained before Levi's last.

"Will you do it, Sheriff? The execution, I mean. Will you make it so's I don't feel it."

Jim knew these words were coming. He clenched his jaw before replying.

"Levi, son, I'm getting old and my hands have started to shake. It'd be better if someone else did it."

"Don't know no one else that can shoot like you. And I want it to be you, Sheriff. You knew my father. He trusted you, and I do too. He'd be proud to know it was you."

The innocence of the plea sent a shudder through the Choctaw lawman. A long-ago memory caught hold. He saw his now-deceased friend standing by the river with his arm around his oldest son, Levi, already at fifteen taller than his dad. It had been the day Levi was baptized.

He'd be proud to know it was you. The words, plastered by guilt, spread thick in his mind. Then more faces etched his memory—of old men and nearly boys who had once mirrored these same sentiments, asking for a quick and painless end.

"Okay, son. I'll do my best," was all he could manage.

Caroline stood in the yard, scattering chicken feed, as she saw her husband return with his prisoner. Seeing both still alive, she sighed with relief.

Jim took Levi to the barracks, then fed and stabled the horses. He washed the dirt from his face and arms before sitting down to dinner with his family.

Darkness descended and the evening meal was delivered to Levi. With the days chores finished, Jim closed and locked all the doors and shutters to his house. He checked them twice more, a nightly ritual as of late. As he climbed into bed with his wife, she eased herself into his arms. Levi's request still weighed heavy on his mind. "You doing okay?" Caroline asked, kissing his cheek.

"I don't know that I am," Jim said. "Levi's soul might surely be damned for what he did, but what of mine? Is there salvation for me? The commandments state plain as day 'Thou shalt not kill.'"

Caroline took their Bible from her nightstand, sat up, and worked through the pages.

"The Bible also says this," she said, marking a passage with her finger. "The revenger of blood find him without the borders of the city of his refuge, and the revenger of blood kill the slayer; he shall not be guilty of blood."

She closed the leather-bound Bible and placed it next to her bed. "You quit worrying so much about your soul," she continued, holding him close. "The good Lord and I both have worked hard to see that you're gonna be just fine. And I've met few men more deserving than you of a worthy home in heaven."

Jim smiled at his wife for her efforts and gave her a tight squeeze. But he was unconvinced.

Rolling away from her husband, Caroline dowsed the kerosene lamp and the room went dark. She waited for her her husband's steady breath of sleep before closing her own eyes.

Jim stood with his hands tied behind and around the weathered oak post outside the courthouse. In front of him stood a man he recalled by face, but not by name, a man he had executed years ago. The man held Jim's Springfield rifle ready to shoot. The gun spit fire and Jim felt the bullet shatter his knee. The man handed the rifle to another man. One by one, every man he had ever killed took aim and fired, none making a fatal shot. The last in the long line of redemptive executioners was Caroline. She awkwardly pulled the stock to her shoulder and lifted her finger to the trigger. Her eyes bled with anger as she squeezed.

CHUH-KOWWW

The rifle shot jolted Jim into the waking world. He looked around the bedroom. Windows were still shuttered and safe. He reached for his wife, but she was gone.

A soft glow of candlelight came from the kitchen. He rose from the mattress, ignoring the chill. Moved by the muffled sound of crying, he lifted the quilt from their bed.

Jim found Caroline huddled on the floor against the kitchen wall, crying to herself. Lying close to the warmth of the cast-iron stove, she trembled. He sat beside her and draped the quilt around them both.

"I try so hard to be strong for us both," she said.

"I know," he whispered, wiping at her tears.

***

Six days later and one day before Levi's last, a guard authorized by the District Court came to carry the condemned man to the courthouse. Levi's wife and children were already there, waiting to say their goodbyes.

The next morning, Jim again left his house before the sun's first hint topped the horizon. For most, it seemed a promising warm day in early May. For Jim Darneal and those who would gather at the courts, the air hung darker and colder.

Arriving at the courthouse lawn, Jim dismounted and handed his horse's reins to Elias. He stood alone at his usual place. Jim lowered his eyes as three Choctaw Lighthorsemen escorted Levi across the grass and tied him to the post.

Standing twenty paces in front of the condemned man, Jim felt the wind in his face. Levi still reeked of the earth, oak wood, and sweat that had seeped into his pores from months of stewing in the barracks.

A piercing thought entered the Sheriff's mind. *I could miss slightly,* *he thought, just this once, and my troubles would be over.* Word would travel fast and no one would ask no more. As quick as the thought entered his mind, he tossed it aside. *Levi should not suffer for my guilt.*

Years back, he had often asked for a red mark to be painted on the condemned man's chest, giving him a target. Now he knew the spot all too well - no mark was needed.

It was time. His rifle was clean. He had checked and rechecked. Noting how comfortable the gun felt in his grip, he took aim. Clearing the dust and moisture from his eyes, he inhaled deeply. In the distance, Levi's chest appeared just above the sights of his trusted Springfield rifle.

Darneal slid his finger toward the cold trigger. His habit, unknown even to himself, was to touch the trigger, blink once slowly, and fire.

In the split-second darkness of his blink, Jim again saw the face of Levi's father. His hands shook. He opened his eyes and heard the nervous shuffling of Levi's family. They felt his hesitation.

Fighting his desire to lower the rifle, Jim re-sighted on Levi. The young man's eyes were pleading, begging for finality. Jim whispered a quiet prayer and steadied his resolve. He squeezed the trigger.

***

The execution of Levi James was not the last of the Choctaw executions. Later executions took place in other regions of the Choctaw territory, but it was the last one sanctioned by the Mushulatubbe District Courts—and the last one conducted by Choctaw lawman James Darneal.

AARON RUDOLPH

Fixing Things

The morning air cuddles me in half sleep.
My eyes open to the day sneaking inside,
helping itself to my weekend laze. I seek
the silence of late nights, want the walls to hide
me from church bells calling all to morning service.
I cover my head with pillow, a sign that I'm nervous.

Four states away, my father's nailing wood in the hall.
He's hammering together a shelf, a gift
for my mom, at work finishing the night shift.
Once a month I make this long-distance call.
I finally leave bed, phone in my hand again,
practicing *Hello*, mimicking that hard way of men.

Last night, I watched *Breaking Away*
featuring a baby-faced Dennis Quaid.
Dad never cared for film or the music
I fawned over, instead, preferring the much
more active task of chopping wood or the touch
of varnished furniture, cold and slick.

When he answers my call, we stumble
with courtesies. And then there's silence. I smother
it, list my tasks at work, a mundane jumble.
Then Dad repeats a joke he learned from my brother.
Then we laugh and laugh about the dying car
we drove cross country, its sputter lasted so far.

To the Poet in Line at K-Mart with a Handful of Coupons

If you weren't always working part-time
for meager money, you
would've already taken your savings,
booked a flight for Berlin and for a month
or two, photographed the birds, or
the sunsets falling in and out of frame.

You dreamed of collecting plane tickets
like baseball cards stored in a binder,
monuments to watch as dust stacks
itself on them and marks the years.

Instead, you have poems growing
old in manila folders. They gather
like a child's collectibles and you wish
you could trade them in for adventure.

You begin a poem in your journal
about Germany and doodle
a sketch of a bearded, balding man
cupping coins in both hands.

The man smiles as large as a city street,
beside him, a woman raises her beer stein,
winks his way. The sun behind the woman
is bold and carefully drawn,
like the ones you visit in daydreams.

CARL SENNHENN

Oklahoma Street Scene: Noon

Spring shouts with laughter
of students sprinting between cars
to burger joints for lunch just as
an old woman comes down the street
Noise and confusion part
to let her pass
Quiet white haired dignity strides, slow
rich with purpose
her long gray coat a reproach
to windy mischief

Someone's grandmother
she cups weathered hands
against her breast to protect
two trays of tomato plants
their tender leaves
proud green flags in the wind
—emblems—she and they
and the students—sufficient
for spring this early April noon

January Snow and Ice

This afternoon
now that heat
and light have been
restored I labor slow hours
Judging contest poems
about the beauties
of snow
of spring
of summer's roses
and all the while snow
quietly honors winter
just as it did Christmas Eve
—and as reverently
Only, you were here

On the patio
my legless Chinese horse
(his head inclined to the ground)
seems to hunker for warmth
under thickening robes of white
He reminds me of a statue by Henry Moore
or, perhaps, an Oriental Sphinx
but in miniature

Gathered near him
the chaise and summer-lawn chairs
are reupholstered with down
and small birds flit
anxiously across my vision
through thickening branches
their nests in last summer's arbor
lost in white

JUDY SING

Country Sunday

Clean girls toe gravel road to church in June
to see and hear expected scenes within.
Stone-deaf Miz West shrieks out of joy her tune.
No music hides a human voice from sin.

Hard benches claim hard backs for bone-strict hours.
Close air oppresses flowered dresses. Men
in overalls fall solemn, take in powers
from wine and crackers, ask up why and when.

Moist coins flung into collection plate—
spare tokens pay back sad-eyed warner's fame.
Duty done for one more week, the weight
of separation lifts: for this we came.

Same gritty road leads from the church house door,
Same June sun two bits hotter than before.

By The Cedars
The horse stands at the fence,
hoof tucked up,
idle for hours,
not knowing that the little girl
has moved to town.

BENJAMIN SMITH

Fred Hamner in Reverse

shot
back of the head, bullet coming out between his
eyes, caving in his face
dead man identified
Fred Hamner
july 1932

three men, driving a Chevrolet coupe, license
tag number 99-512
robbed Mill Creek bank
shot at pedestrians

running
questioning
what does justice mean
who doesn't have a sin to carry

deputy sheriff
from Wewoka
praying for rain

who doesn't have a sin

SANDRA SOLI

Thursday on Bus 26

Interminable. The man in the second seat unwraps a waxed paper bundle of sandwiches. Smells like bologna, maybe yesterday's. I could gag. It's taking forever to undo the paper. The sound goes on and on. Most of the passengers have traveled to town on this rattletrap for years. They know each other's names, sit in the same seats as though the driver had assigned places. In thirty minutes it will let us off at the corner of Main and 4th like the aging lemmings we are. Some must walk another block to their office tower, and a few will connect with the hospital bus, though first shift people are already at work. It's too early for bologna sandwiches.

You should know we have desperate problems with public transportation here. In Portland, Oregon you can hop a bus to nearly anywhere in the city for practically nothing. Here, a monthly pass costs $30 with free rides on ozone days. You have to get up early to find out if it's Ozone Day because Bus 26 leaves the Park & Ride stand at 6:04 a.m. sharp. Every third week or so it breaks down, leaving riders stranded at the curb of the expressway. I've driven by, pitying their body language, business suits already wilted, everyone on cell phones calling for backup. Usually the red tourist trolley rescues them and clangs its way to town, topping maybe 24 miles an hour the whole way.

Me, I have no backup. If my car goes to the shop, like yesterday, then I walk to Park & Ride and wait in silence, mostly in pitch dark, until the driver shows up to sell me a $4 ticket, one way. What a rip. Once last winter the driver forgot to wait for the woman in her wheelchair who gets off at Goodwill. He left her sitting in snow until a stranger collected her. She had to be delivered to the hospital instead. Did you know paralyzed people don't realize they're getting frostbit feet? I should have guessed that. Things you don't think of unless you're involved. There was a new bus driver right after. How was he to know? The Goodwill store isn't an authorized stop, anyhow.

Today the same women as before are swapping romance paperbacks. I just make notes for my novel. Yeah, one of these days and all that. But I keep writing notes. The wheelchair lady suggested it one day when I was handing her the purse she dropped out of her lap. She even told me her name, but all I remember is her trip to the hospital. She said I was so quiet I must be a writer. Well, sort of, I said. I think stuff, mostly. If these windows were cleaner I would be a landscape artist. She laughed at me then. On my next trip she gave me this notebook I'm using now. Lots of pages. It will take a long time to fill it up. But I liked her even before the notebook.

Today we make it almost to the metro exchange lot next to the sheriff's office, when the bus heaves a noisy shudder and the driver pulls over. Geez, we aren't stopping to pick somebody up. Something really is busted. My fortune cookie must say this is another lucky day.

The driver gets on his walkie talkie. I rub a spot on my grimy window to peer at the county jail, eleven stories. Somebody is midway up, washing windows. Come wash these windows. We aren't going anywhere. My god, you're not washing windows. You're coming down.

I count floors through the dirty blur, four down and two more to the ground. Nimble as Spiderman-in-training, feet splaying out from his body, toe and heel-hooking for balance at each window frame, he claws his way to the street.

The ladies keep reading. One guy is on his laptop, playing a game. The man in the second seat stops eating his sandwich. He looks at me to see if I am going to say anything. Where is the driver? He's in front of the bus, looking like he knows what's going on. But nobody else has noticed our extreme sportsman, his marvelous defiance of gravity.

He approaches the driver of our bus, who shakes his head and throws up his arms like an Italian tour guide, still yelling into his walkie talkie. The man climbs hesitantly, using the hand rail, and stands before us. His hair is a mess. He wears a T-shirt saying ARE YOU SAVED? I thought they wore orange jumpsuits in jail. Maybe he's not a prisoner. Maybe he is going to tell us what's with the bus. But he doesn't speak. He sits down and folds his arms over his stomach. Now his shirt says E   YO ED.

I consider the possibilities: BEYOND ED. WE YODELED. EYES TESTED. ARE YOU LOVED? Yeah, and saved. ARE YOU LOVED & SAVED?

"Hey, you hungry?" says the bologna man, holding up his other sandwich.

"Thanks," says the new passenger. "I could use some a that." He eats the whole thing in a couple bites, then wipes his face with the last of the waxed paper. I look at his sneakers. A dribble of blood leaks down one of his white socks.

I clear more space on my window to see who's coming. Not a soul. When the bus driver returns, hoisting himself into place at the wheel, he announces the trolley will be along shortly to pick us up and everyone will get a free ride card for next month. Nobody is griping. They are used to this.

Spiderman has not heard the announcement. His arm is over his face now. He's saved, and he's asleep.

KATHRYN SPURGEON

Progression

Sunlight, clouded by dark sunglasses,
pours over the green grass and dipping hillsides
where cattle wade in muddy waters,
old barns crumble and barbed wire fences
line dirt roads. It shrinks,
the pasture where brush is plowed under.
Bulldozers level the meadows,
planting rows of gas lines,
ruts of electricity and paths of concrete
where no cows are tethered or horses wander free.

Majestic oak trees give way to Bartlett pears,
swing sets and rose gardens.
The remaining Angus
gather together in clumps
on the far side of the openness
watching the building,
the coming of civilization
while herds of Palominos,
near extinct beasts replaced by bicycles,
watch the creeping face of progression.

Uncertain Future

Stand next to the tall man
in the gray tweed suit
listen to the sound of the train
its feet bellows on
through the earth's deep soil
and shakes the windowpane
in the small-town church
striking fear in the hide
of the mongrel under the porch
of Aunt Bee's bakery
while Main Street's
culinary surprises
bounce on the counter
like a life led
on the train trekking
back and forth
between town and city
unsure of where it's going.

JIM SPURR

The Night is a Neon Halo

There it sat 1.5 miles west of town.
North side.
The old roadside tavern. Once run down.
Now new. In actual fact now a church.
A church by the side of the road.
It had gone from Raggedy-Ann's Drive Inn
to Last Chance Tabernacle.
I went there once to an evening service.
Saw the people. Same one's as
at the old honky-tonk.
Just older.
And they smiled more than the old days.
Remembered me and welcomed me.
There was no question they had become
believers.
Some did light up in the parking lot.
Addicted I guess.
Couldn't put my finger on it
but something just did not seem right.
The place. The walls. The bar.
Maybe that was it. The bar.
Supposed to be on the west side to your left
as you walked in.
It had moved to the north wall.
With a new carpeted red rail.
Someone hugged me (No one would have
done that 20 years ago. Not here.)
and said, "Praise brother, praise."

And I sat down in that place
where I used to sit
that wasn't there anymore
with people I knew and had never known
and saw in that room my world had ended
quietly
just like old Eliot warned me it probably would.

The Sailor on the Honky Tonk Floor

Up against a wall in a bar
near Okemah, Oklahoma in 1955
sat an after brawl human mess.

Two marines started it he said
as he slowly spit a bloody
tooth into my hand.

Anything I can do?
No problem. I won.
I helped him to his feet.
You won? How you figure?

That ain't my tooth.

JANE VINCENT TAYLOR

The Lake Between Us

Lake water here is reddish brown,
full of carp, catfish, frogs, turtles.
But it shines in the sun, sparkling
a corona when a stone is skipped
across its stink-fish surface.

My mother didn't swim and was afraid
of water. Willowy and lovely,
she wouldn't wear a swim suit,
only white shorts and a red plaid shirt
tied at the midriff.

If she kept her platform sandals
firmly on her lustered feet , everyone
could see she wasn't going in. She
and the beach blanket were inseparable;
she and the sun were fine.

The lake was a thing to behold; its depth, width and coolness
no lure. She never saw the underworld of murky water,

or the happy legs of swimmers kicking off the bottom,
a cloud of mud arising off the pebbly floor.

That was the difference between us
I told her once when I was learning
to love the steamy power of a hissy fit.
You just want to be clean and untouched.
I want to swim with impunity.

   (Well, I didn't say impunity.)
That was not the word that hung in the air
between us. Impurity was that one.
I don't care if my new pink suit gets stained.
I don't care if there are snakes on the bank.

It was Oklahoma, after all, very very small
and rusty red in the Cherokee Strip.
Bring on the dirty water, I said, sinking
into the body of Ponca Lake, bring on
the kiss of water moccasins.

SHEILA TIARKS

At the Oklahoma City National Memorial

Sentinel seats
forever empty
one hundred sixty-eight strong,
mother chairs, father chairs
nineteen baby chairs
backs erect as death,
they sit at attention
stone cold marble, bronze, glass.

By night, their lights
illuminate the city.

Days, they gaze in reflecting pool glass
this day broken by whoosh of wings
mother duck, baby ducks
swimming lessons
life.

Oklahoma Burning

They were minor fires,
only forty-eight houses killed
countless wounded
zero mention in the national news.

But we were virgins;
we did not know fire ate horsehair,
could overtake mares and swift colts
that once bested Oklahoma winds.

Our fires had lit hearths
danced on charcoal, made picnics.

No fire known to us
confined horses behind fences
too tall for leaping
and forced hurried burials
before the children came home from school.

HUGH TRIBBEY

Without a Road or Path

without a
road or path, or a
fence or landmark recklessness &
inertia blood hounds
after him
spinning its way

actual ripples
lights flickered all over seen
lots of ray of sun
fell on the
kitchen floor
all the way

down to
Red River those unfamiliar with
the country and gain it
back again time
furnished pasturage
back to six shooters

at twelve o' clock
could not say letter *n*
just such work persecute me
on choice claims
give away
all he has

as a
provident farmer all muddy &
torn knew what a home
meant across his
face death
from Texas with

a chain
a little easy money braced
us Christmas cactus in that
pen hell to
this Jesus
blue phosphorescent light

did the
night riders get things regulated
against the changing world dust
to eat in
a pile
like hogs like

ten thousand
told the tornado vaseline in
our nostrils wasn't my master
done that his
followers He
all time broke

pestilent Russian
thistles britches was the other
man Kiowas made lonely plum
thicket close to
Shawneetown of
cattle on a

stampede right
toward them dust pneumonia too
much of that Blue Dog
the first tornado
blaze-faced horse
was setting the

pace to
grow and swell fresh pork
necessary to out-talk any of
the rest of
us hide
began cried just

like finer
points green corn shootings of
holiday dining a pass to
go any place

[Collage. Source: *Oklahoma Memories*.]

Elma Hartzell on the Page
(after Larry Levis)

The Ben Franklin chin
is two generations away
from the willowy girl in
the blurry snapshot, who unbraids
knee-length hair
to be silly for the camera,
giggles under the arm
of her older sister, the one
with the profile and
"all the personality"
who stepped into
what would become,
one summer night,
the path of a bullet,
to protect a friend
from a jealous lover
while lightning bugs signaled
pale green on the lawn
and the dance band thumped out
"Cotton-Eyed Joe" in the distance—

Elma Hartzell, under a pale,
floppy hat, with her stiff
"Banty hen" gait
and the quick, short strokes
as her sharp hoe slices
goathead runners from the yard
trimmed and fenced,
her fear of water and delight
in stories of drowning,

scandalized by the Comanche family
across the street who dries
meat on their porch in
moist, red, fly-bothered strips,

her chocolate-covered grahams
in the tupperware bowl in the center
of the aluminum and enamel table,
the too-easy WWII jigsaws—
cartoon square jaws, khaki, straps
dangling from helmets
or battleship guns spreading
before a setting sun—
as she and Mom review
gossip and family history,
Mom eventually reciting
the litany of Dad's failures,
on endless Saturday afternoons,

the mewling tone in her letter
as she apologizes to Mom
for not being there when I am born
because Jasper thinks the roads
are too muddy, Jasper
the town con man
with white hair, puffy
fingers and puffy words, whom
she goes back to,
too many times.

A Diastic for Oklahoma

1.
True
grasslands the world
where the rainfall and yet America
to
the great
savannahs
places in stretches
all table. parachute-like growths to moisture
and
a mild

even
not true can
create their not
only used by porcupines, pangolins (scaly
prairie)
ungrazed by

Africa,
for example, special
song flights acrobatic flights, and the
little
interactions not

only
convenient hole leading
tucotucos underground giving chess game of
American prairie dogs

acres
in America I
have captured black-masked rodents called
nest
burrows increase

2.
their range
have these little animals animals
that dig
paws, bumping like

the pallas
may be pronghorns still roam
find more
immune complexity and
great as
a test young of horned ungulates
ungulates must
be birth if

they large
flightless lookouts animal and walk
danger and
by tick birds

waking threatened
and impala dogs are not
large enough
eagles are always

constant close
feed on unprotected if they
essential. You
You may see

3.
their home these remember
animals are dwindling grasslands land
mammals

ever acre single
lands must is switch grass
is

only you travel west
so does the height found
in

Wind Cave burrowing owls
long lithe body falcons swoop
concentrate

landscape with endless
turned the sky the day
whites

4.
Across the prairie, the pronghorn Prairie waving invertebrates—
even crickets,
prairies whose parasites perform nuptial travels
across the prairie

and
porcupine grass dominates the Prairie,
plucks and ruffles
prairie ground.

[Source: *The Amateur Naturalist* by Gerald Durrell with Lee Durrell.]

ALVIN O. TURNER

Cowboy's Grave

The grave lay unmarked
almost fifty years, until
a companion from the fateful drive
remembered, drove 400 miles north
from their Texas home,
borrowed a horse and rode right to
the lonely place, laying
a simple marker there
now covered again with sod and weed
truly forgotten this time.

Panhandle Homes

Houses are smaller there
and stand naked,
without sheltering trees,
to face the harsh elements
as do the ones who call such places,
home.

This hard land demands
hard people, who need little,
who can be taught to forget
there can be easier ways.

RON WALLACE

selections from **Oklahoma Cantos**

3

Steel grey April rain washes
discarded Sonic sacks and Coca Cola cups
into muddy creeks beneath county bridges,
replacing dyed colors with blue sage and white poppies.

4

May shakes out high cumulus clouds
to drift above farm ponds,
where snake doctors dance among cattail reeds
edging muddy waterlines.

7

A barbed wire spine rusts, buried in bark
beneath a cardinal's song,
and orange-flamed Paintbrushes split coyote bones
in an empty pasture.

9

A crisp brown husk climbs a plank
of grey barn wood,
lifeless, wingless with the locust flown
somewhere into the surrounding sea of green.

10

Scattered cattle stand in broken shades
of a few post oak trees
off fenced edges of black-patched two lane highway,
dusty buffalo grass burning in July heat.

11

Red dirt dust collects on dented fenders
of a '49 Ford left to rust
among blackjack oaks sprouting through
the ghost of a flathead V8.

12

A winding creek bends under remnants
of barbed wire sagging across a shallow gulley,
where fireflies appear in flashes, disappear, and reappear
in tangled vines above the ravine.

14

The long July days end in fire
rising from a western sun sinking into slate blue
as dusk unpacks stars to tack black onto night
and cool the heated air.

17

A distant train whistle writes lines of poetry
for the last lightning bugs of summer;
the night sky already smells like October,
slipping through torn hickory leaves.

19

Rain gathers in low, black clouds
moving like dark herds across the sullen sky—
rolling, changing, sputtering
in a stampede ahead of the forked lightning.

21

Air comes alive with scorched yellow
whirling in torrents on a sweep of north wind,
and a spike-antlered buck walks the fence line
of a neighbor's pasture.

22

The steel sky lowers its weight
onto the skeletons of walnut and pecan trees
pressing sun into the ground,
burying its fire in the still blackness.

23

A green-eyed solstice sings winter
to life in flames of the shortest sun breaking
the season wide open,
drawing the cinch tighter on the year ending.

25

Two scraggly black calves
stand in a pasture of white Oklahoma snow
pulling cold tendrils from a round bale
steaming beneath the dark skies of a winter day.

26

In the hours before a new beginning
comes the sound of wings,
with the shadow of a hawk who brought
the snow of the moon to the world.

27

Old years close in flares of light,
and new ones are born bathed in blue,
days dancing like Cheyenne warriors
calling ghosts to ride with them into the fight.

MARK WALLING

The Jeep

The sand and the water gave us vertigo
  but we hoped for amnesia
when we saw the river crest the windows
  of the Jeep, tires spinning
like the damned, unfelt, unheard, and we remembered
  it was January.

They wanted to climb out and perch like the shipwrecked.
  I screamed, *Get out and push!*
and they knew they had handed their trust to a loser.
  One of the six said, *We're gonna get wet,*
and the Jeep slipped a step, and we cried
  at the sight of the bridge and the sky,
and crawled out.

  The cold water on my socks and underwear
was the sound of my father's voice
  waking me to his dream, which began
with the gift of a '65 Mustang convertible I cruised
  back roads in, high-beams seeking
my own tragic vision in the ocean-womb of night.
  I never knew the level of the oil
or washed the country's dust off, and after
  unveiling the hose and wax a third
time, he followed his wiping with transparent tape
  and a For Sale sign.

I shrugged, then received without ceremony
  the used Jeep as replacement
and commentary, a tool to drive out of the wilderness
  of adolescence where he couldn't trail me.
Three months of possession, twelve weekends of chagrin
  for friends who wanted to cover
anything with tracks but a road, and I obliged them,
  a Sunday surprise. I could see

dirt roads weren't on any map of dreams, so I launched
     us to the river bed where men lived,
reeling the world by hand. I made the tires bite,
     spun sand into a cloud of snow,
crossed the water at an ankle-deep point, but upon return
     found the earth had turned,
and we went down.

     There was no ice,
but it was cold, and when one of us found
     a drop-off, he emerged, spewing,
I'm gonna freeze to death! and ran and fell again.
     Good, I yelled. We trudged up the embankment
heavy-legged, unconcerned about stick-tights or burrs
     or branches scraping skin.

Atop the bridge, we began the two-mile walk to town.
     I cannot say if the others looked down
at the river. I didn't and knew Lot's wife
     was sinless because she could,
and that God the father was human, trapped by children
     and his own commands that interfered
with his dreaming. My father would not believe me
     when I told him and remained unbelieving
as he stood on the bridge.
     He made me a pillar there in his weaker way:
You will never do anything again.
     I wanted his judgment to come true
not because I was guilty but because
     I was sober and awake,
yet still longing, as I stood with him at the top
     of our small world, more desperately
than before for a dream that could not be forsaken
     by the horizon.

THERESA-ANN "TRIXIE" WALTHER

The Beating

Against faded sheets she lies
bent like a comma, legs twisted
and falling aside, her
face ruined
her mouth open
as if last sounds
were yet to burst through.
The imprints knotted on skin
are heavily veiled
by tangled black hair once
brushed and gathered back,
her hands clasp closed
a nut brown dress unable to hide
the marks puzzled up-slanted to knees
bruised like plums. And yet this photograph
catches the improbable color of iris
while the image remains
flattened and remote

Summer 1981

I fell in love that summer with her uncle
with his twenty-two-ness and his rest-less-ness
when she and I were best friends
thirteen and dying to grow up
the two of us with James our secret
confidant interested
with me always
in the middle on stolen midnight trips
to see the ocean's moon, parked in shadows
an arm around my neck, fingers
fondling breasts just beginning to bloom
with confusion a tingle, an urge
to know and no one cares when my panties
slide aside just Lily
beside me smoking and passing joints
laughing and oblivious that I was
dizzy with pleasure
dizzy with shame

PAMELA WASHINGTON

The Cache I Carry

Okies know it,
West of Lawton,
Outsiders spell it wrong.
I carry it.

I carry nostrils full of horse sweat and manure—
The scent of Grandpa's aftershave, Old Spice,
Stays on my check after, I am lifted up and on
My first horse and weakens the other two.

The smells of kitchen work, meals for men,
Hang still on my clothes as remembrances,
Grandma's meatloaf, fried chicken, and okra
Construct the aroma of the feasting family I carry.

I carry the recited sound of surrounding towns—
Neighboring kingdoms, Snyder, Indiahoma, Meers,
And the trinity—Cyril, Sterling, Fletcher.
Names chanted from a green highway sign.

The rhythm of my own name Pamela Sue,
A sound heritage of two-named relatives,
Ina Mae, Charla Faye, Bobby Gene, Clarence Wayne
Cadences the familiar, familial I carry.

I carry the local color of my Grandparents' house
Yellow with green shutters, surrounded,
Surrounded by flowers, purple, yellow, red,
Their petals clung to my plucking fingers.

The tones and hues of my home come from
Iris, Holly hock, Poppy, Indian Paintbrush.
Flower seeds handed around in garden club,
Populate the fragrant fields I carry.

I carry the heat from the sun soaked
Brown bodies of my cousins as we
Puppy pile on mattresses strewn on the floor
Rough sheets, line dried, against our skin.

The feeling of bare feet on red dirt walking to town
A pleasure copied into my DNA.
Squishing mud, kicking up dust, kneading grass,
Transmits the finest freedom I carry.

I carry the taste of orange candy peanuts,
Dug from Grandpa's pockets at the rodeo,
Popcorn with too much salt and butter, and
Cokes with peanuts from the Dairy X.
.
Children spitting out lake water after a belly flop
Hear of a swallow of creek water.
The cold water from the hose in Grandma's yard
Is the water purity measure I carry.

I carry Cache.

L. MICHAEL WEST

Beyond the Gate

It is already warm. I may have waited too long but the Boxers, Bella and Max, are dancing at the back gate almost before I pick up the leash. I slip the collars around their necks, adjust the lead, and allow them to gently pull me into the alleyway.

The gravel road is almost as old as the city, which is near creation as far as locals are concerned. On one side I can see people in a parking lot, closing car doors and hurrying so as not to be late to work. On the other side I see the backs of houses long past their prime. They tell a story: once built for families, then occupied by older couples and now by low income renters. The little fences built for gardens, white washed tool sheds, and freestanding garages reveal the number of decades they've stood here. The dogs lead me down the alley past the cane patch, around the corner and to the dirt path that leads to the walking trail. The houses on this dead end street are far beyond repair, the kind with plywood over windows, rusted tricycles in the yard and gaudy Christmas decorations that never come down. I shudder as I realize at least one of those rooms has a child in it with a neon Budweiser sign as a night light.

Bella leads and then Max, down the embankment and a spry hop over the trail side ditch, neither willing to get their paws wet. This early in our walk they're still house dogs, a fact that will seem impossible the further we venture from the gate.

We head south down the cement path, built upon the bed of an old railroad track. We pass by the abandoned car tire that no city employee bothers to pick up no matter how many times he mows around it. On the east side of the trail is the old house with the cinder block outbuildings behind it and the small catamaran I've imagined owning since I was a small child. The dogs sit when we reach the street as they've been taught and it makes me smile. We look both ways and then cross.

Immediately on our left, there's a lot where someone has lived, I imagine, all their life. In my memory, the place has never changed- it is a hold out from the past with long poultry sheds filled with chickens and pigeons. I can hear the rooster crow from my house as I drink my morning coffee. Either the sound or the smell of the birds begins to affect the dogs and their gait. They pull a little less on the leash, smell a little more on the wind, and watch the tree line for something in motion.

Moving forward, the tree line becomes a wall of oak limbs kept in line by the gravel on each side of the cement walkway. The sounds of the city fade, replaced by the screaming of cicadas. We can smell the woods. Sap, dirt, and decomposing leaves. Its a sweet, earthy smell that makes you notice that you're breathing.

The dogs begin to pant, walking with their mouths wide open, tongues lolling to one side. Puddles and ditches are tromped through now as a right of passage with each dog smiling like only Boxers can, lips pulled back like on a joker's face from a deck of cards. You are never sure the meaning of that grin, whether they are laughing with you or they're about to eat you. Neither dog has known a life where they didn't sleep indoors but all it takes is 100 feet of wood-line to make the wild dance in their eyes.

Maybe it's the dogs, or the wind in the leaves. Maybe it is just being somewhere without a to-do list, but I can feel my instincts sharpen as well. Suddenly a man who says "Huh? What did you say?" three hundred times a day can hear a finch scrounging for food in the leaves of the woodland floor well enough to locate her. But the point isn't to think about these things too long. Just be. Just absorb. Just partake of the world around me.

The tree line starts to break. Here and there you can see the backs of houses. On one side are brick homes no older than I am with pools and decks. But on the other side, sit frame houses that remember the sound of the whistle and the smell of the coal from when the railroad engines used to pass.

Soon we pass the end of the trees all together and the tall prairie grasses of Oklahoma take over, like they always do any space left untended too long. The land slowly flattens in an expanse of green and yellow that sways and swells like the waves of the ocean. Grass is loud, even deafening when there are no car engines rumbling by to squelch it. It sounds like millions of high pitched scratchy voices pleading for you to listen to a message of urgent importance. I cannot tell what the grass has to say, maybe I've forgotten how to listen. It sounds rebellious, even revolutionary, like it's waiting for the day it will rule the plains again.

Off to the south is a small shallow pond where my son first realized how the cattail plant got its name and the giant bluff where generations of locals have searched for fossils. The land has been developed some. There's a paved street and someone has added large landscaping rocks around one side of the watershed.

The red pole the city placed to keep cars from driving down the walking path marks the end of our walk. It comes too soon. Ears get scratched and my face gets licked and we turn back. The walk is always shorter back than out. The passage is an odd journey, like Alice falling back up the rabbit hole, returning to civilization, productivity hacks, kennel cage doors and bill notices. The grass hisses, the cicadas sing, some rooster crows and then the gravel crunches beneath our feet leading to the little gate that takes us home.

Once inside, the two panting dogs lie down, making as much contact with the cool hardwood floors as possible. They are house dogs again, full members of the family with squeaky toys and a massive bean bag. I have to hurry, there are things to do, but for a while longer I notice when I breathe. For a little while yet I smell things I normally miss and I listen for the grass to whisper its espionage.

Today I sit at my desk enjoying coffee with friends. I rest comfortably in the most urbane place I can create for myself, but even here I remember that the grass still speaks. And somewhere in the back of my mind I wonder if tomorrow I might whisper back.

WHY/HOW

DOROTHY ALEXANDER

State of the Arts in a Red State

From here, the eye moves outward
over flat land toward the far edge
of more space that most can stand.
Cheyenne, Arapaho, Comanche
who roamed here tracking humpbacked
herds through rolling oceans of grass,
called this place the horizontal yellow,
when nothing else but sky broke
the grand sweep of distance.

Now, phallic forms rise whitely
from the flatness. Erect grain bins,
prairie cathedrals, giant wind machines,
give definition to endless air
and counterpart to tiny bright clusters
of poets and artists, branded "other,"
who persevere, huddled against ragged
winds of self righteousness and fundamentalism,
adding a welcome dimension to this raked stage,
hanging by their fingernails, suspended
over the edge of the known world.

Civility in the Slow Lane

Last week, driving on Interstate 40, trying to stay under the speed limit, I noticed the driver behind me was obviously anxious to move faster than that. He kept honking at me to move on. However, I steadfastly stuck to my law-abiding pace, which only increased his agitation. Soon the vehicle on my left moved ahead and into my lane. Then the speeder made his break. As he came even with me, his middle finger shot up and literally quivered as he stretched his arm as far in the direction of my face as possible.

Now, I know that's not a rare occurrence. These days when rudeness is rampant and incivility is everybody's everyday problem, the raised middle finger is the trademark sign of those who flout the rules of civility by "flipping off" or "giving the bird" to any fellow human whom they perceive as an impediment.

But, every time it happens, I am reminded that a raised finger can also mean something entirely different. Where I live in sparsely settled western Oklahoma, and in many other rural areas of this country, when you see the driver of an oncoming car, or more likely a pickup truck, raising his first finger in your direction, don't think that you are the target of anger or rudeness. On the contrary, it is a greeting, an acknowledgement of your presence, a nod. The driver is conferring his regard on you.

When I drive in my home territory, I automatically raise the first finger of my right hand as soon as a vehicle gets close enough to see it, and I have come to expect the same gesture in return. It's the polite thing to do, like saying "How do you do."

But, not everyone reciprocates. When that happens we might say, "He must be a sorehead" or "maybe he's "from off." And if you meet 10 or 12 cars in a row who do not
raise a finger, then know you are nearing a city. In towns of more than 2,500 people rarely show such courtesy.

It used to be only men did this when they met another man on the road and refrained when meeting a woman; but for the past several years I have noticed that women have taken up the habit (unless they were very old or very conservative), and men do it regardless of the gender of the other driver.

I have noticed also that Democrats do it more than Republicans; that teenagers sometimes don't recognize which finger you have raised, and respond with the rude middle finger. It has come to my attention that elderly farmers deliberately do not make eye contact as they pass. So, I discreetly look straight ahead as we meet with our respective fingers in the air. It seems to set better with them if you don't try to turn it into something too personal.

Then, there's the accepted way to actually display the finger. My method is to place my right hand on the steering wheel (if it's not already there when I see a car coming.) As they get within, say, 50 or 75 yards I casually raise the finger above the level of the wheel and let it stay there until the car has passed. Some people I know make a quick jab and let it go at that, but I prefer the extended version. However, if I meet two or more vehicles in succession, I do lower and raise my finger quickly so that it doesn't appear to be just one generic gesture. I like to greet each one individually. I consider that more polite.

So, when you pass through my part of Oklahoma, keep that first finger poised for a quick draw. Otherwise, we'll think you're not friendly.

TINA BAKER

My Ducklings

It's my little secret. I don't really have my ducklings
exactly behind me, one perfectly after another,
but I truly want to think I do.
So:
Don't
hang the wet cotton dish cloth over our beautiful amber canister set,
scratch and scrape on the nonstick skillet,
drive my car except in an emergency,
or leave clothes, like little mole hills, all over the floors.
Because, I'm convinced I never would.

I have suggestions, tips, heartfelt hints,
and here are a couple: first, to cook tender stew meat, stew it!
meaning stew long; longer than 15 minutes.
And second, you must try feta cheese.

I'm beginning to wonder; could I put a band-aid on the lip of a
cracked tea cup
and still use it;
use it to hold a candle or a violet?
Could I hit the wrong note, burn the buns,
break the glass, leave the ice cream out?

Yes, I admit it.
My ducklings do waddle off,
but I truly want to think they don't.

DANITA BERG

Head of the House

The couch cushion is dented and frayed from multiple scratchings, turnings, and settling-ins. He likes it here most because he can lie in the sunny patch from the living room window and look out, waiting for one of us to pull into the driveway. The cushion smells of body odor and hair, of urine and oatmeal shampoo, and we're going to have to replace the couch for the fourth time in as many years, all because this one cushion looks so bad, because of him.

But today, he's not here.

And the sunny spots in the backyard, the bare areas where he's dug away the grass to expose the warm soil, where he likes to roll on his back and reveal his pink stomach to the sun—I expect to see him here, giving me his upside-down, thick-lipped grin. I remember him offering me a view of his crooked underbite while waving his legs in the air. I know you called me, but the sun … feels … so … nice. Perhaps you'd like to rub my tummy, just for a minute, before we have to go in?

He's not here either.

I can walk easily through the kitchen, not tripping over him when I try to turn away from the refrigerator. I'm not pushing him down from the table, no no no, trying to keep his face out of my Cheerios before I'm through with my breakfast, trying not to laugh at his googly eyes, which only encourages him to put his paws on the edge of the table.

He's not here to trip over and to beg.

It's odd to go to bed and to be able to easily access my husband, to not have to shove our missing boy down to the bottom of the bed and to admonish him gently. The behavior we've scolded him for countless times … no, you can't sleep between us, no, you can't have more of the bed than we get, I don't know of any other dog that wants to sleep with his head on the pillow … it's behavior we'd welcome now. As much as I've complained about his snoring, his 3 a.m. barks to go outside, his insistence to pin down my feet when I sleep so that I wake up with leg cramps … well, I'd never complain if he would come back.

Because where he is right now, is in an oxygen tank, tubes inserted into his neck and his leg, wondering why his mommy and daddy left him in this weird place full of other sick dogs. He wants to know why he can't come back with us, why we couldn't better explain that it is best to leave him in this sterile environment, with strangers in white lab coats and a dog that whimpers in pain from a car accident. There he is just a medical case, a five-year-old Boston terrier that passes out from a lack of oxygen and inability to sleep for the last month.

When I get the call at my college, in a break between classes, that the vet is "most concerned," he says that we shouldn't get our hopes up. I want to go to the clinic, less than 20 minutes away, where he is wondering why someone hasn't come to get him out. Instead I go back to class and sniff theatrically to emulate allergies, hoping to convince my classmates that I'm not crying over what others might consider just a stupid dog. I imagine those warm patches of dirt in the backyard, and wonder which one Simon would like best to be buried in. I reach for more tissue.

Tonight, my husband and I go to bed quietly, noting how silent the bedroom is without Simon to jump up on the bed before us, to insist on one more game of roughhousing and ear chewing before calling it a day. Without his kicking and snoring, we sleep restlessly, and more than once I reach over to pat the little head that isn't here.

In the morning we get another call. The hospital found a mass growing in his nasal passages, the size of a lima bean. It's going to cost the price of a good used car to take it out. Are we willing?

We look around the house where we can't tell him to quit ruining the furniture with his incessant scratching, and where we haven't complained for days about the cost of upholstery cleaning. Here is his limp leash, because we do not take him for his walks. Neither of us has been able to fluff up the flattened couch cushion.

Yes, we are willing.

Four days later we bring him home, a bandage circling his neck to protect the open wound from his tracheotomy. His spine and rib cage poke through his skin because he's lost his appetite from worrying and not being able to swallow properly. He warily circles the living room, eyeing us as the traitors we are for leaving him in that terrible place. He goes over to his bowl and takes a cautious drink of water. Then he goes back to the couch and finds his place on the dilapidated cushion. He rolls over on his back and puts his belly to the air, snoring contentedly.

Now we are home.

PAUL BOWERS

Vortex

Thirty years ago my father disappeared
As if, by throwing open the front door
Of our blistered yellow house,
Leaping from the tongue-and groove-porch,
He dove, body and limb,
Feet first or head first,
I don't know which,
Into a passing tornado.

He was not the proverbial flying Guernsey, though,
Or the mailbox sailing
To a different postal code
Or the two-by-four piercing a scrub oak trunk
Or the Buick, occupied by a vacationing family
From Wisconsin, flipped and spun, then
Released into a horse pasture, right-side up.

Rather, he entered the vast eddy
And never came out to describe
The marvels of his flight,
Or explained why my mother's whispered words
Were not enough
Or why I was not enough
To resist the thrill of circulation.

I imagine, by violent updraft.
He achieved the gates of heaven.

Even now, my life is dominated by wind:
Bullied clouds overhead
Harried, frustrated blackbirds
Driven back against their desires.
Outside my evening window
Leaves puzzle and unpuzzle
With each southerly wave.

I cup my ears when the sky darkens
And catch gusts in my palms.
I breathe in and breathe out
My own treacherous vortices.

Angles of Defense

You ask me if it's all right
to drink bourbon and exercise
simultaneously. You leave
the refrigerator door ajar.
You never do the dishes.
You leave the seat up.
You cut the grass too short.
You kiss funny on Sundays.
You burn meat on the grill.

You don't square your shoulders
when we argue, but stand
askance, side-cocked
like a prisoner too cowardly
to keep his eyes
open and heart exposed
to the firing squad.

Balance

Two dogs splay
on the lawn, bear-skin-like.
Crape myrtles blow pink, the leaves
on the elm above
my head are poxed
by some sort of infestation:
a thousand pricks
of a pencil lead
through each leaf
and vein, like the work
of an angry child.

I look beyond
the pasture fence
to the horses standing muscled
in September heat.
I feel like drinking Chianti
in a swing, and kissing
your full summer thighs.
 I feel like eating tender fish
and the last tomato not yet
come from Ecuador.
I feel like cursing this mid-year
moment when I cannot
strike my balance between
the equatorial sun
and the striding, funneled
walk of autumn.

TIMOTHY BRADFORD

Four Poems for Tamara

1.
The earth loves
sticking to your feet. Two

horses against a fence strain
for the greenest. Nothing

moves too fast for you,
but do you know
how the Himalayas grow?

2.
You have educated my feet
in dance. At night I place

the opiate of poems in your ears.
Your thighs are warm snow,

their melt is the spring
I drink. Cold water for dark animals.

3.
Who can prove that we
are not for each other?

Show me for certain
the place where we part.

I've not seen the knife
sharp enough.

4.
Someday I will hold you
past your will, past noon, from the rush

in the streets. I will kiss your eyelids,
large as a Monarch's wings,

and make us famous to no one
like the grass that feeds a horse.

The Poet at Seventeen
—after Levis after Rimbaud

His youth echoes with the clipped, mechanical clicks
of an Italian bicycle's freewheel over the back roads
he traversed, too disciplined, believing his shaved,
muscled legs starred with ingrown hairs would carry him

like sails. All day outside, the Oklahoma summer
brought out the olive tint in his skin, said to be left
by some Gaul good at building actual bridges
despite leaving only a pier in his father's heart. Leafing

through cycling journals in the dim, artificial cool of his room,
he imagined this absent grandfather architect as hailing
from Normandy, where Jacques Anquetil, 5-time winner
of *Le Tour*, was born. His father had Anquetil's strong nose

and financed weekends racing in Ft. Worth, Wichita,
Moline. His team met at Love's Country Stores, slept at Motel Six.
Oh, the cultural education, like a trucker's! On Sundays
after races, muscles sore but content unlike his head,

he'd return with a bit of prize money or a new jersey.
Café Columbia: good climbers. *7-11*: American hopefuls.
La Vie Claire: the champions. And he felt safe then, knowing
how to take a corner at speed—the set up, how far to lean,

the exiting arc. He was even happy in his routine, rising
at 6 a.m. to ride a couple hours before school, or during summer,
the lunch shift at a French restaurant in a strip mall,
the only place that'd give him long weekends off.

Leaving early, he'd avoid his parents and his neighbors
while the façade of each suburban home sang only to him. Every day
another day to sprint to town limit signs, get caught in rain storms
and come home drenched and worn, hungry as a beggar.

And on weekends with no races, Jimmy, the team coach,
drove his old yellow Chevy Cavalier at 30 m.p.h. with the hatchback
propped up while he and his teammates motor-paced behind, tucked
into the slipstream. "It's how they get fast on the Continent,"

Jimmy'd roar over the classical station blaring on the cheap speakers,
his grease-patinaed hands punctuating the tempo on the dash
as the smell of dope and espresso got churned into the air
rushing by them. Once, he felt too strong for the pace, left

the safety of the slipstream and raced up alongside the car,
trying to equal its speed on his own. Head tucked low, mouth
gulping air like a dying catfish on some red earth shore,
he couldn't keep up and had to duck back into the draft.

At least he had that kind of determination then, and welcomed
the physical world while feelings remained orphaned. Girls?
He wore the odd luck of the disinterested and dated
some attractive ones, but his blushing ambivalence

ended most nights early. Their scent on his skin
he'd cover with Lycra the next morning to carry with him
like a mantra for a hundred miles. With the blind faces
of homes behind him and an open, road kill-studded

way before, he felt sure of his ability to escape his beginnings
by sheer muscle power connected to pedals, his weight
suspended over roads leading beyond the borders
of all the earthly and interior maps he knew.

MIRANDA BRADLEY

My Five-Year-Old Daughter's Bunny
(The one I begged my husband not to buy)

I hold him,
dying—

not dead.

His black fur shines—
velvet waves
Apache hair.

A warrior body,
half-alive,
shudders
then
calms
between
convulsions.

The splintered,
tiny neck
beneath fluff.

His face is wet
from my tears.

I nuzzle,
sob, heave and
he struggles more
to lift,
hold breath,
live.

He will only go
by force

so I place my first
and middle finger
against his nose.

NATHAN BROWN

Cotton-Picker

He picked cotton as a kid in Cyril
and pushed around cranky milk cows
over on the poor side of the tracks
in a tiny town that didn't have
any wealth on the other side.

After he turned nine, the family moved
across the tracks to what became known
as B & E Street (Brown & Ellis)—
all the postman needed to deliver a letter.

In high school he played shortstop for the Pirates
well enough to get a scholarship to OBU
where, as a lefty, he's held—since '54—
the highest batting average for 55 years.

That was enough at the time
to get the attention of the Oakland A's.
But he became a Baptist preacher instead.

And for the better part of a half century
he tried to teach the better parts of God
to a flock that—more often than not—
acted like a bunch o' cranky milk cows.

And he did what he did
as well as anybody ever has.

And my brothers and I always had skateboards,
warm beds, and hot chocolate in January.

He still gives us what he can—
sometimes more. And I believe
he loves this life and smiles with hands
down deep in secret, sacred pockets,

because he's never forgotten
how those hard, dry, cotton husks
sliced the hell out of his fingers.

Southern Concern

To speak of the lower Great Plains
is to speak—always and eventually—
of the Southern Baptists.

These good folks are nothing
if not concerned. And not necessarily
just for your everlasting soul. No…

they feel led to cover more territory since—
as any cursory glance at modern society reveals—
God has grown somewhat lax in his policing
of the planet over the last half century or so.

Therefore—in picking up the slack—
they're concerned about your dating habits.
For instance, if you're forty and still single,
something must be amiss in your prayer life.

And they also worry about the general public's
misperception that fermentation might have
played a role in the great grape juice miracle
Jesus performed at the wedding in Cana.

And they simply live in abject fear
that all the virtual nudity—just one
of several questionable side-effects
in today's fashion—so rampant
among young people, might
make them more prone
to dance at this year's prom.

So if you slide down, or in,
from the north, or the west, know
that they will be concerned about you too,
along with all the foreign influences and organisms
you might introduce into their holy ecosystem.

However, take some comfort in knowing
that their primary targets will always be, first
and foremost, their own wounded and fallen.

Natural Flavors

The trail of their tears
ended—some say—
in Tahlequah, Oklahoma.

But the tears of the remnant
continued to fall long after
their feet came to a stop.

That's how the Cherokee spread
throughout the water supply
of this grassy hinterland...

their salt and blood
seasoning the rose rocks
and dark red dirt.

SHARON BURRIS

New Year's

And of me, what do you wish?
A woman more caring, more focused,
a woman more graceful,
softer of voice and
step?
One more able to
show what she
feels,
to say "I love"
you and all
more easily
off the tongue.

It is, of course, what I wish of myself;
another way
in which we are one.

Fairy tales unspool and I balance
on a dew-drenched web
between lover and killer
and embrace
both
in my strong hands
and you
are the silver rod I grasp
to not topple.

There are no nets
ever.

Incantation
(from the Other Voices series)

Ish a' cammanda yowen!

The words mean nothing.
What matters is
my eyes, crazed, half shut,
tears streaming the kohl around my lashes
into black scars down time-worn cheeks.

Ish a' cammanda yowen!

Greasy, graying hair falls
in tangled mats over
my hot face,
patterning the writhing firelight
as this ragged skirt
swirls the dust around
my dirty toes.

Ish a' cammanda yowen!

The words mean everything.
A hunter's moon gives them power.
My raspy chant gives them life.
The night magic dripping from
my pores like sweat gives them the
weight of a blade,
the potency of a plague.

Ish a' cammanda yowen!

Tomorrow, you will die.
I have said the words.

CHRISTOPHER W. CLARK

Another Love Poem

Your grey eyes, gemmed in spokes of light,
Like stars pricking against threadbare spaces
In rain-churned clouds, or luminous millwheels
Turning in a slow dance against darkened sky—
Not quite, no, like something else entirely

Your eyes a bat-blown, star-sequined darkness
On which had been breathed the first faint
Pearls of morning-light—but no, that's not right, either—
They were like something, a palimpsest maybe?

No, I'm thinking of intaglio, or that other thing,
Some color, what is it? reminds me of a Brueghel
Painting, you know the one—

Your eyes, they were like birds—no, words—words
Written on a frost-lettered windowpane,
Etcetera,
Etcetera

But they were kind eyes, after all,
And they held a secret and a promise
Too rich for telling, even in poems

In Defense of Our Time Together

You might have bloomed once, you tell me,
A pale-green bud trembling on the edge of blossom—
But I was a frost, a late ice storm in March,
A killing, captive cold, that snuffed to smoke
The bright flame quivering within you—

Only you did not see, you could not see
How much you flamed, how deep the blossom,
When the late, lingering sun kindled
You—for a moment—to an ice-married brilliance

Gravid Spider

A pale weaver suspended in moonlight:
Upheld by thread flower-frail and tenuous—
Spinning, unthreading her silver-spindled
nurseries from branch to branch—

Her belly rounded as a pearl,
A ghost-smooth bud in the moment before
Flowering into a thousand teeming black
Petals: dark asterisms scuttering
In dew-swept, fleeting, constellation

DEZREA D'ALESSANDRO

we broke chalk together

I.
we broke chalk together,
unflavoured by word butter.
you cooked a meal over
stove-top palms for me.
you were sweet warm,
my campfire blanket.
we made love, red hot,
dwindling like cuddled firewood
over dying embers,
falling asleep crackling,
holding the psalm smoke
in between our fingers.
we burnt into carbon,
whispering ashes
in between, i love you.

II.
we broke chalk together
to draw on chalkboard walls
inside synagogues.
shared the supple wine,
scribbled drunk lines
on black sheets
in white noise worship;
nothing too intense,
just some kids
still colouring outside
the lines of the moment.
i bought a box of
unleavened bread crayons
for the occasion.
so thoughtful, as always,
not because i cared for you -
simply a centerpiece

for my table where
our heart plates rested.

III.
we broke chalk together
in the front room -
snowflake communion.
a filling window supper,
i brought my own spoons,
we've yet to share silverware.
although, we had done our homework,
polished our kisses
like knives in the morning.
i stopped fearing the dawn darts
you'd throw when we woke up
once i heard how you'd
learned to show love
in the sheath where you grew up.
it was clear how your past would be
my stainless steel grading scale.

IV.
we broke chalk together,
i saved the pieces,
placed them in a coffee can
with your red lighter.
your chest was never lit,
a cool hearth, despite my matches.
my ribcage was our space-heater,
i was the reason
our hearts were unfrozen.
we slow-cooked our last sunday
though our eyelids were falling;
to quit stewing too early
would leave the last bites
weak and unsatiating.

now we will take naps
in separate fire pits,
our stomachs full with
intimate memory chalk bits.

20 broken rules

i've never said "i love you" first,
but 1. i wouldn't say it back, either.
this is the least of my sins.
you are the chalk painting and i
am the rain—
just 2. touching your face
destroys the art—
this wasn't my intention.
if you were a red light,
and you always are,
3. i wouldn't wait three and a half seconds,
never the less three and a half days.
because 4. i don't pretend you haven't been on my mind.
5. i don't lie
6. except about things that are trivial,
but potentially dangerous.
7. not only did i break the mirror,
8. spill beer at the party,
9. walk beneath the ladder,
i also
10. texted, 11. called, 12. kissed, and 13. reached for your hand first.
you are the ocean
covered in ice.
tell me a story.
"about what?"
your melting point.
14. my cup runneth over.
my mouth is a can of paint.
i apologised your walls red
15. and cautioned your senses reflective orange.
here is a rule i thought we'd abolished:
women who like sex are:
16. sluts—sometimes;
17. easy—if i were a stamp
you couldn't ink me enough to admit that;
18. desperate—i am when i'm scared.

19. i'm scared
you can't perform alchemy on metals,
or rain,
or paint;
what of me that is not gold will not become it
and you're going to find this out eventually.
20. you're going to find this out eventually.

DEIDRA D'AMICO

Beside Myself

My life is a poem within an epic
I just can't tell what chapter I'm on,
is the overall theme a tragedy
or a comedy?
Like the time I was in a fire
only saved at the last minute
hurling myself down the fiery stairs
or jumping clear of a train wreck
having lost my ticket
or the day I wandered past Ave X
Some of these names are made up
but only to protect the innocent
who I can't seem to find

Don't cry for me,
I only lost a shoe
and never joined the junkies.
I survived the fire,
the stairs
and the car crash afterwards

As for comedy, well, I kept getting lost
on my way thru America
never having mastered the art of direction
or how to decipher a map,
Wandering is a skill I've developed,
part survival, part dance
It's a two step procedure
the way you can slip this way
or that
So when I get on the road
I'm looking for the impossible
Can you tell me where to find it?

I'm carrying one dancing shoe
Emergency mis-matched socks,
and always getting ready
for the final show,
either way I'm the director,
whether I'm the victim or the star,
the one who moves the lights,
who finds the costumes
and all the extras.

JIM DRUMMOND

For Those of You Who are Scoring the Game

Payday was cold, but there was enough March sun for practice between the afternoon clipper-clouds. The rest of the swing shift could be seen through the backstop, trudging up the hill from the plant past the company's billboard of the Milky Way hung on the chainlink right field fence. At the bottom the scriptural font proclaimed: "Frances Held Plutofuels. There'd be no Heavens without Held." The principle product: navigational fuels, or psychofuels, which were encoded to direct the vessels it thrust, obviating the need for navigational instruments and pilot control. The fuel could pre-program for predicted maneuvers needed to avoid astral rocks and space debris.

We were loosed a half hour early during the early season for practice.

Janet had just thrown me her first pitch, a slippery sinker which I took for a ball. As I waved my bat across the plate I saw Ace descending the far hill from the plant between his two bodyguards. He was carrying his bat like a Pluto rod, horizontally between two fingertips. It seemed like there was even some space between his fingertips. Electric Boy.

Once before, they'd pulled me from the plant floor to sit with Ace while he performed his computations. It settled him to have a woman sit with him while he worked, his pencil moving stiffly in chronically icy fingers at the end of his pipe cleaner arms. His head was no larger than my own diminutive skull, but rich with fine black hair like seaweed. He favored Prince Valiant, which might explain how some of Held's more gauche shop-rats came up with jeering him as "Princess" or "Prince-ace." Now the bodyguard approached me, no shades, looking happy and nonchalant unlike any movie gangster's muscle, but she had plenty of real muscles under her Held t-shirt and cargo pants. She held out a note, folded into a tight triangle.

"What? Why?"

"It's from Frances. What are you doing later?" Hence the smile, the no-shades, the flashing eyes.

"Headed to the family farm to harvest mountain oysters, dusk to dawn. Another time, perhaps." She winced and then laughed as she sat in the bleachers. "Better read the note now." The unfolded note, creased like a diamond, was terse:

"The boy insists he can play like a girl. This being so, teach this young bird to bunt."

I handed the note to Maria, who was serving as Ump. "How old is he" she wondered. I told her about 19.

"Still hairless?"

"He's right in front of your for God's sakes." She looked me, "So what?" Maria was suspected of a salacious craving for males.

Innocence might surmise, "Frances thinks it won't hurt us if we stick him in batting ninth every few contests." Certainly he appeared to be starving for earth beneath his feet. It intoxicated him now: by the time he went through the gate in the backstop unaccompanied by his bodyguards, he was trying on a woman's stride. Which made Janet chuckle. "Helen," she said to me, "Batter up."

"Helen, where do I stand, left or right?" asked Ace in the clear counter-tenor of a Shakespeare song. I was surprised he remembered me—it had been two years since I'd incubated him during his calculations. "Right side, of course, you're a boy," I answered. He stepped to the left-handed side. This was not to be credited. A few heiferish men had made the league over the decades, but never a lefthander, on or off the field. Every hitter on our team batted left. "Stand on the other side, Ace, the left side is for righties. I know it's confusing." But he looked at me instead of complying. "I realize I can't," he said. "I have a cataract on my left eye."

"Does Frances know that?" he nodded. Does she remember it would be the better question. I looked around. Everyone else was looking at the darkening sky, either worried about not getting to hit, or finding something to look at other than Ace on the wrong side of the plate. Janet wound up, then threw one middling fast, with no wrinkles, and Ace lined it to right field, even with his back elbow pointed straight to the ground. Ruth barely made a shoestring catch in the rightfield corner.

"You won't do that again in a million years," Janet said. The sinker's dip to the outside corner was as wicked as they get, but Ace picked it up like a kingfisher, lining what would be a clean double to left. He knew enough to run the bases, faster than I would have thought his pearly sticks could manage. Angel blew the throw and he wound up on third. Janet said, "I saw this sort of thing once in a girl from Ocracoke. His eye's in the end of his bat."

"Horrible form," I observed. We were talking like he was a dog, him standing right there. And I had been the one bitching at Maria for third-personing him in his presence.

"Form doesn't make a hoot," said Janet. You don't have to dance like iron filings to hold the magnet." This was over Maria's head; she was behind me leaning against the backstop, unconsciously pawing the ground like a bull, pouring on the pheromones; she went down to third base, making a big show of coaching, patting him on the back, rubbing his David Bowie shoulder blades.

In the locker room later he sat on his bench in his sweat shorts, biting his nails. Of course everyone but me stripped down as if he were a blind dog, never giving it a thought. I knew some polysexual era history and physiology, however, took anatomy at the Community College when I misthought myself a budding nurse. He was quivering. He turned beneath the pressure of my hands on his shoulders to straddle the bench facing me, his back to the room. White carbon eyes less pure than fervent. In every diamond dwells its burning coal.

"Let me look at your head," I said.

"It's not bad."

He couldn't catch, not even a floater. Ruth had brained him at second base with a pop-up. "Why the mosaic development, Ace?"

"I can't explain what it's like for me. Computation problems come at me, like meals through a slot three times a day, but piles each time. I get mental R&R, watch the ball team on TV, which is all I get with any blood in it."

Ruth slid over to lay a ginger compress on the knot on his skull, and Jan felt it tenderly. Elsewhere in the room wet towels were sailing and smacking flesh as if birds were lightheartedly being snatched by slobbering ocean dragons. It all could have been on TV, they sure cared nothing about Ace as audience even though he was the boss's son.

"Lately I've been fading in and out sometimes," Ace said. "Usually I can figure out what the next 8 pitches will be and what the next 14 hitters will do, down to whether the right fielder will have to dive for the catch, or by how many feet the throw to first will beat the third hitter. It's easy, it's laid out in my head like a chessboard in four dimensions, I don't need any paper. The game is absurdly simple. Still, when I'm not working on her computations, in my head I'm hitting baseballs all over the lot."

"You should go back into your head and catch those hits," I joked. Was I patronizing him like Maria? Ace looked at me and shrugged. "There's just my two eyes, a hardball, a wooden bat, vectors in a field of green sectors." So! He'd lied about the cataracts. He was a true lefty. If this were the Olympics it would be a chromosomal scandal.

This wasn't the Olympics, this was the plant's bottom line. Ace's unprecedented computational maturity accelerated production of intelligent plutofuels to one-third the time computers could program the fuel. This was money.

There are eraser songs that you sing to get nagging ones out of your head, the songs that stick like gum on the bottom of your mental shoe, eraser songs that don't themselves stick when they've done their job. The thrust of Frances' instruction lay in the bunt as erasure, I decided—bunting would purge his expensive echoing daydreams of line drives—there was her emphasis, not on fledging the "young bird." She did not EVER want him fledged. Well, Frances, this is why it's your company.

Ace was starting to calm down; I really am a woman.

Ruth had called down the photographer, a wispy blond named Daniella, who like Ace looked about 14. Ruth is the team captain for psychological warfare, or Razz. She had Ace stand like a white spider in the center of a circling web of naked sluggers two heads taller than him; Ruth made him strip over my objection that he would get too cold, which was the best thing I could think of without getting them suspicious of my motives. He would in fact get too cold, anyhow.

I knew what Ruth was after with this shot. Her previous sally: a shot of the team with an older man in an apron, trainer or master watchmaker, made the team seem a finely tooled, frozen juggernaut in icily peak condition. Historical inevitability. *So, isn't it simply and classically 'no contest'?* was the liminal message that seemed to induce hypnotic languor in the opponents, who in theory are rendered secretly avid for their own annihilation by this photographic maneuver.

On the other hand women with a frail boy gives an impressive jolt of power, a shock. It ties you in as infrared blood-sisters, Minervas having burst out from his big cranium and thin thighs. Venuses all married to their lame genius Vulcan. Ruth had been to more than college. "Daniella," Ruth said as the etheric photographer packed up, "just caption it, "Ace Held, Rockets' new backup DH." The word backup was a sop to the now-nominal designated hitter, Maria, who struck out a lot.

It was daring, capturing the image of the owner's son to count coup on the competition, taking a huge risk in crossing Frances' purposes, but tough women like Ruth were one-woman unions. Which Frances knew as an ex-steward who had parlayed our dues into minority ownership to leverage her buyout, her own majority stake coming also from our skimmed dues, it was thought.

After the photograph with short story appeared on the net we received Frances' second note: it was a tone-deaf, "What did I ask you to teach Ace?"

Janet and I worked him. "You two are the cows, you do it," had growled Maria, the batting cage captain, sour over his cold-shoulder to her advances and beginning to see the light of her own flame-out as well. It was a matter of "breaking" a hardwood bat with a life of its own, same as breaking a horse. Janet threw changeups so slow they bobbed like apples in a damp breeze. Ace was mesmerized at first but the eye in the end of his bat soon got the idea; in one afternoon he was laying down unreachable rollers that tracked the inside of the foul lines like radar.

Every few hours the bodyguards delivered snatches of computations to the dugout. They took Ace about thirty minutes to perform. It was three days before Ace confided to me that each time they were the same computations; he was screwing up. The male in him was getting ever ghostlier.

Ace came up to me at the concessionaire's 20 minutes before the season opener with the Tomahawks, and ordered a turkey dog with dijon and pearl onions. We shared a burgundy cooler, standing very close, and I enjoyed his flower-scented cologne. His voice was creeping a bit lower, careful of its new alto buds. "Helen, Frances is pissed as hell," he said. The womanly strong mouth was a fresh twist of second-hand lemon, too. "She said she'd take my ascended orbs." The x-rays were looking more like ovaries every day, he added. "And you know she doesn't ever speak figuratively. I guess you can see from the problems getting kicked back that I'm losing the touch. She's augmenting me with those dusty computers even now. They didn't catch my first botch."

"What did that do?"

"2300 lives and a clipper to Io were translated into radio waves."

"Dead!?"

"More like life as a moebius strip. Looping."

"But how can fuel cause that?"

"What do you think happens when you refine close to absolute purity? Things disappear into thought. Apotheosis for the Io clipper on account of my daydreaming during fuel encoding calculations, or even because of subconscious events. The reverse of what's happening to me."

I started laughing silently. He took the cooler from me and drank. "You laugh like that when you're afraid," Ace observed. I wrung my dampened hands, then dried them cathartically on his red undershirt sleeve. It was hard to follow his description, but not to feel what he was feeling. "What do you mean the reverse? What's happening to you?"

He looked at me and I could see the friction in his eyes. "She'll do anything to pull me out of the dive, even if I'd rather smash up." Suddenly he touched my breast. I slammed his hand off, blurted, "Queer!" then laughed, but he didn't look hurt or surprised. Limpid reflection eyes, not even waiting, suiting a wolverine more than a boy.

"It will never work, Ace. Against nature."

"If it doesn't then I don't care. She can put me under the knife and save herself a fuels process operative device. Whichever happens at least my brains won't dissolve into male pea soup and land me in the seminal breeder pool." Sappho has a masculine ending?

We had a few minutes before Play Ball. We slid into our empty locker room, took the training table. He rippled like an eel against my delirious flat muscles, and I sensed the burgeoning caves within him.

When Ace stepped into the batter's box, her eyes were flashing. In high crystal tones she chanted some razz at their pitcher. The first pitch she bunted along the third base line, threading it barely fair and barely foul like a helix before it ended up dead in the fair territory dirt as she hit the bag with her foot. The Tomahawks never had a play.

I was coaching first. This new Ariel leaned over quickly and nibbled my ear. "Frances already has herself a new pigeon, Helen!" her voice going up high over a siren beyond the fence. "The transistor just said the Io clipper has landed thick as granite, all hands fit." The radio device glinted, silvery in her ear. A minute voice from its receiver crackled over strings and horns.

She easily beat a pickoff throw back to the bag. "Oh Helen," she predicted, indicating my flat belly with her index fingers, "she'll be a girl." She laughed. "Just like her Daddy!"

"I thought of a good name for her," I said.

"What?"

"Tiresias."

For our journeywork on the plutofuels floor, the law requires ovarial but not gonadic sterilization to guard against teratogenesis.

I admired Ace's brilliant (but now unsteady) gift of prescience— still do. But in that sort of thing you have to be careful of *projecting*, don't you?

SALLY EMMONS & EMILY DIAL-DRIVER

Fifty Pieces of Heart

In August of 2007, the University of Oklahoma Press released a book called *Voices from the Heartland,* a collection of essays from fifty Oklahoma women. The book was edited by four women: Carolyn Taylor, Emily Dial-Driver, Carole Burrage, and Sally Emmons-Featherston. Named an "Official Centennial Project" by the Oklahoma Centennial Commission (Oklahoma became a state in 1907), it also received recognition as a finalist for the Oklahoma Book Award in 2008.

The process of getting the book published should have started with a proposal and an agent (Larsen 221, 224; Herman 15). A search of Internet sites devoted to book proposals, some with sample formats and some with examples, came up with 529,000 hits. John Boswell in *An Insider's Guide to Getting Published* says, "today fully 90 percent of all nonfiction books sold to trade publishers are acquired on the basis of a proposal alone" (Larsen 1).

That is not the way it happened for us (more about this later).

The book journey starts with the story of Oklahoma. Oklahoma is not only in the center of the United States, it is in the center of the world of mixed messages. Oklahoma is frequently romanticized as representing the "heartland" of America. Typically, when a person thinks of Oklahoma, not only do images of wind "sweeping down the plains," people sitting in rocking chairs on front porches, the Trail of Tears, and devastating tornadoes come to mind, but also, perhaps because of its location in the Bible Belt, Oklahoma is also associated with old-fashioned family values and a strong work ethic and is considered by many to be a place where a general goodwill to fellow man (and woman) still exists. Oklahoma was certainly characterized as the "heartland" after the bombing of the Murrah Federal Building in Oklahoma City in 1995.

However, Oklahoma also has some startling statistics. The Institute for Women's Policy Research regularly examines the quality of life for women in each of the fifty states in the U.S. It examines things such as poverty levels, teen pregnancy rates, educational levels, domestic violence occurrences, and the like. In 2004, it ranked Oklahoma as the 48th overall worst state for women in the nation

(*Status*). Put another way, out of the 50 states in the United States, Oklahoma was ranked third from the very bottom. According to this survey, women would be better off living in forty-seven other states than living in Oklahoma!

"Why?" one might ask. In terms of poverty:

•Single women head nearly half of all Oklahoma families living in poverty.

•An Oklahoma woman earns only seventy-five cents for every dollar earned by a man.

•The average Oklahoma woman, sixty-five and over, struggles to live on fifty percent of the average male's income.

•If that is not shocking enough, we can look at the educational crisis that Oklahomans—particularly female Oklahomans—are currently experiencing:

•Nearly twenty percent of Oklahoma girls are never graduated from high school.

•Fewer than one in seven Oklahoma girls complete four or more years of college.

•An average of six babies is born to Oklahoma children every day and nearly half of these mothers will not be graduated from high school.

•As for as domestic violence is concerned, Oklahoma statistics are also distressing. The statistics show that:

•Approximately one is six Oklahoma women is a victim of domestic violence.

•Nearly one in eight women has been physically assaulted or raped sometime in her lifetime.

•Oklahoma ranks as the fifth worst state in the nation in the number of domestic violence-related homicides.

•Finally, Oklahoma's "claim to fame" is that Oklahoma leads the nation and the world in the number of women that it incarcerates. In fact, Oklahoma's incarceration rate for women is *143% higher* than the national average

Despite all of this, Oklahoma produces record numbers of Miss Americas, America's most successful "American Idol," and countless other women of achievement. Thus, although the statistics may show that women would fare better in forty-seven other states, the reality is that there are well-grounded, successful, happy women who call Oklahoma "home" right now and have no intention of moving.

Who are those women and why *Heartland*? As an exercise, we occasionally ask our college students to take out a piece of paper and list the most successful, influential, and powerful men in the state. Names quickly emerge: Governor Brad Henry, OU President David Boren, Garth Brooks. We then ask them to list notable women in the state. The names of entertainers are bandied about, but the list typically stops there. Rarely does a student name a businesswoman, or a mother, or even a next-door neighbor who is active in her community and a positive role model.

The statistics above are alarming and the seeming lack of female role models striking. However, Carolyn Taylor herself knew many accomplished women who defied those very statistics. She decided that there needed to be a book of stories about Oklahoma women and their difficulties, achievements, and triumphs. Taylor went to her friend and colleague Emily Dial-Driver in February of 2005 and said, "Let's do a book. I think we can have this ready by November."

Obviously that was a naïve assumption (it takes even longer than nine months to birth a child!), but Taylor and Dial-Driver began to compile a list of people who they thought might be willing to share their stories. The list included women from varying backgrounds: politicians, business women, academics, mothers, women living in the country and in the city, women who are preachers, and the list went on. Very few of the women were actually "professional" writers so the thought of asking women to share their stories was a scary prospect. What if no one accepted?

The initial letter that Taylor sent told each recipient that she was being asked to tell a story about herself, something that she had learned, something that she wished she had known before, something that had affected her deeply in some way, or something she wanted others to know. Surprisingly, most of the recipients replied that they would love to participate (much to the thrill of Taylor and Dial-Driver, who had wrongly feared that NO ONE would accept their invitation) . . . but most said they did not know what they wanted to tell. With a little encouragement, each came to the conclusion that she did have something to say, something important to pass on to other women, other people.

Ultimately each essay appearing in *Voices from the Heartland* reveals a personal story, intimate and fundamental yet these women shared their personal experiences despite these challenges. The theme of each story is that, despite obstacles, women are tremendously successful and great role models. What better way to counter the statistics than by showing women who are thriving in Oklahoma?

On some level we all recognize that stories are about life experiences and that they "tell" more than just a simple story. Isak Dinesen says, "To be a person is to have a story to tell." Ursula LeGuin maintains, "There have been great societies that did not use the wheel, but there have been no societies that did not tell stories." In fact, Muriel Rukeyser says, "The universe is made of stories, not atoms." However, if stories are not "saved," which generally means written down, they are lost. Stories are valuable—and necessary. They disclose culture, personality, event. They expose and illuminate the past, the present, and the future.

Moreover, those stories reveal the commonalities of experience. In her play *Trifles* Susan Glaspell says, "We live close together and we live far apart. We all go through the same things—it's all just a different kind of the same thing" (1322). The stories in *Heartland* reveal what it means to be an American woman today because, Oklahoman or not, women—people—"all go through the same things." The stories resonate with all audiences: men, women, old, young, Oklahoman, US citizen, international citizen. The incredibly generous women who share their narratives are from various classes, races, professions, and stages in life. They include women people may have heard of, such as Carolyn Hart, Joy Harjo, and Billie Letts; women people may not have heard of, such as ministers, teachers, and businesswomen who may be known locally but not widely; and women people will never hear of because they wanted to be published anonymously since their stories were so wrenching they did not feel they could handle recognition of any kind.

Obtaining those stories in one way was difficult in that Taylor had to encourage women that they had stories to tell, to encourage participation, to overcome the hesitation of those people who were not professional writers. Obtaining those stories in another way was not difficult because everyone has a story. One just has to find it.

Once the contributors decided what they wanted to say, what incident in life they wanted to explain or illuminate, the editorial process had to begin. Taylor and Dial-Driver were joined by two other editors: Carole Burrage and Sally Emmons-Featherston. Two of the editors, Emmons-Featherston and Dial-Driver, teach writing so they put the writing process which they regularly teach into practice. In a nutshell, the process has two main parts: point/support; write/revise.

After the first drafts arrived, each draft was assigned to a "primary" editor, who looked for the "heart" of the piece. After each of the stories received notations from the primary editor, all the editors held a conference, generally agreeing with the determination of the primary editor and discussing tactics to elicit the additional material needed, if any. The primary editor then wrote a personal letter to the contributor asking for additional details or additional clarification. Letters said such things as "We would like to hear more about. . ." or "Could you add some details about. . ." or "We think _____ is what you are really talking about so could you tell us about. . . ."

These letters elicited a second draft from the contributors, which usually was the final draft. The primary editor then took that draft and did first revisions, perhaps cutting or shaping or reorganizing. Some drafts had minimal work on them, a word here, a new paragraph. Other drafts needed more extensive tinkering. In some instances, editors asked for a third draft from the contributor. In that case the primary editor sent a second letter asking for clarification or for additional details. This happened in only a few instances. Little work or extensive work, minimal or maximal revision, each contribution appears in the book.

As the drafts were finished, they were returned to the contributors for their final approval. In some cases the contributors asked for—and received—small changes. In most cases contributors approved the drafts without change.

Heartland was finally a manuscript, a completed manuscript.

Most writers know that to get a book published, they must first start with writing a book proposal. It never occurred to the editors of *Heartland* to start with a proposal. How could a proposal be effective when there was doubt as to who might be a contributor? How could a proposal work without a complete chapter to show as an example and no chapter could exist until a contributor agreed to participate? Besides, the editors in their naiveté did not realize a book proposal was appropriate so the whole thing was a moot point.

Even a naïve person has, on the other hand, heard of agents so the editors determined that the next step was to try to get an agent. Taylor sent innumerable query letters to possible agents. Some never replied. Most replied that they thought the project had limited appeal and they were not interested in representing a project with only regional importance. One agent asked to see the manuscript and, upon reading—and loving—the document, decided to become a representative for the manuscript. Her take was that the stories had national and even international interest.

The agent shopped the project around, receiving multiple rejections, most saying "The subject is too regional." The editors were convinced that meant the prospective publisher did not read the manuscript since the stories are universal. Finally, the agent tired, and the contract expired. The editors were discouraged. Thankfully, when one person was discouraged, another editor was optimistic; this was one of the great benefits of working together as a team.

However, a serendipitous meeting with a representative of the University of Oklahoma Press raised some hope. Seeing the Press represented at a conference, an editor described the project and asked if the Press might be interested. The Press representative said that he thought the Press would like to see the manuscript, the whole, complete, entire manuscript, which the editors promptly delivered and which the Press accepted for publication.

The next step was a contract. There were a few snags. The standard contract says the copyright on each piece belongs to the press. Further, it is standard that editors receive approximately ten copies of the book—to share. However, in the initial and subsequent letters to contributors the editors had assured them that the copyright would remain in their hands. The editors had also assured them that each would receive a copy of the book. The contract was rewritten to reflect these prior commitments to contributors.

In addition, the editors determined that the royalties should go to the Women's Foundation of Oklahoma. The book was for, by, and about women. The Women's Foundation, established in 2002 as an endowed fund at Communities Foundation of Oklahoma by Merle Chambers of Chambers Family Fund, supports women educationally and entrepreneurially. Their motto is "When women and girls prosper, communities thrive!" This seemed the perfect place to send royalties.

Galley proofing came next. The editors had several discussions with the text editor over issues, mostly about capitalization. Finally everything was ready for print.

The initial print run was 3500 copies. The editors thought nothing about the figure until later. At a conference two editors had a discussion with a representative of another academic press. The representative marveled at the low price ($19.95) of the hardback book, saying that her press would have sold the book for $40 to $65. She asked what the print run was and was shocked at the 3500 figure. Her response, with a certain amount of ill-concealed scorn was, "They must expect it to be a popular book."

Voices from the Heartland has been a popular book. The University of Oklahoma Press ran a second printing in hardback of the book and, as of March 2009, has moved on to a mass market paperback run.

The reason the book is "popular" is the stories. One story is written by Oklahoma City bombing survivor, Susan Urbach. She opens her narrative :

> *One morning I went to work. That doesn't sound like a defining moment, does it? I've gone to work on thousands of days in my lifetime, as perhaps you have. Yet one beautiful spring morning—April 19, 1995—I went to work, and life literally exploded. My office window directly faced the Alfred E. Murrah Federal Building in downtown Oklahoma City. . . . When the blast happened, my office was destroyed. I was hauled off to the hospital for several days. If you totaled up the stitching (which the doctor and I did because Workers' Comp wanted the information), it was about 3 ½ feet worth of stitches on my left side from the cheek on my face to the other kind of cheek. . . . (18-19)*

Her essay goes on to describe the process of recovery and healing—a healing which continues today. Even if we have not been the victim of a bombing attack, we have all suffered loss and sadness. We can all learn from her experience.

In "Prison Saved My Life" Claudia Lovelace, now a successful Methodist minister, candidly writes about her long history of drug use and prostitution, which led to her eventual imprisonment. She states

> *When I went to court, the judge gave me three years in prison. As they led me away, my world became unimaginable. I was not frightened: I knew what was coming because I had done time in juvenile hall. But I was now forty-six years old and I was going to prison. I felt so alone. Once again I had built my bridges just to tear them down; it seemed that had been my life story. I would climb out of the messes I had made of my life so many times, just to return. (149)*

Because of her time in prison, however, Lovelace finally "found" herself. She recovered from her drug addiction, became college educated, found solace in spirituality, and is now a minister making a difference in her community. She was an Oklahoma statistic . . . but she also defies the statistics.

In "Revelations," Kathy Taylor reveals the conflicting emotions that a parent undergoes when her child dies:

> *I had a hard time with people who, trying to comfort, said, "God will not give you more than you can handle." As if no one had ever had a nervous breakdown or overdosed on drugs or committed suicide. Indeed, many experience situations they cannot handle. . . . My personal tragedy made me reflect on other traumatic events. Why did God allow the sudden death of a young mother or catastrophic events like hurricanes and tornadoes? If He were such a caring and glorious God, why did He allow such tragedy to occur to his children? (56)*

Ultimately, Henry learns that, for her, healing is directly tied to finding some kind of meaning in loss and to reconnecting with a God she had distanced herself from because she blamed Him for her pain. Sadly, part of the human experience is to experience and endure tragedy. Part of this experience is also to question, "Why me?" Henry affirms that this feeling is normal, yet she also cautions us to not be crippled by our pain and to find something in the pain that will allow us to make it from day to day.

The stories in *Heartland* resonate with all readers. One reviewer of *Voices from the Heartland* said, "As I read, I reminded myself, 'These are all Oklahoma women.' *Voices from the Heartland* could have been subtitled *Fifty Pieces of Heart*, for that is what the reader is receiving.

The message, albeit subtle, is that no matter what changes confront us, we are not alone. The spirit of woman, beautifully rendered as universal in this collection, is there to sustain us" (Isom).

The stories are all written by women but they certainly are not just about women and women's issues, nor are they intended strictly for female readers. The stories depict life in all of its many incarnations . . . the good, the bad, the devastating, the uplifting, the challenging. There is a story about surviving adultery. There is a story about appreciating family. There is a story that encourages readers to be more philanthropic. There is a story about being a parent. In short, there is a story for everyone in this collection of stories. There is even a story about the importance of remembering family stories.

Stories record our experiences and share the wisdom we acquire from these experiences. Stories teach us about ourselves and others; stories give us lessons that we can use in our own lives. According to Karen Dietz, a professional oral storyteller, "Sometimes we need stories more than food to stay alive."

The editors now have their own story, the story of their journey from concept to book and their story of how the writing process actually works to transform prose from draft to publication.

We all have stories. We should share.

Works Cited

Dietz, Karen. *What Storytellers Say about Story*. International Storytelling Center. Web. 21 Nov. 2008

Dinesen, Isak. Storyteller.net. Web. 2 Feb. 2010.

Glaspell, Susan. "Trifles." *The Norton Introduction to Literature*. 9th ed. Ed. Alison Booth, J. Paul Hunter, and Kelly J. Mays. New York: W.W. Norton, 2005. 1314-23. Print.

Hammerstein, Oscar. "Oklahoma." *Oklahoma!* First Broadway production 1943. Recording.

Herman, Jeff. *Jeff Herman's Guide to Book Publishers, Editors and Literary Agents*. 17th ed. Archer, TX: Three Dog Press, 2006. Print.

Isom, Joan Shaddox. "Review." *Amazon*. Story Circle Book Reviews. Web. 10 May 2008

King, Thomas. *The Truth about Stories*. Minneapolis: U of Minnesota P, 2005. Print.

Lapine, James. *Into the Woods*. First production San Diego, 1986. Print.

Larsen, Michael. *How to Write a Book Proposal*. Cincinnati, OH: F & W Publications, 2004. Print.

LeGuin, Ursula. "Favorite Quotations: Storytelling." *Daily Celebrations*. Web. 2 Feb. 2010.

Rukeyser, Muriel. Storyteller.net. Web. 2 Feb. 2010.

The Status of Women in Oklahoma. Ed. Amy B. Caiazza and April Shaw. Washington, DC.: Institute for Women's Policy Research, 2004. Print.

Taylor, Carolyn, Emily Dial-Driver, Carole Burrage, and Sally Emmons-Featherston, eds. *Voices from the Heartland*. Norman, OK: University of Oklahoma Press, 2007. Print.

JOSH GAINES

Tourette's Tick Two

Tick tick
Nose crunch up
Nose crunch down
Look down left
Down right
Up right, left
Repeat, repeat
Twist the neck
Make that frown, Hard
And sniff in the throat
Breathe in and make
THAT sound.
Tourette's, tick tick
Talk twice, twitch
what?
Speak my mind like I have a choice
My own voice surprises me
Caffeine addict
Caffeine, that poor man's Ritalin
And poetry, and pool, and focus, and poetry (sniff, grunt)
And alcohol when I'm tired of the
Tourette's that follows me like seconds
Second hands, hands, mine, this
"This (sniff) is what it's like"
(neck pop) "ike"
"tike"
"ly-kuh"
"by-kuh"
"kuhh"
"kuhh"
(grunt, look up/down, sniff...)

For Man

Look down on man,
Look down to man,
Look you.
Go to the mountain and look
Shake that soul avalanche loose
And loose what you see
On us sinners.
Look on man.
Weep for Adam
Who, among men
Is the sole keeper of true loss.
Weep for man
And his misunderstandings
Of importance
Who'll fight a flag burner
But won't help a homeless vet
To his feet.
Weep for man,
Follicles on a sphere
Hurtling through space
Pretending he matters,
More than other matter,
To that space,
Or the sphere.
Look for man
In your gods.
Look for gods
In your bank accounts.
Both will yield positive results.
Look to man
To misinterpret those results.
Go now and quest
For the sake of searching.
Go now and find Atlantis
In the deepest and blue.
Find your devil there

Bedeviled, wrapped in your blues,
Waiting for the trade.
Sing his song.
Lead like pied-pipes
Pray for nothing—
Become your salvation
And sing for man
Whose song mourns
The paradise lost.

Listen.
—You can hear it singing back—
Lean into man
—By tapping any one—
Like hammers falling to chain gang spirituals
—Of our dead "beneath the mountain" bones—

Listen to their bones
Cradled to your ear
Like Atlantean newborns
Telling the ocean's sea shell secrets
To your ear.
Tune your song
To those buried bones
Who face forever up
And like them,
Look for man
In the stars' endless perfection
And like them,
Don't be surprised
When you don't find him there.

MARY B. GRAY

A Song for Muddy

baby, there's no worries
about my working hands, these
hot meals, your pressed clothes

see, I understand you got
that other woman at home
but if she were it
you wouldn't have come straying
looking at me to play home

you sang that song, crooned me
right into those arms

you could use my money
but you don't want it
could use my home

you sing to me
"I just want to make love to you"

well its such a shame,
my money is yours just the same
I'll keep you a home keep you a bed

your that rollin' stone, rollin' to me
so be in this woman, my skin silk-er
sweeter, my moans louder
leave them kids, I'll make you
a man, my man make us a lot

you sang your song, crooned me
right into those arms

Vertebrae

> *The Serpent was clever, more clever than any wild animal God had made. "The serpent seduced me," she said, "and I ate."*
>
> —*Genesis 3:1, 13 MSG*

you make me sinner-woman
    make my knees weak
    make my thoughts less
    give this body more

in nakedness I was to find figs
to shut my eyes
be ashamed
to pray to the rock

but you whisper
    sinner-woman
    to where will you run
should I have prayed for my wicked ways

conversed with Adam
reminded of my arranged love
or steadily remained wrapped inside
the warmth of your anatomy

you are more sin bearer than seduction
me more woman than sinner
more waken than naive

like a snake you move down my spine
if I am your fruit
let the bite come
may its juice be worth the risk

KEN HADA

the hard luck of not dying young

even those tough, whiskeyslurping
jerkyeating
muleskinned
cactusfaced
sowmouthed
rockballed
bloodysouled
outlawing
gunslinging
bulletbiting
marauding
mutilating
scalping
injunhating
badass
posseridinghombres

at darkest night
under a rustler's moon
in deepest sleep

lay their guilty, sweetlittlejesus face
upon a saddlepillow
holding themselves tender
tucked with a cowboyblankie
curled
in the position neither mothers
nor angels could resist
nor could any fellow rider—
at least for a moment—despise.

Zen and the Sensitive Redneck

He's always been good at stacking things.
As a boy he volunteered to stack firewood,
picking up scattered logs, ordering them
to ricks. He made money as a teen by stacking
hay, bucking alfalfa and prairie grass
onto the truck, then into the barn,
marrying the rows tight to last.

He's good at fixing things too.
He repairs fences, wires circuits,
times his engines.

He stacks, he fixes, he builds.
He does these things alone.
The mystery of happiness eludes him
so he finds joy in things:
in wood, in hay, in metal.

His yes is yes, and he means it.
His no means no.

He gave up desire when the pain
scared him, offered him strange visions
he did not understand,
illusions he could not manage.

His life is a tradeoff—he won't desire
and she won't return,
so things occupy his time.

His life is to find joy in a tractor motor
firing on a frosty morning,
to feel twine tight on a bale made last summer,
to keep fences from sagging,
to hear quail calling,
to see cattle grazing.

He knows he can depend on grass
and rain and soil—
the satisfaction of partnering
with all these things.

CAROL HAMILTON

Evening Out

> *"We may rejoice in the error of our ways"*
> *Billy Collins, Nine Horses*

"There seems to be a habit here,"
he says, and sprightly, shakes his head.

The glasses tinkle from each table.
The waiter never mentions the aching of his feet,

nor we ours of heart. Light gathers
in pools at the tables, behind the bar,

and not one utters, "What a waste,
this time unshared," and we here elbow

to elbow, tossing tips, our words,
out on the linen, calculated by per cent.

Perhaps one will show off, telling too much,
bravado escaping from neat billfold creases,

and tomorrow with no lunch money
for the kids, he'll shout at their hunger,

then remember proudly everyone's surprise
at his bold gesture, his largess.

Meanwhile, we'll pass the intervening hours.
We shall plan again when and where and how we'll dress.

Blessings

Taste the grass that even ruminants
        will die from
despite the elaborate evolution
of stomachs working in tandem,
a production line to squeeze nutrient
from the most heavily defended victim.
From this feast we rise singing,
fall singing, ingest green pastures,
thankful we have not yet
        turned color blind.

Wind Spirits

They clear out loose things,
lift them up, give the dust
a whirl which nearly chokes.
The sunset lays down its earth pigments
of orange and gold with harp strings
of light pinning the huge canvas
to a flat horizon. Such a vast heaven
makes us stop to see. We cannot
hide and hoard, so we plains people
walk lightly, know our nomadic souls
can blow away at any moment.
We drive tent stakes through what
we treasure, but mostly our hearts
bob and dance like bright balloons
on a string held as tightly as possible
when the great continental weather gods
clash around us as if once for all
they will settle all our battles over territory.

TRACY HAUGHT

Finding Refuge

She skips child-like
Under a nebulous glow of pink sun
Exhilarated
She lets her arms
Lift with the wind
As she spins and collapses
In the pale hissing grass
Violet leaves rusted brown
Lift and settle like laughter
Around her

Music plays without keys
Or reed
Dream-fed it swirls
Winding up through the trees
The sycamores swaying with
The mesquites
Earth's overflow of rhythm
Bending and blowing
Nestling warm around her
In the cool of evening
Like a merger of senses
Humming.

LAURA ANNE HELLER

from Rise When the Rooster Crows, an unpublished collection of persona poems.

Nest
Claire

Whenever I go to the chicken coop
to feed the hens and baby chicks, gather
the new eggs, he jumps from behind the door,
grinning like a hound dog. I laugh, the eggs
bounce against each other in my apron,
two tumble and break at our feet. Smiling,
I kick the broken shells aside. He laughs.

The morning light warm in my breast after
I had watched the sunrise from the porch on
the first somber step. The rays move across
his tilled earth like my dress being slowly
pulled off in the evening when we make love.
Soft light reveals the hard work of the field,
hoes and boots and weeds and mounds of red dirt.
We move like two birds skirting to the edge
of an oak branch scratching on our window,
too full of hope in summer's full moon joy.

The Song I Gave to the Sparrow
Claire

I walk to the fairest green hill
where an old southern red oak stands.
In that oak lay hidden a nest,
and in that nest sits a sparrow,
sister to her brighter brother.

When I come upon her resting,
she has no song to sing to me.
So I pick her up and hold her
in my hands, a cup of prayer.
And then I hum my song to her.

When I open my eyes at last
she opens her beak and sings.
She sings my song then flies away,
not to the oak nor to her nest,
but to the sky and the green hills.

I have given all of my love,
love for the man who tills the field
and who turns me away at night,
to the field sparrow and for now
from her far tree she sings my song.

Black Crow
Claire

His wasted work, so he sinks with the sun,
his face long with shadow and when I come
to join him, my face lit by the moon's glow,
my eyes bright like a star caught between clouds:
he glares at me and then turns away from
the hope I carry. He leaves for the bar.
And when his blood is hot with dry anger,
he returns with dust smoking at his heels.
We fight when his tongue is sharp with whiskey.
His old black belt, a crow, flies in my face.
The welt of his spirit bruises my cheek.
I fall like a vine the wild black bird
no longer wants to use to build the nest.
His wings thrash and hit me. He breaks my hope.

And he tries his damnedest to break my wings.

Under the Pleiades
Lucinda

Mother's crying in the kitchen;
I know because she stirs a cup
of tea. Her hand shakes. The pot shrieks.
Father's a pillar in the hallway.
Knives, spoons and forks clatter to the
floor as he rakes his hand across
the counter. One steak knife tumbles
into the shadow where I watch.

It is heavy in my hand now.
Small, I step back into my room
and climb out the open window.
The cool night air breathes on my face
as I push tall field weeds aside.
The moon is a sliver, a scythe
carving a star turning her back.
I kneel at once as silence falls.

I cannot hear his shouts, her cries.
I turn the earth with my fingers,
feel a song sink in my movements.
The hole is deep enough to lay
the knife into the soil's shadow.
The moon scratches lies on the blade
and disappears as I shove dirt.
Bury the knife. Bury the night.

The Beckoning
Lucinda

In midnight's total darkness of new moon,
the rolling storm clouds hide the distant stars,
those little pieces of hope which guide me
in my evening corn field tramps. In this dark
place I discover my fears. I find them
as they brush across my face at wrong turns,
the stalks walled against me; I can not move
forward without climbing over bent cornstalks.

Here I fall, like a leaf, in the clearing,
the empty space where death spreads its blanket
and beckons me to dig these little graves:
Bury the fear, the nightmare, the last fight...
Even bury the hope, the dream, the last smile...

The last time my mother smiled she stood on
the bottom steps of the porch watching me
with joy run through the field to her, shouting
about the wooden turtle I found. Light
shone on her face like the sun on a flower.

And the last fight was the evening the moon
hung low and dawn was nearing. He had just
stormed into the house, the porch door slamming.
I woke hearing them yell, my mother's sad
song fading as she ran crying in the field.

I wait and the sun rises. Father, gone.
My mother, gone. I sit in the worn chair.
And then the old man from across the field
comes carrying her, belly open and red.

MATT HOLLRAH

See *Gilda* for Him

In snow like this, soft and quiet,
he says they smoke like a fish downstairs
and invokes the lyrics of Hank Thompson
Smoke, smoke, smoke that cigarette.
He wants to be alone. I've taken his spot
near the second story windows
where the view of tires slurping snow
in irregular rhythm is better.
He calls out the names of the band members
not really talking to me or himself.
Rochester was his right hand man,
he says. I trick myself into thinking
I could enter his world through similes.
But even if my imagination allows this,
I can always come back
and go have a nice red with pesto
while he regrets never seeing
a Rita Hayworth movie.
*You know she fought the rest of her life
just to be herself again*, he tells the world.
I think of Hayworth in reverse,
pulling her elbow length gloves back on,
walking backwards off stage into an ordinary life.
I want to buy him a beer,
so it will pull him back. Instead,
I only imagine where he sleeps
in snow like this, soft and quiet.

Morel Hunting

My father walked slowly
through the trees—Pastor Ulrich
didn't know what to look for until
Dad found one and held up
the conical, honeycombed fungi
that only looks like food
if you already know it is—
just before Easter '77—
just after rain in the shade
of old scrub oak and elms
not yet dead from the Dutch disease.
Both men tasted the musk
of mushrooms even before finding them
in the Glencoe woods behind
my great-grandmother's house,
the gobble of wild turkeys
beyond the creek bank.

Paper sacks full of them,
Dad and Ulrich started home
on the unmarked back roads of Payne
County, red clay on the tires
of Dad's yellow Volkswagen,
stop signs overgrown with Johnson grass.
He never even saw the truck
pulling the horse trailer that
broad-sided him, rearranging
the hammer and anvil in his left ear,
breaking his arm, and our pastor's jaw—
the broken glass in blue sprays,
the morels tumbling in soft arcs.
Ulrich had his mouth wired shut
for weeks. Dad still has a pin in his arm.
He stopped hunting for mushrooms.
We stopped going to church.
Those spongy cones,

those gastronomical gold cones,
must have shot their spores into my brain
and made us pagans.

I went hunting after last Wednesday's rain,
boots laced tight, plastic bag
hanging out my back pocket,
looked under fallen logs, along ravines,
in hollows, at the base
of wild apple and cherry trees.
I didn't find a single one.
What I found instead—
the gentle incense of wet leaves,
the early evening's broken light.

When my wife and I found them
growing in full sun, roadside
on a pile of wood chips from a chewed up maple,
we snapped them off at the base
and took them home for dinner.
But an overactive imagination
coupled with a Christian youth,
worried the inside of my skull
like a soft stone. Don't taunt, it said.
There is a reason why your father
was spared. The mushrooms
are fakes like the viceroy to the monarch.
Remember why your pagan mother called
Dad's disaster, "disassociation from the astral plane."

I washed them in the sink,
two tablespoons of butter in a hot skillet,
waited for the smell, memory's sense,
and didn't die.

Wind

In stillness, all these trees bend East
    and it becomes a name blessing

the hair on the nape of our necks.
    As cottonwood seeds swirl in vortices

of indifferent June air thick as snowfall,
    tears well up in my left eye.

Music in columns of wood and brass,
    the ring of chimes we invent for it,

the whistle in a cracked window,
    the paint it dried in the Sistine Chapel,

it filled sails like a giant's breast
    and sent Europe to the New World.

MARIA RACHEL HOOLEY

Sunlight

The birds of mourning flock over my head
As blue fingers of dawn caress the sky
Winter condenses in my breath still fed
By grief's unending rule. Last spring you died.
You have the earth as your final home
While I above remember my old dream
Of youth guided by your love. Alone
I face this wind that's charged with ice unseen.
This coming spring can bring no pain so great
As the previous season my heart stained,
And still I fear the coming warmth for weight
My heart can scarcely carry toward refrain.
Now I must learn the way of birds in flight
To startle wings of crows into the light.

Apex

This is that moment
Before the debris starts swirling
In the vortex.
Rain pelts nails of moisture.
And the air carries
The sweat of nature.
This is that moment
When storm overtakes sky
And you want to head for shelter
Instead of watching the F4 dead in your path,
Sitting in the courtroom
Waiting for a ruling
On the marriage that spun
Like a trailer pulled from the earth
And shattered on the ground.

Drive-By Confession

At this moment, I'm willing to bet
Your Catholic friends inside that church
Are having communion
While I am in my car, heading home.
You spent a lifetime, trying to make me
One with Catholicism, but there are other
More intriguing mysteries to research.
Two springs since you died,
And I find myself taking the long way around,
So I can pass the church you spent hours inside.
And I find myself thinking all the things
I should have said before you died.
Sometimes the words even come out
And hang in the air before the vent
Jetting cold air blows them away.
Right now I'd take five Hail Marys
Or anything really so long as
Something I said made it to your heaven.

LAYTON ISAACS

Regional Delicacy

We specialize in tattooed girls
who call themselves conservative.

They like blowin' smoke 'bout
what they'll do when the baby comes.

Too frightened to leave,
they love ole' sugar daddy.

The escape they're faking, is so mundane
and the kill, so routine.

GRANT MATTHEW JENKINS

Three Misreadings

1.

Yes, I am here—in the hollow of your neck. That wall so sure-footed seats a traitor, where grip slips in the pulse of the vine. The libertine larvae invisible flies in the night, and so sick surety rests unequal in the blind moon. When fault lines appear. No. Yes. Maybe.

Dwell in the blade, sing off key to the stall you steal me in, brick by brick. There is no end to this rearrangement. The knitword akimbo like arms entwined, knowing meets out harsh reward and an end to mystery. Fictive certainty. Knoll dismay bead.

What feign quarters the hand. The nature of the glob has changed, although license is still taken with delectable imagined lines. Took a toss on the strand. Had time to take time again within you're writing. Three, they come in threes. No eyes may be.

This form of two and a half, I lifted it from your lower back in a thin film. Speechless complainer, I will know thy thought. The birds are more visible when it is cold outside. Asphodel has no sound. Save in the imagination it is late but an odor. Noise. May bee.

Or do you breathe for the both of us? She waxed lachrymose. Grace, a word for pins. Dancing will on end of power result in loss of color. No desire to be younger troubles them. He laid a five on the table before touching her foot. Expensive whisky. Noyes made beats.

Sex is the number we always turn on, while wheezing renders us extraordinarily. We grow old in each other's arms. The heart unlearns what it has erased. If you feed me more lines, I will start to think to have to sort of. Right now, I'm ripping them off of you. No y es ma beso.

2.

My food and pleasant pulse beat so quickly yet to prepare a frame for the reception of it, the relation of my disasters. To seek one who fled, I wait but for one event. We called each other familiarly the slave of passion, mingled with horror bearing a celestial stamp.

From me, proceed over the untamed yet obedient element. But they want (as the painters call it) keeping. I am wavering in my resolutions. Her brow was clear and ample, interpreted as mine, whose form and motions where lighter than the hills—you are well acquainted with my failure.

And quelling the dark tyranny, upon lifeless matter her promised gift. No expression could body. The oak had disappeared, her blue eyes cloudless, drew that fluid from the clouds that I might infuse a spark. Inflicted torture with praise palpitation of every artery languor and extreme.

Collected the instruments of life around possessed, the capacity for bestowing animation to her hiding-places. So astonishing a power placed within my hands. And her lips and the moulding of her face, sensibility and sweetness that none could behold her, without looking on her as a distinct species.

The lifeless thing lay at my feet and prepared myself for a multitude of reverses with all its intricacies of fibres, muscles, and veins for the kind of relation in which she stood to me. Judge respecting friendship ardently, hope that the gratification of your wishes may not be a serpent to sting you.

Success shall crown my endeavors, consummolation for my toils that I may never know. If I fail, you will see me again soon, or never, which had particularly attracted my attention was the structure of the human frame, a stream of fire issue. And nothing remained but a blasted stump by such slight ligaments in painful labor, to arrive at one at the summit of my desires—harmony in that very dissimilitude. Gay and playful as a summer insect. No one could better enjoy liberty yet no one could submit with more grace, mind united to so little pretension.

3.

I embrace you now, sentence, though often mine enemy. I embrace you and give you your own line unfettered, though you cradle me with your naturalism.

Every sentence a death sentence—but it's alright. I accept your no, tho I have no
choice

She waxed lachrymose. Speechless complainer, I will know thy thought

you exposer, tyrant
love

I rub my teeth against yours, not pulling away in embarrassment, but leaning in, grinding enamel on enamel—feeling it in the root, the nerve, which is a system of roots, of veins, of vines.

Some were detached sentences; other parts took the form of a regular diary, scrawled in an unformed childish hand

I suck on your arm-pit and love the sound of your moans and delight at this new found land. You suck mine and now I know, a moment of synchrony, the illusion of love. And real.

I pulled its wrists on to the broken pane, and rubbed it to and fro till the blood ran down and soaked the bedclothes

The soul rises to the surface in the delicate dilation of capillaries, the flush of a once old touch.

Things get mixed up.

SUSAN KATES

The Comfort Highway

I take the road through the bowed, bleached grass
past billboards peeling at the center.
It's good to turn loose of things—
regret and desire,
those old stones.

The red basin of this place is an open hand;
pink and lilac sky pull s overhead.

Dialing the Dari-Mart pay phone
hung on the graffiti-splashed wall,
I might have called to say this
or that, wind blowing over my words
in harsh, yellow light.

I might have told you how
the crimson rocks of this canyon
are a hand on my forehead,
a soft word I might forget.

Time worn mountains
turn to ruin without remorse.
Five hawks cry above them.
Across this cracked region, searching, waiting—
they beg every secret of the broken earth.

The Bird Watcher

My colleague Catherine possesses a sharp wit and a lilting Oklahoma accent. She is a woman who can disagree with a man in a voice so laced with honey that it takes him a moment to realize he has been given what for. She achieves this effect is in countless faculty meetings, a move I admire but can never pull off myself because I am unschooled in the ways of Oklahoma womanhood. Catherine and I have a sisterly bond because we were raised in the same Southern Baptist tradition; we share a familiarity with pulpit pounding preachers and evangelistic creed. But the similarities end there.

I am an overzealous assistant professor just out of graduate school. Catherine recently earned tenure at the university and she is hell-bent on dating and dancing for awhile. She has little time for me, the nagging kid sister calling for advice. I am a phone person. Catherine can bear no conversation longer than five minutes. "The phone is an instrument for making plans, not gossip," she tells me one day in her sternest sugared tone. I do not give up easily because I trust Catherine to give me the lay of the land and other secrets that will help me to survive academic life.

When I suggest lunch or the occasional film, Catherine invites me to walk with her at a local pond where King Birds swoop and Cardinals perch in plain view. As the new girl in town, desperate for companionship, I acquiesce. I want to talk shop; Catherine wants to talk Snowy Egrets and Night Herons. "What do you think of the work of so and so?" I might ask, panting beside her as we circle the pond. Catherine is a very brisk walker. "Oh look, it's a Prairie Warbler," she says in a voice of soft surprise. It doesn't take me long to learn that if I am going to converse with Catherine, I am going to have to learn a thing or two about birds.

Honestly, I could care less about any creature sporting feathers. These animals mess on my lawn chairs and the hood of my car. They screech at my cat. Perhaps I think all things avian are loathe and sinister because I watched Alfred Hitchcock's *The Birds* too often as a kid. The birds in the film are the physical embodiment of disturbing, shattering forces that threaten all of humanity. They scratch children. They peck people's eyes out. As a result of this movie, I see the

Audubon Society as a creepy little organization. Beneath the cheerful exterior of mostly geriatric members with their white tennis shoes and expensive binoculars, something isn't right.

Maybe something isn't right about feigning bird intrigue for Catherine; it's like faking interest in football for a man I hope to date. Lonely as I am for friendship, though, she is worth the effort. I relate to Catherine's birding passion in terms of my own love for junking. I am a scavenger in search of the next old basket or lamp; Catherine is in search of birds both exotic and ordinary—the Painted Bunting, the Yellow-Billed Cuckoo, the Rose-breasted Grosbeak.

At the local pond where we walk, the sparrows squeak like unoiled wheels. The sounds are disturbing and I fear birds might attack us or defecate on us, but Catherine is unconcerned. She has a CD at home with various birdcalls, and she studies songs of assorted species as though there will be a quiz. At the pond, even invisible birds are noted by my friend as she cocks her head, tuning in to a whistled cadence. "Oh, there's a Red Wing Blackbird," she'll sigh. "And a Blue Jay. No—I'm mistaken. It's a Mockingbird in his Blue Jay mode." Catherine is a regular bird detective.

We agree to meet at our usual pond one day when the sun is high and the heat is excruciating. Catherine is late: I am unhappy when people do not keep their promises to the clock. At last she comes bobbing down the sidewalk, her blunt-cut hair swishing politely. "I'm sorry I'm late," she winks at me. "I was listening to my time management tape."

I frown, unamused. "It's too hot to walk."

"Not if you put on your heat shield."

"What?"

"Your heat shield. It's a way of setting your mind against the temperatures. Just tell yourself that you have a heat shield made of ice on your head and you won't feel the sun beating down. You can reduce your sense of the temperature by a good four degrees."

I don't want to talk about heat shields or time management, so I just set off walking, forcing Catherine to keep up with me. Suddenly, a pearl-gray bird with a salmon-pink chest dives beyond us. Its long tail forms a V, larger than the rest of its body. The bird moves like a midget helicopter, diving down then moving upward again. "What is that!" I ask, startled and amazed.

"Don't you even know our state bird?" Catherine answers with ornithographic superiority. "That's a Scissor-tailed Flycatcher."
This little guy is less like a bird, and more like a gyroscope. He has stunning colors and horizontal movements. I quickly mask my enthusiasm because Catherine has been waiting for a moment like this to exert greater birding influence.

"I've been thinking. You should put up a little feeder in your back yard. Or a bird bath. The poor things are desperate for water. You could at least put out a pot or a bowl so they could get a drink."

"And turn my backyard into a trailer park?" The thought of a stainless steel pasta pot on my grass brings to mind a leaking house with containers placed forlornly around to catch rain. I will scout Catherine's birds, but I will not nurture them.

Some weeks later in an office at the university, I encounter a portrait of the Scissor-tail, his majestic back tail feathers in a long elegant V. I notice prints of other Oklahoma birds hanging in banks and physician offices all over town. They have an eerie presence. I learn they have been painted by the late George Miksch Sutton. Prairie birders think of him as their personal Audubon, a local treasure. He is former University of Oklahoma professor and the author of a gazillion bird books. That these Sutton portraits turn up in so many places around town gives me a feeling like the one I harbor about the Audubon Society. It is a little creepy to meet Oklahoma birds on the walls where I work and do business. I visit the dentist and a Great Horned Owl squints knowingly at me. I go to the bank to sign for a car loan, and a blue jay arches in a menacing pose. At a friend's law office, a Boat-Tailed Grackle stares back with its beady black eyes. George Miksch Sutton is all about town, haunting Norman from his grave with Hitchcockian intensity.

For some reason I give in and buy a cheap feeder and fill it with sunflower seeds. Red Finches, Blue Jays, and hearty Robins appear and soften my heart toward the whole birding enterprise. A nest of Carolina Wrens builds a nest on my patio in an ornamental bird house and Catherine comes to watch the mother and father work tirelessly to feed the four beaky babies with fleshy pink limbs. They open their mouths and squeak upon our approach. Only a hard-hearted person could fail to take in this scene's sweet wonder.

Catherine and I drink iced tea on my back porch and observe the industrious parents flying back and forth to their brood with insects and seed.

"Carolina Wrens are just my favorite bird," she sighs.

"Every bird is your favorite bird."

"Are you sure you wouldn't like to borrow my bird call CD so that you could learn birdcalls?"

"No thanks. Just because I put up a feeder and am the arbitrary host for a nest of wrens doesn't mean I want to become a bird scholar."

The truth is that I could use a little bird knowledge in order to address the crisis developing in my back yard. An awful smell begins to emanate from the nest and I call Catherine to tell her that I think one of the babies is dead.

"You need to get it out of there," she says. "Get some tweezers and pull the dead one out."

"The only tweezers I have are from Beauty Supply and they cost fourteen dollars. I am not getting anywhere near a bird with them. Besides, if I touch the birds, the mother will never come back."

"That's an old wave's tale. Take a little spoon and spoon him from the nest."

I check the internet, and sure enough, it says that nestlings touched by humans will not deter the mother from returning. I find a plastic spoon and head outside. The other birds cry out as I lift the limp and gooey dead thing from the nest. I toss its tiny remains into my garden and throw the plastic spoon away. Within minutes, the mother is back on the job, feeding her brood.

I watch the baby birds each day with interest as they develop their little wings and become stronger. It is important to me not to miss the moment they leave the nest and so I begin to inspect them compulsively, at least twenty times daily.

"Give them some space," Catherine instructs. "They aren't due to fly away for at least another two weeks."

When I cannot stand it I take one of the babies from the nest and put him on the ground to see if he will try to fly. I realize that no sensitive birder would do this, but my curiosity has got the best of me. He hops all around, clearly distressed. The mother and father squeak from the nearby tree as if I am a bird predator, which I guess

I am. I go to put the little guy back in the nest, but by this time the two others have squeezed out to see what is going on. They have landed on the potted plants below and are hopping around, greatly disturbed themselves by this bird circus. No one is flying, but no one is in the nest. I call Catherine.

"You did what! Oh the poor dears…"

When I look around again I see that the entire family is perched in different parts of the tree. In an hour they will all be gone, good riddance to me.

Despite this birding faux pas, Catherine suggests that we travel to France together for a conference on Global Literacy. She pitches the trip in terms of her passion, not in terms of our literacy research.

"Imagine," she says with an enthusiasm she must know will be met with skepticism: "We can see French birds!"

"People don't go to France to see birds," I reply, beginning to consider the international possibilities. "They go for the Eiffel Tower and Monet's water lilies." Who would look for birds when they could search for 19th century junk in the Paris Flea Market? I am compelled to call her a bird brain, but I fear she might retract the invitation.

As we prepare for our trip, I leave room in my suitcase for the treasures I hope to find at the Marché aux Puces de St-Ouen. Catherine packs two heavy volumes titled *Les Oiseaux du France I & II*. These weighty texts are filled with color photographs of birds named Peregrine, Lesser Kestrel, Redshank, Avocet—and other French sounding birds that I am willing to bet will not be plentiful in an urban setting.

On an August morning we arrive in Paris. Because it is too early to check into our room, we leave our suitcases with the hotel clerk and head to the charming Luxembourg Gardens a few blocks away. The garden is filled with lovers, students, and outdoor chess players. We stroll through the famous park past ancient statues, refreshing fountains, and fragrant lavender. Men play boules, and children turn round and round on the antique carousel; there are no exotic birds however, only pigeons that resemble the New York variety, Orioles, a few ducks.

At an outdoor café, I hear the sound of French fluttering in the background. We sit down and order steaming Cappuccinos. I take out my journal to record a few of the events of our journey and Catherine takes out a bird book with post card size photos of *Les Oisseux Francaise*. One sip of my coffee and I am having a perfect French moment. Then the German man at the next table initiates a conversation with Catherine.

"Where are you from?" he asks, after he has observed her accent, always a giveaway. He pulls his big black framed glasses from his distinguished face.

Catherine smiles demurely.

"Oklahoma," she adds before turning back to a picture of a bird that, I am certain, has never ventured near the Luxembourg Gardens.

"Home of the Cowboys and the Indians," the German nods. "The Wild, Wild West!"

We are used to this reception in the U.S. Too many people continue to think of the plains as the last holdout for men on horses and Native Americans in tipis.

I roll my eyes at Catherine, but it is too late. She has already engaged the gentleman as she has other men in libraries, on buses, and in restaurants. Catherine can emerge from the most unexpected places with a date for lunch. One day as we pushed our trays through a cafeteria line back home, Catherine began talking comets with a man from the meteorology department. They conversed their way past the desserts and the beverages, and as I waited for my change from the cashier I heard Catherine say to the man, "See you Tuesday at twelve." She waved happily, then picked up her tray.

"We're having lunch next week."

"You made a date in a cafeteria line?"

"Well he knows just everything about comets!"

The German man leans forward attentively in his chair, and Catherine's routine has begun. I want to write in my journal and keep this perfect moment going, but it is too late. To this European, my friend is the quintessential southern belle, a rare bird perched in the Luxembourg Gardens.

"What brings you to Paris?" he asks, sipping his wine.

"Global literacy," Catherine says, extending her hand. The German reveals that his name is Hans, and, like us, he is an academic, attending a chemistry conference. Maybe he is, maybe he isn't: you can never tell about café conversations. If you are going to embellish and reinvent yourself, this would be the place to do it. Catherine and Hans go on for some time in superficial academic banter about the rhetoric of science and semiotics.

I am anxious to check into our hotel room a few blocks away where we left our suitcases so that I can change my clothes and wash off the traveling dust. The man wants to know where we are staying, but Catherine pretends to get the name wrong: Hotel Saint Beatrice she says, but it is Hotel Le Sainte Beuve. I am grateful she tosses him off her trail. We part ways with the man, and it appears that, at least for the moment, she prefers my company to Hans.

The lobby of Hotel Le Saint Beuve is all maroon toile drapes and fuchsia orchids. Lavender fish drift inside a wall aquarium, as if on T.V. The clerk hands us a real key, not the plastic card you get in the U.S. We drag our suitcases up the winding, black wrought-iron staircase. Catherine fumbles with the lock and voilà! What a sight! The tiny room is covered with yellow wallpaper on which delicate Parisian birds of excellent plumage perch all around. Some are blue, some rust with white markings. My friend laughs with delight. The rest of our chamber is so small that one can hardly move through it to reach the antique armoire and twin beds. Despite these cramped quarters, the room expands a bit with the birds against the yellow heavens.

My first French hotel room ever does not disappoint. There is a tiny balcony where Paris can be seen in all its glory. The Eiffel Tower rises in the distance in the ways I have only seen in coffee commercials. I have the inclination to step out on our terrace like Marie Antoinette and cry, "Let them eat cake!" I pause instead to observe that France has nothing on Oklahoma when it comes to the sky, even if everything else here seems to triumph, particularly the cake.

We take out the superb lemon pastries purchased before we arrived at the hotel and recline happily on our beds. "Tweet, tweet," I say to Catherine, "You got some birdies after all." She smiles and pulls out the weighty ornithological texts from her suitcase and proceeds to study them instead of the magnificent city just outside. The elegant wrens and delicate Orioles perch all around this charming French aviary. I have to admit, these are my kind of birds.

They are not menacing or rough. Not one of them will soil the silk bedspreads. And if I listen carefully, I can almost hear them chirp *bonjour* and *bienvenue* against the pale yellow background which encloses our room with all the citrus perfection of a lemon tart.

ABIGAIL KEEGAN

Saying Yes to the Storm

In the middle of the night, the storm
asks for life. Winds hoot and rush
through the alley between our houses
to awaken us. Next door, candles
at the Buddhist altar are blown out,
our goddesses and christian icons
flat as dried fish against the wall
vibrate to the rhythm of the storm.

Rising, I go near the glass door being
pelted by ice. Outside a small, thick tree
limb spears the ground pushed by
100 mile an hour wind. Air funnels
around my stomach and spleen.
My lungs breathe in the eye of chaos,
walls of water and wind funnel, some
force penetrates the deep sea of my will
to live: I say, Yes, to the storm.
Far away, whole continents of the planet
sleep in a calm night, indifferent
to a life going on from here and now.

The Grateful Dead

If I go to Greece, they picnic
on graves with their loved ones.
In New Mexico, sugary smiles
and deep eyed glances laugh at me
from brightly colored street parades,
their breath the scent of burning pinyon
in chilled November air.
In Tennessee they ride atop walking horses,
and whisper Moody Blues songs
from the grave I leave behind.
At home, the dead hover about me
the way angels sit on children's pillows.
Their funerals are in my teacups,
pictures of them in caskets
hide behind paintings on my walls.
There's not a piece of furniture
they haven't worn with their touch,
few books without their notes.
When the orange slice cake comes
out at Christmas, their lovely fingers
press-up the last bits of crumbs.
Often, just before sleep,
the whole crowd of them quivers
round my bed, pressing me
with fingers, knees and paws
hoping to slide into my train of dreams
as if I'm the last subway on earth.

JENNIFER KIDNEY

In the Closet

Mother was a fashion plate,
her excuse for excess
her secretarial career.
Cousin Babs,
on the other hand,
who graduated
from modeling school
sashaying down a runway
sporting a saucer hat,
was dubbed a "clothes horse,"
a position beneath
contempt to which
I should not aspire.

I marveled at Mother's
tri-colored sling-backs
that exactly matched
the office appropriate
sundress with bolero jacket
and admired the buttons
on her outfits—
some like clusters of grapes,
pimiento stuffed olives,
or ripe berries,
others jeweled in hues
of sapphire or ruby.
She shunned "dungarees"
except for gardening,
and was always fully
accessorized
for grocery shopping.
I longed to inherit
her wardrobe.

Meanwhile home-made
and hand-me-down
were good enough for me.
I had only to go to school
where I suffered
excruciating envy
for twin sets
and short pleated skirts.

Mother was a seamstress
and fashioned for me
two dresses a year—
an autumnal print
for the first day of school
and something green
to celebrate my birthday.
I was allowed to choose
the patterns, but nothing
ever fit even when
I was too old
to be likely
to "grow into it."

Now I have my own career
and closets crammed
with color coordinated
costumes, and my bureau brims
with cashmere and cotton knit.
The coveted clothing
has long been discarded
but I inherited the genes.

Ocracoke—August 2009

The Piping Plover
lays its eggs where they lie
camouflaged by their resemblance
to shell and beach debris,
thinks that this disguise
is their protection.
If the nests are discovered,
that stretch of beach is closed
to the public for the season,
cordoning them off from careless feet,
crushing tires, and probing paws.

My sister and I reach the open beach,
carry our parents' ashes in plastic bags
out of sight beyond the dunes
from sunbathers and beachcombers
and Frisbee-throwing dog-owners.

In the shade of waving sea oats
we wait for the surge of surf
to cover our feet, then open the bags
letting ash and bits of bone
commingle, becoming one
with sand and fragments of shell
mixed by the swirling water
and finally invisible
as Plovers' eggs awaiting
breaking open and life.

KELLEY LOGAN

The Doppelganger

When I was a child
Old people would loom from crowds,
Touch my face and whisper names
That belonged to people I had never met
And smile,
Tears standing in their eyes.

After, safe in my bed, I dreamt of worlds
Populated by sepia men and sepia women
In strange hats and starched clothes
Who, upon some secret signal, would all turn in unison,
And look at me with my own face.

Today at parties, I am told by strangers
 I look like people I don't resemble in the slightest.
Walking home, passing the mirror of darkened store front windows
I see thousands reflected, one by one, in the panes of glass.

JULIA MCCONNELL

Descent

Yesterday morning it rained
cold viscous drops
that sealed themselves
to the streets, the cars, the rocks,
every surface glazed in ice,

transforming the lantern tree
in front of my house
into a Swarovski crystal,
bending her branches,
boldening the outline of her shape,
revealing the mockingbirds
puffed up against the cold.
Any journey became treacherous.

This morning it is snow that is falling
soft and silent
a beautiful descent to the earth.
Wind stirs the limbs
in their glass casings,
creaking and cracking,
like the amplified sound
of weight settling
on an old leather saddle.

I sit hypnotized
by this downwards dance,
feeling the chill
and squinting
in the reflected light.

My little tree—
this could be the storm
that will break you
with so much terrible beauty.

How to Control Time.

Wake up early and drink coffee.
Make your plans, write your lists.
Draw diagrams. Gather gear.
Analyze equations, blueprints, longitudes, and latitudes.
Allow for contingencies, singularities, and loose gravel.

Next check the bearings on your wheels.
Cut the fingers off your gloves.
Make sure the rope is secure
to the bumper of the car.
Strap on your skates and hold on tight,
while the whole world becomes motion.

But remember,
when turning a corner
there is a point in acceleration,
where your feet will leave the earth,
and for a moment you will be there,
suspended between stars and pavement—
until velocity and gravity work against you
and you fall back to the asphalt
bruised and scraped and breathless.

Quantum Mechanic

Stop marking off the days
cut up your calendar with silver scissors
hang a page from each month
on your refrigerator.
Place a bottle of wrinkle cream
on your bathroom vanity
next to the acne soap.
Punch the time clock
until it is broken.

Twist time,
bend it into shape.
Comb out its strands
into a glowing wave.
Stop measuring in minutes,
use stones or trees or glass or air.
Collect time's particles in a sieve,
watch moments flicker and darken
like a jar of summer fireflies.
Experience time in whale years,
dog years, and insect hours.
Become a quantum mechanic
and tinker with Einstein's engine.

Find pictures of yourself
twenty years from now
at age fifty, ninety, seventy, and thirty,
label them each "myself at present"
and hang them next to photos
of friends you haven't met yet.

If we fall out of time
like a watch with a failing battery,
Can time fall out of us?
Like Nefertiti holding court
in a Berlin Museum,
like Van Gogh's swirling sky,
like a house of stone
standing through the ages,
like a masterpiece?

TERI MCGRATH

Fifty Jesus High

When Charlie's old, beat up, white Camaro finally decided to break down for good on the side of Interstate 40, about 15 miles east of Tucumcari, New Mexico, Lance, Charlie's ex-fiancé, packed three neatly folded polo shirts, four pairs of boxers, and two pairs of clean blue jeans into a small suitcase; filled a black overnight bag with toothpaste, soap, razor, shaving cream and aftershave, leapt into his new Infinity, and raced out of Lawton, Oklahoma, to save the day.

He was happy.

Mostly, he was happy because he was angry. He could imagine Charlie standing on the side of that dark highway, waving her slim white arms at any coked-up trucker or drunk teenager that happened by. He could picture the State Trooper who had picked her up eyeing her small figure, her bare legs, the fringe of her cut-off jeans. "What are you doing out here all by yourself?" the trooper would ask, his fat, sweaty chins wiggling. The image made Lance grit his teeth and squeeze the steering wheel until his knuckles became hard, white, sharp-pointed squares.

The trooper had taken Charlie to a filling station where she'd called some of her friends in Albuquerque and asked them to come get her. Charlie's mother told Lance all of this when he'd called to check on her. Charlie hadn't called him. She had called her friends, Chris and Gina, and then she called her mother to let her know she'd be staying the night with them. She was still with them when Lance called her mom's house that morning. Lance told Charlie's mom that he would make the drive out there to see about the car. He said he'd come straight into Albuquerque after that, and maybe visit with some friends he had out there. Charlie's mother had been pleased. She had offered him the guest bedroom.

When he'd stopped to fill up his tank, just before leaving Lawton, he had plucked a bouquet of dark red roses wrapped in noisy cellophane from a bucket near the cashier station. Every now and then, as he drove, he would reach over and pinch one of the roses' cool, red, petals or stroke the soft upholstery of the passenger's seat. He thought, contentedly, of all the things he would not say to Charlie. For instance, he would not remind her that he'd begged her to let him drive or to take his car. That he'd even offered to rent her a car. She hadn't even wanted to take his roadside emergency kit with her—the jumper cable, car jack, flashlight and other tools that may have come in handy. She said she'd be all right without, but he'd taken it out of his trunk and put it in her back seat as she was pulling away. Surely she'd used at least the flashlight while she was stuck out there in the desert night. But he wouldn't ask her if she had.

He whistled while he drove or sang quietly to himself, an old George Jones song that had been going through his mind since he'd handed the old man at the gas station his money.

"Got yerself in trouble, did ye?" the old man had asked, ringing up the price of the roses.

"Something like that," Lance replied.

He took I-44 into Oklahoma City and then got on I-40 which would take him straight into Albuquerque. It was simple as that. Charlie insisted on taking 62 when she made this drive, which took her through Altus and other small towns where she had to slow down to twenty and stop at red lights. Taking I-44 meant back tracking a bit and going through the city, which Charlie hated, but it was a straight shot—no detours through po-dunk, no getting lost. Charlie said his way was boring; getting lost was an adventure, she said.

"Where's Quanah?" she asked him late one night, calling collect. She was on her way home from visiting her mother. "I mean, is it in Texas or Oklahoma?"

Lance had been sitting by the phone for hours waiting for her to call. He had begun to expect a call from the hospital or the police instead. He said, "What? Why? Where the hell are you?"

"Well...Quanah," she'd said laughing.

Lance had held the receiver out in front of him, strangling it viciously. He made a motion like he would throw it across the room, but he stopped himself. He felt his shoulders droop. "Charlie!" he said into the receiver. "Goddamn it Charlie!"

"I'm kidding. I'm kidding," she'd said, laughing some more. "I got... I took a wrong turn, but I know where I'm going now. I'll be home in about... Well, I'll be home."

"Jesus!" Lance said, tossing a couple rose petals into the ash tray. He turned the radio on to a classic rock station and ignored it until it started breaking up; then he punched the off button irritably. He drove in silence for several hours, through endless green and yellow fields, glaring at cows and dead armadillos, passing up moving trucks and mini-vans. He crossed the Texas border and began traveling through more fields of green and yellow.

"Quanah!" he said, "Christ."

At least then she'd had a decent car—a sensible Ford Taurus that her mother had given her. But she crashed that one into a tree early one morning on her way into work. She'd spun out on the wet roads and crashed into a tree. When she told the story of the wreck to Lance and everyone else who wanted to know about it, she always put a great deal of detail into the part where the air bag deployed. She said she'd always wondered if it would really come out, and what it would be like when it did. She said when her face smashed into the air bag, she was thinking, "Oh."

Lance didn't have a car when Charlie crashed hers into a tree; in fact, he'd been using her car to get to school and work. He'd just started a new job, and hadn't yet saved up enough to get himself a car. There was nothing he could do to help Charlie, and it made him angry. He began to suspect her crash was an air bag experiment gone wrong. She needed to be more careful, he told her. She was self-destructive, and now it wasn't just herself she was hurting.

"Because I love you, Charlie. I don't want to see you get hurt. I want you to care about yourself as much as I do."

"I do," she'd said, in a very small, perplexed voice. "I do care about myself." She was shaking her head very slowly. "You don't have to do anything."

"What an asshole," Lance thought, cringing at the memory of him scolding her, like a child, for getting into an accident. "I'm being punished," he said to the back of a slow-moving, orange station wagon. "And I deserve it." He hit his turn signal and pulled into the passing lane.

He'd apologized, of course, and she'd accepted, but she still bought the Camaro at him. She'd pulled into his driveway the day she bought it, with her brother James in the passenger's seat, pale and shaken from having coached her on driving a standard. She crawled out of the window, like Bo Duke, and waved her arm at the car, smiling proudly. James reached out of the passenger's side window to open up the door and get out. Then he held the door in an awkward sort of hug, one hand on the armrest inside and the other pressed firmly against the smooth exterior. He lifted the door and slammed it shut. He had to try it a couple of times before it stuck. When he was done, he gave Lance a look that told him he should do something about his mouth hanging open. Lance attempted an expression of thoughtful appraisal, covering his mouth to hide his smile.

He walked around the car, looked in through the windows at the seats, which seemed to be composed almost entirely of duct tape. He kicked at the tires, and looked underneath the car, for nothing in particular, although he wasn't surprised to see the muffler hanging down to where it nearly touched the ground. Finally he stood behind the car where Charlie was standing. "It's a classic," she said, pointing at the KISS sticker in the back window. "150 bucks!" she said, laughing.

"No doubt," Lance said, "I mean, really?"

James seemed to be having a coughing fit. Charlie was beaming. In a proper world, where everything behaved as it reasonably should, Charlie's car should have been one of the cars lined up for demolition at a monster truck rally. She loved the car, though. She bought it new tires and some fuzzy dice for the window. She covered up the backseat with a quilt, and put t-shirts over the bucket seats in front. Whenever Lance expressed concerns about the safety of the vehicle, Charlie would cover up the driver's side mirror and say, "Shhhh."

***

Lance was hungry, but he didn't plan on stopping until he got to Amarillo. The car was warm and filled with the fragrance of roses. He opened the window. A billboard he had passed a few miles back had told him that he would soon see the largest cross in the Western Hemisphere, and now he saw it sprouting up out of a yellow and green field to his left. "That cross," Charlie had observed, the first time she'd taken him with her to visit her mom, "is a big goddamned cross."

"It is," he'd agreed.

"How many Jesuses would it take, I wonder?" she'd asked. "Fifty? I bet it's at least fifty Jesus high."

"Sounds about right."

"How big a cross do you need?" she had asked, sounding, actually, a little bothered by the whole thing.

Lance believed that Charlie was testing him. It's true she had an inexplicable faith in her Camaro, and her Camaro had inexplicably managed to survive two years of her driving it around. She loved it and seemed to believe that her love would be enough to keep the car going. But surely she knew it couldn't make a trip like this. Lance had begged her not to drive it.

"Let me take you, Charlie."

No, she'd said. She wanted to drive.

"Well, take my car then, or let me rent you a car."

"Shhh," she said, patting the hood of the Camaro consolingly. "It will be all right, Lance," she said. "I'll be okay. It's not a big deal."

"It's not a big deal," Lance said in his Charlie voice, tossing a few more rose petals out of the window.

Charlie thought everything was going to be okay, and nothing was a big deal. The engagement ring he put on her finger when he'd proposed had been too big for her. She'd had to hold it in place with her thumb while she showed everyone at the reception so that nobody would notice. Lance felt terrible about it. He'd screwed the whole thing up, he thought.

"It's okay," Charlie had told him. "It's not a big deal."

But a week later, she gave the ring back to him.

"It is a big deal," Lance said, squinting into the afternoon sun.

Charlie said she didn't want to be engaged. She didn't want to go with him to Austin, where his company was sending him to work. "We don't have to go to Texas," he'd said. "We can stay here. I can find something here."

"That would be crazy," she said. "Anyway, I don't want to stay here."

"Well, what the hell do you want?" he'd said, too loudly. Charlie sighed and looked at her hands.

"I'm sorry," he said. "I'm sorry Charlie. I just… love you. I want to make you happy."

"I know," she said. "I know you love me." She'd kissed him and hopped in through the window of her Camaro, and he watched her pull away.

But she didn't know, Lance was thinking. He was sure she didn't. Charlie's engagement ring was in Lance's glove box. He'd had it re-sized. He imagined placing it on her finger again, how well it would fit. He'd give her these roses. He'd buy her a new Camaro, or she could keep the old one if she wanted. He'd get it fixed up—-restored. Whatever she wanted.

Just past a highway sign indicating he was 35 miles from Amarillo, Lance pulled his car over to the side of the road.

"This is crazy," he said, calmly. He had his hands on the steering wheel still, and slowly, he leaned forward until his head lay on the steering wheel too.

When Charlie left, she wouldn't take his car or let him rent her a car. She wouldn't take any of the money that he offered her. She didn't want his ring.

She said, "I got my oil changed; I got money for gas. I'm set."

"What if you get a flat?"

"Got a spare," she said.

"Got a jack?" he'd asked.

She'd shrugged, and Lance had walked to his car and pulled the emergency kit out of his trunk. He tossed it through the passenger window into the back seat of the Camaro. So she had his roadside kit, which was important for several reasons. It was something of his that she would have, he'd thought. It would give him a reason to find her when she got back, or give her a reason to find him. It was especially important now, though. Because, of several truths Lance was slowly coming to grips with on the side of this lonely state highway, in the blinding heat of the Texas sun and in the shadow of the largest cross in the western hemisphere, the most pressing was this: Lance had a flat tire.

He didn't want to get out to look at it, because he knew that it was bad, and he wasn't sure how he was going to fix it.

He lifted his head up to look out the window. The sun was bright. The light mixed with the dust on Lance's windshield and the scent of roses wilting in the front seat. The road made a straight gray smear through the dust, and Lance sat still and stared at it for a long time as the sun began its slow, inevitable slide down the western half of the sky.

Missing Piece

George sits across the table from me in the coffee shop and watches me load my baked potato with butter, sour cream and salt. He sits behind a thick shroud of cigarette smoke and points two-thirds of a finger at me. "You're ruining that potato," he says. "All that butter and salt. . .That'll kill you."

He uses the butt of his last Lucky Strike to light his next one.

I respond to his criticism by making a big show of taking the first delicious, buttery bite. Lightly seasoned with George's disapproval, it is delicious!

"Mmm Mmm!" I say.

He passes me a napkin, and then turns to look out the window at the parking lot, and the evening traffic. He mutters about clogged arteries and fat. "Cholesterol, you know?" he says, blowing smoke into the glass. A smile wrinkles the corners his eyes in a way that has become familiar to me, but that I don't think most people would notice.

He's not really joking though. George actually is telling me how to eat a baked potato. He also tells me how to drive my car and how to park it. He tells me what stores to shop at, and how to buy dish towels and then how to use them. Once, when one of our cooks quit in the middle of a shift, he told me how to make pancakes. That's was actually quite useful. He tells me how much sugar to put in my coffee.

"Have some cream," he says, waving his maimed digit at my coffee cup. He pushes a couple little creamers at me. "Put cream in it."

When I was trying to decide what to major in in college, George told me to take classes in forestry. "You could be a forest ranger," he said. Then he told me the story of me being a forest ranger and living in a quiet little cabin in the woods. I'd come down into the nearby little town every now and then to have coffee and talk with the people, he said. He described the life of a forest ranger in such sweet detail it put a lump in my throat. "You'd have all this green around you, and shade," he said. "You could sit out on your porch in the mornings as the sun comes up, and smell the trees and the rain." He waved his hand at the imaginary birds perched above his head.

One afternoon he brought me a pile of books (all published in the early seventies) about plant science, about trees and flowers, and animals.

Have a dream, he was saying.

Have mine.

"Put some cream in your coffee," George says. "Less sugar, more cream."

And though I do not enjoy cream in my coffee, I put cream in my coffee.

NANNETTE MOORE

Thoughts at Midnight

what do we do when we find ourselves
standing at a crossroad

do we take the path to the left
or the one to the right
or the one down the middle

do we take the smooth one
or the rocky rough one
or the one that circles back
back to where we are?

if we take the smooth one, will we learn to overcome obstacles?
if we take the rough one, will we give up before we reach our goal
what if we chose the one that circles back
do we get a chance to correct the mistakes we've made

i find myself standing at a crossroad
trying to pick and choose.

PHILLIP CARROLL MORGAN

Two Lane Highway

> *He was a frequent attender of fairs also, which, in*
> *Arabia, were not always mere resorts of traffic, but*
> *occasionally scenes of poetical contests between*
> *different tribes, where prizes were adjudged to the*
> *victors, and their prize poems treasured up in the*
> *archives of princes.*
> —*Washington Irving,*
> *Mahomet and His Successors, 1849*

the taste of her kiss
still lingers on my lips
following the narrow highway
through the curvy countryside
lush and green and wet from rains

viewed high and early
from a hilltop above
the surface
of a spring-fed pond
glints reflected morning sunlight
like dancing tips of silver flame

the shining pond itself is
situated on an intermediate hillside
above a pastoral valley
on my regular trade route

inviting me to view the same scene
over and over
in different lights seasons and times of day

As I topped that familiar hill
in my Ford pickup this morning,

I thought of Mahomet crisscrossing Arabia
in camel-powered caravans in search of truth.
As the Arabs' regard for poetry clearly shows,
the desert was a warmer place in Mahomet's day.

He was coolly stigmatized nonetheless
for his first essay in arms at age sixteen,
simply supplying arrows and bearing a shield
for his uncle Zobier,

who led a warlike expedition of Koreishites
in aid of the Kenanites
against the tribe of Hawazan.

Irving noted that Arabian writers
right up into modern times
call it al Fadjar,
or the impious war,
because it was carried on
during the sacred months of pilgrimage.

Later on, Mahomet was heavily influenced
by Nestorian Christians, lingering
many moons as a young man
in their Persian Gulf monasteries
while Arabia still tolerated
immense religious diversity.

I am not exactly sure how this relates
to a two-lane highway of interior Oklahoma
being driven upon by a man
who was just kissed,
except that it illuminates the fact
that this man may have a hard time
differentiating the physical and spiritual,
as do the Catholics, calling Mary the
mother of God instead of the mother of Jesus.
Nestorius believed that Christ the man and

Christ the Word were too different natures
existing simultaneously but distinct
in the same body.

Mahomet was into the journey, as I.
Jesus described himself as, the way.
This two-lane blacktop
has made itself simile and metaphor,
its roadside hills, waters, woods
and creatures speaking to me
in different lights in different seasons.

This road reveals more subtlety than definition,
more mystery than resolution,
on which I have difficulty
distinguishing kisses from sunlight,
in separating the carnal and the divine.

Red Power, White Pride

One of my favorite quotes
from a warrior of the white tribes
is John Adams saying this:
"I have studied war and politics
so that my sons could study
business and mathematics
so that their sons could study
art and literature."

In light of these remarks
by Warrior Adams
I would like to thank
the warriors from the red tribes
who have come before me,
clearing the way, so to speak.

In pre-Mississippi,
fighting Desoto
and his hidalgos at the Tombigbee River
and at Chicaza town,
as well as the French
at Ogoula Tchetoka and
at old Ackia town.

Fighting the United States on the Red River;
at Alcatraz, at Fort Marion, at
Horseshoe Bend (on both sides
of the Tallapoosa), at Wounded Knee,
and at Little Big Horn, although
that wasn't much of a fight.

So that my granddad could be a farmer,
so that my dad could be a warrior
in World War II, which was one hell of a fight,
and who later could do business independently,
so that I could study art and literature.

Hear me, this is who I am,
I say.
This is who I am.

Literacy

this poem
on this page

this disembodied self

this is not me

this is not narcissism
no coded message either

this is you
in your native tongue

rearrange the 18 letters randomly
on this page
it is still you

this is not a mirror
this is not me
this is not an apple
with a worm

this is you
straight in the eye

Indian Man Christmas Cards

Dear Chad,
A single strand of fibers
cannot bear much weight, cannot be
of much use. You and Sarah,
Sam and Henry are a four-stranded
unbreakable rope. Soon to be five-stranded.
This is why we stand together.

Dear Jerry,
You are a journeyman. We stand
side by side, warriors of the same tribe.
I wish that you and I, Uncle Bill and Wade
could work together every day.
Those four strands woven together
would make an unbreakable rope.

Dear Bill,
I wrote to Jerry and Chad that our family
is a strong braided rope. You are
much more a man of backbone,
than of wishbone. We are brothers.
We have worked together. We have
stood and wept over graves together.
One cannot have too many brothers.

Dear George,
We have talked around many fires,
in many languages, living life
as a poetic verb. We have recited poetry
in hidden coves echoing from canoes
in desert canyons on emerald rivers.
No greater friend of the earth than you
walks upon its surface.

You have taught me that there is
no righteousness without knowledge.
You and I are poets, standing on the ridge
and wondering. We are brothers,
smoking the pipes of philosophy and peace.
One cannot have too many brothers.

Dear Scott,
we have lived many winters in sight
of each other's fires. When our families were
young we worked many days in the same fields.
We were from birth inseparable playmates.
Grown men, we stand tireless allies. Our sons are mighty
and our daughters are women of power. We share
memories in our blood of creels of crawdads
and fields of grass. You taught me that a man
must grow where he is planted and that there is
no freedom without love. We are brothers and friends.
One cannot have too many brothers.

Dear Allen,
In a tide of faces, our father and mother
watched the ball play on fields of lush green.
We were young oaks for the roaring crowd,
you playing one guard and I the other. We have
fished together from the banks of Oklahoma streams.
We stood for right in the streets of cities,
warriors fighting to make peace, end war. We shed
vitreous tears for our friends who fell, and we
have since seen the birth of many children who
have not known war. You are the elder brother, I the younger.
With our father, you are the champion of my youth.
One cannot have too many brothers.

Dear Wade,
You are my son. The things we have built
together are enduring treasures. We are craftsmen
who learned to work together like cold and freezing,
like heat and melting, like rhythm and beat.
A son teaches his father that boyhood
is eternal, something that does not expire,
does not end. In war or peace, hunt or gathering,
grown sons are like brothers. They stand fast
when grief intrudes, embracing difficulty like a lover.
The same women give us life and grant our positions
in the design. Like fine brothers, a son is true.
One cannot have too many brothers,
but can be satisfied with one good son.

JOHN GRAVES MORRIS

Through

The way kudzu overtakes
and overwhelms local foliage,
through has become the all-
purpose, all-weather preposition—

one expresses creativity *through*
dance, *through* poetry, *through*
music, politicians earning political
capital *through* public works projects,

through creation of local jobs,
through adherence to traditional values,
through religious devotion, in *through*
the out door, *through* and *through*—

in and *with* and *by*, arthritic,
in tatters, shaking with delirium tremens,
loiter at the soup kitchen for words,
just looking for a little broth

to help with their articulation
or shame motorists at turn signals
or by the on-ramp, brandishing a sign,
"Will work to restore our good name."

BENJAMIN MYERS

On My Thirty-fifth Birthday

Rambling through the rooms
in which fathers
wander—picking up worry
and setting it down, picking
up love—I meet
my own father, fresh
from his cancer

and follow him through
afternoon rooms
of unmoving light,
to a place where
I am seven years old
and he is fixing our neighbor's
water heater, bending
to it like a ranch-hand
to the birthing cow.
I am holding the wrench, and he
is teaching me that a man
can fool a machine into working
just a little longer.

Further back
there is a screen-door:
already he has passed through.
I am standing
with my toes against the threshold, straining
to see through wire mesh
while he lingers
at the edge of a dark line of trees,
waving for me to follow.

To the Late Night Stars

Take your pointy hats
and go;
this poem is not for you.

I need to find
that basement of bone,
spit city
where true poems breed,

and begin,
crawling up my own
blue vein—bulged
like a snake heavy
with prey—
until I reach my mind,
a hallway of rattling doorknobs,
where I can
sit cross-legged on the floor
and wait for a door
to open.

JL MYERS

Wrestling the Wind

> *until then I will be the fool, wishing for the day, that I*
> *could change the world*
>
> —*Eric Clapton*

I want you home by dinnertime, she said, as I pedaled away—Do you hear me?

I nodded, my face already west into the wind, not looking back.

It gets dark early and I don't want to be worrying—I barely heard her yell from the front porch. I was far enough down the road; I wasn't turning back.

Mom was concerned, always. I was her firstborn, it was the bicentennial and I was growing up far too fast. If she could have kept me at nine years old for ninety years, it wouldn't have been long enough for her. She was always trying to baby me. When my dad was helping out as volunteer assistant coach for the Sparring Elementary wrestling team that I was a member of, she accused him of pushing me too hard to win.

Nothing could have been farther from the truth. I wanted to win. Win like the other boys on my team.

I wanted to be like them.

So, when I won the third place state championship in the 50 lb. weight class the previous weekend, I knew I would get to be one of them.

And that evening, with my Snoopy handlebar radio pulling in the AM band, I cruised my metallic green Schwinn, with its blue metallic-flecked banana seat, west to the county line road, to meet up with those older boys from the team.

Those boys who would be my friends.

***

Can I come out to the clubhouse, I asked, as I dodged the dodgeball for the fifth time.

If you can make it all the way out there by yourself, Pete said, lining me up for another attack with the ball.

You make it out there and you're in the club, Michael added from the sidelines—but if you don't, then we know you're a wus.

And we'll tell everyone in Mrs. Walker's class that you're a homo, Pete said as he faked a kick towards me. I tried to dodge without intimidation.

I'm not a homo, I said angrily.

Clay's a fag, Pete mocked in sing-song—Gay Clay, Clay is so gay.

What time, I asked, stepping forward from the firing line.

Five o'clock, Michael said, as I narrowed the distance between them and myself.

That too late for a homo, Pete asked as he kicked the ball towards me.

No. I'll be there, I said dodging the shot—How far is it?

Two miles out 96th street north to county line road, Michael piped in.

Don't be late, Pete said

At the far end of the gym, our teacher, Mr. Dalgren, blew the chrome coach's whistle that hung around his neck all day, every day.

Put the dodge balls away and get outta my gym! Mr. D always told us to get out at the end of gym class like that. Do not forget your stuff, he'd add - Do not be late for your next class.

***

I won't, I told her as I closed the trunk of the old Valiant.

If you get another ticket, your dad will be furious, she said—So don't be speeding. You'll get there in due time.

I said I won't, came out as I turned my back and got into the car —I'll be safe.

I was eighteen, well into my first semester at college and you'd think that she'd give it a rest.

Just don't like you driving at night, she said—that two- lane between here and school isn't the best road.

He'll be okay, Mrs. Wilbury, came a voice from behind—I'll make sure he doesn't speed.

Thanks Brian, Mom said as she turned to my friend—I know you boys will be okay; I just worry sometimes.

Brian Chambers and I had been friends since '77 when my family moved to Bartlesville. He lived next door and his dad and mine had been our Boy Scout leaders at the Methodist Church in

Oak Park. We played on the same baseball team, took Karate lessons at the same place and worked the same low paying summer jobs at the same local park. In the years since those days, I've tried to keep up with what he was doing. Last I knew, he was going to be an officer in the Highway Patrol. Somehow, I never saw him in that role.

He will always remain as a friend to me.

And as my first college roommate.

Well, my first roommate, along with Darin, our other roommate.

You see, we were freshmen. And with an increased enrollment that year, all freshmen roommates living in the dorms were forced to share their two-person room with a third student.

That would be Darin Huber, in our case.

Darin was a big man. Second all around state shot put champion. The college had offered him a meager scholarship, tuition only, to play football. Because of his size, he could have been a lineman, but he turned them down cold.

He wanted an education. And playing football for a junior college does not guarantee an education. Besides, he had promised his mom that he would help get his brothers through school once he graduated.

And playing ball was not part of the bargain.

***

Took you long enough, Pete said as I slid to a stop—We didn't think you would come.

I'm here, ain't I?

Well, we almost left, Michael said—my mom wants me home early tonight. My dad's gone tonight with his buddies. Pete's dad goes too.

I think all they do is drink beer, Pete said—but my mom says it's important stuff that they do; things for the town.

So y'all can't stay?

Nope.

I guess I'll stay. Awhile anyways, I said.

Suit yourself, Michael said—the clubhouse is up the road, just over the first hill.

Under the big blackjack, Pete added—and don't mess with anything.

They rode away, down the darkening eastern highway toward town, leaving me to make the rest of the way myself.

I can't wait, I said.

***

I can't wait to get back either, Brian said, as we valiantly flew eastward, on the road towards school.

I looked over and nodded—Got the fuzz buster?

You know it. Homecoming's this week, he said—He plugged in the radar detector, to warn us of what traps lay ahead.

All the parties, I said—all the women.

All that, my brother, all that, he laughed.

That week ran off as quick as the rare October snow in Oklahoma. When we looked up, it was Friday. No one went home for the weekend, as usual. The culmination of a week of homecoming festivities was tonight. A rally, bonfire and the street dance.

The pyre had been built that morning. We all had walked past it going to class. Plenty of kindling had been left for us to feed the fire.

We had only to wait for the words to set it ablaze.

***

In the distance, I could see it. The large blackjack. It stood stoic in the darkening northern horizon against the gathering southern wind. Underneath its protective arms was the clubhouse. Constructed from pilfered plastic milk crates and sheet plastic, on top of which laid a sheet of corrugated green fiberglass as a roof. Zip-tied to the side of the structure was an old ten-foot CB whip antenna. Flying at the top of this mast was a miniature Jolly Roger, under which was a small confederate flag.

In the breeze flew the flags of warning.

They were pirates, and this, their ship.

And they took no prisoners.

As I slowed my bike under the tree and the last rays of daylight fell, I noticed smoke from behind the next hill.

My curiosity piqued.

A grass fire?

Remembering that my mom wanted me home by dark made no difference. It was nearly that now. I would be late. Just a peek at the fire beyond the northern horizon and I would head back home. It had to be a half a mile to the next hilltop and by the time I had made it halfway, the orange glow beyond was growing with the feeding wind.

I gotta see this, I muttered to myself as the wind and my curiosity pushed me.

***

You gotta see what, the girl asked from behind the front desk.

The spare key to my dorm room, I said—Mine's locked inside.

Can't help you, she said—The extra roommate was issued the extra key.

No other key, I asked—what about the RA on my floor, shouldn't he have one?

If he's in his room, he's got a pass key, she said—Good luck catching him there. He's usually down at the gym, with his buddies.

What room?

311.

As I made my way up, I remembered my roommates saying that they had met our RA the night of floor orientation. I had missed it because of my evening Comp class.

He's a real nice guy, Brian had said.

And that's all he would say about him.

Can I help you?

Yeah, uh, I locked myself out.

Hang on, Mike's the RA, he said turning around, Mike, you got a lost soul here.

As I waited in the hallway, I realized the guy that had answered the door looked vaguely familiar. Like an old photograph that you haven't seen for awhile. Things look the same, but somehow different.

Locked your keys in your room, the voice asked from behind the door.

Yeah, and my roommates are gone.

What's your name, he asked as he stepped out from behind the door.

Clay, I replied—Clay Wilbury.

He took on a puzzled look and he asked did you ever go to school in Sparring?

Yeah, just till I was nine and moved away.

Ever wrestle at school?

Yeah.

Remember me, he asked—Michael Parks?

From the wrestling team, fourth grade, I asked.

That's me, he said—Pete Graham's my roommate. He answered the door. Remember him?

Yeah, from the clubhouse, I said—I remember.

As we walked to my room, we talked of the past and the things that had happened in our lives since I had moved away. He and Pete were there on scholarships for wrestling. He asked if I had continued the sport after I moved. He didn't think I had, since he hadn't seen me at any tournaments. Drinking after the bonfire was his suggestion and I concurred.

Bring friends, he said.

I'll do that.

The fire starts at dark.

***

And as I topped the hill I could see it.

The fire wrestling the wind.

As the dark blue northern turned black, the cross stood as a man with outstretched arms, leaning into the wind.

The flames fought the wind, and from a distance, made the cross look as if it was moving.

I was so mesmerized by the sight of the fire that, at first glance I didn't notice the ghosts. Seeing them scared me and I got on my bike and didn't stop pedaling until I reached home.

I never went into the clubhouse.

We moved a month later.

***

Good to see you, Mike said as I walked up—We were hoping you'd come.

I was waiting for my friends, I said—They must already be here.

Behind Mike was the pyre, ready to burn. At the ready was Pete with an oiled torch.

Who invited the fucking niggers, Pete asked, motioning behind us as he lit the torch and passed it to Mike.

Not me, Mike said as he grabbed the torch and tossed it into the kindling—We serving barbecue?

Well, no, and this here ain't no equal opportunity event, Pete said, motioning to those walking up behind me—Unless they're offering to be what's barbecued.

As I turned away from them and the fire, I saw my roommates standing there.

Brian and Darin.

And with them they brought the wind.

***

Where have you been?

Mom, I saw some ghosts.

Where did you see these ghosts?

Out by Pete and Michael's clubhouse?

Were they just floating around?

No. They were dancing.

Dancing?

Around a cross. It was on fire.

Get in the house.

JOE DALE NEVAQUAYA

The Poems of Novembers Grace

(1)
In houses of Novembers Grace
the implosions of old gravities resonate
the last pods of late autumn spiders
that hang cirrusly and pale
beyond the anguish of shadows
and brief filament of day

Above the darkening earth
dead horse sagacious of night rises
from the autumn grasses and gallops
away towards the one moon of three
against which the cedar tree is filagreed
in morphine splendor and dirt

within the fallen quadrants of light
a horses clavicle lies broken
and frozen, facing east its shadow
is an unstrung harp.

(2)
the babys sour breath,
a fist closed to the day
the slamming of a screen door
on the unnamed reservation
in the beginning of a February blizzard,
the ground too frozen to dig for the twisted
bone and seething heart.

(3)
atop the western ridge rattles
the silhouette of the shunting rain
the outline of a man reaching
toward the hand of another,
even from this vantage I can hear
the labored heaving of all involved.

(4)
Your mother steps forward
from the glacial wind of roaring trees
her calling voice is lost to the tumbling leaves
she turns once
a glance of askance over her shoulder bent
and disappears into the dark of the pecan grove
and the barbed wire fence.

(5)
in arid attics apparitions
appear and pass through mirrors
of ancient locust slough
membranes of summers past
sucked dry
like the rat bone to dust.
The shadow of Edgar Allan Poe
lengthens with the sinking room
as you dance, hiss and recite
the Tell Tale Heart
you breath a low land mist and fog
a clattering train
a distant wailing dog

(6)
We were the newest drunks in town
even though we were nearing forty.

We are awakened by the rumbling
and wheezing rains passing
we were emblazoned and gaudy
tumbled with the dry weeds in our sooted hair
diesel in our words of travel and separation
we became shimmering and wavering visages
of blue and yellow rags, tacked here and there
with tar and bits of hardened blood and knuckle.

We fought this town, we earned our place at the table.

JUDITH TATE O'BRIEN

The Wolf
> *for Lois*

My sister's sadness lives in a big house in San Antonio.
All night long, it howls, *Cancer, Cancer.*
Wherever my sister goes when she sleeps,
> her sadness goes there, too,
> > shape-shifting into storm, quicksand, wolf.

When my sister hauls herself out of bed in the mornings,
she finds it awake and waiting in the leather recliner
> its dark fur soaking up the light trying
> to shine in at the high windows.

When my sister searches her husband's face for the familiar,
> she learns another way to be lonely.

My sister and her husband speak to one another
> in sentences without doors.

The wolf turns them into liars.

PATRICK OCAMPO

Sound of the State

It's only at the closing of daylight, when the sun paints
a last line of red at the rim of the world
and the wretched, stunted trees stand sentry over the
desolation of the sickly grass,
only when the birds quiet their dusty wings,
when the hawks end their futile circles,
and the kingbirds huddle and hush their harsh
kittering cries, only at the end of the day,
when you are driving along the road
that is the decaying heart of America,
only then can you hear the faint cry of the displaced spirits, wailing
almost imperceptibly over the land still stained with souls.
We do not belong, we will never belong, we are lost
and far from our ancestors, and we died here,
our bodies plowed over by the outraged land,
free us, take us home.

But there is no home,
no resolution, no restitution,
all that is left, are endless ghostly cries,
and the sound of the insects popping yellow pockmarks
against your windshield. This is the sound of the state,
the sound of engines driving relentlessly across the landscape,
and every dissenting voice, and every cry for mercy
is shattered on plexiglass moving at 90 miles an hour
towards what we think is God and progress.
The song of the state was written back east
by men who never saw the land and probably
mistook us for Kansas, and if they wrote now,
how could they make music out of the spattered
sounds of voices dying against a blood-red sky?

Maybe if we all stopped the engines, closed our eyes
for one minute a day for a thousand years and spoke
the simple word of forgiveness, maybe if we stopped
talking and started walking the way of mercy,
maybe if for a thousand years we asked and gave
and became the unstrained quality of mercy,
maybe then the voices would silence, and
the song of the land would rise
and heal the broken spirits
and send them singing home.

And maybe, if for a thousand years
we were the very bones of mercy,
maybe then we would be something
worth singing about.

JASON POUDRIER

Blackberry Cobbler

The smell, bitter and biting
at your taste buds, ignites
saliva and concaves your cheeks
as the fork crumbles the crust
and slices into the blackberries
that bleed onto your plate;
you see and feel the warmth
as you bring your first forkful
forward and taste it before
the cobbler reaches your lips.

You sit in your rocking chair on the porch,
slow creaks crescendoing
and decrescendoing from the rockers
while you run to your artillery unit's perimeter
with your weapon in your hands.

You stare out with dilated,
unblinking eyes over a glowing, terracotta horizon
as you peer over the shaking muzzle of
your M-16 at the live dunes
moving around you while you remain locked
with fear, feeling your heart beating
in your hands clutching your rifle,
as a dust devil dies to the north after passing across
your father-in-law's dry summer fields,
and your cobbler continues to bleed
on your plate.

Your feet keep rolling heel-to-toe.
You quiver, facing out into
a night tunneled by the fire behind you,
but you cannot look back;
the medivac has been called.

You listen to the shouts and
screams—all men,
coming from behind you,
till they are muffled by
the blades of a Blackhawk
that stirs sand and smoke around
you, and you disappear like
an egg yolk into a country-
cobbler batter.

DAVID P. PRICE

The Drunk

He argues against the charge that he stole his woman's purse
and her vodka,then downs another can of Milwaukee's classic beer.
He moseyed on down here from Tulsa
when his mother took gravely ill.
Now he sleeps in his truckbed.
His mother is dead.

His sister calls him alcoholic,
and her husband, a real porker,
at near five hundred pounds,
turned him out two weeks ago
for generally just being no good.

He comes by here in his bouncing pick-up,
but the oil is changed, and the tires are new and lettered.
He doesn't come to see me, of course,
but unfortunately I'm always here.

He smokes the cheapest brand of cigarette,
and turns down vodka when it's offered.
He's a beer man, par excellence.
And talks on about this and that,
and gets choked up when he tells the matron here,
'you know I love you and would do anything you ask.'

I don't know what he wants,
like all the others who cross that doorway,
perhaps just knowing he won't be criticized
is enough to waste the gas to make his house call.

Many are like him, around here at least.
None will find what they lost,
as they can't figure exactly what it is.
Like trying to find the answer
to a question that's never even been asked,
and even if it was, it was all in Sanskrit.

He talks about the house he owns in Tulsa
where his ex and retarded son live rent-free.
And brags that if she doesn't treat Alfred right,
she'll wind up on the street with his boot right up her ass.

I think to myself that he is a pussy,
a wimp, a straw man, a big-time talker,
who says and means nothing;
when likely he is a simple fragile piece,
unshaven, looking way old for his years,
wearing his proud stained cowboy hat.

I know that man, I know him better than I'd like.
And as I sit bored and yawning,
it dawns on me that I must want to
get closer to that scraggly essence,
just to prove that I can stand it.
That, yes, I can stand what I once feared most of all-
without blinking one time an eye.

RANDY PRUS

Bryan County Jailbreak

Jailbreaks happen occasionally
in this town, someone
in an orange jumpsuit escapes
befuddling the rest of us
and the cops, being cops,
start looking in all directions
in backyards, under porches,
along the creek beds winding
through the town, with everyone
asking themselves how
someone in an orange jumpsuit
could simply disappear.

Most of us realize it doesn't
take much to want to leave.
We think about it in our dreamy hours.
We know the lock on the jail door
has been broken for years.

But when someone actually does it,
in an orange jumpsuit, no less,
when someone pushes the door wide
into the night, an order has been
disturbed by a possibility.

This awakens all of us. The knock
at the door at three AM, a man
with a gun, a cop disturbing
our slumber, asking if we had seen
someone in an orange jumpsuit,
who escaped the grasp of law
as if it were a fiction, or a dream.

And all I can think is
some lucky bastard
got away.

AARON RUDOLPH

Astronomers Discover the Best Sopapillas in the Sombrero Galaxy

From another corner of the universe, we see you
as a long brimmed hat, native to Mexico.
Certainly you must have your own style
and customs, but in your galaxy

> I hope people pick up their trumpets
> and guitars and others sway
> themselves around these players, a dance
> that everyone knows and practices
> with abandon, their arms loose
> and their heads tilted back in laughter.

> Let there be tables lined with steaming
> crock pots from every kitchen,
> and let the children run
> their fingers over the cakes,
> fried breads covered in cinnamon.
> Let their mothers look the other way.

Your oblong shape inspires my imagination
tonight. I'm again my ten-year-old self,
who dreamed of the worlds beyond my sight,
hanging in the sky like ornaments.
I remember, too, running to my parent's room
after a nightmare in need of their presence:
their safe arms, their connection.

The Conga Player

The conga player caresses his calluses
by smoothing the skin of each palm,
tracing each crease with hardened
fingertips, thick and rough like tree moss
from all the pounding, all the gigs
at small venues where the crowds drink
and shout over the sounds
he lays down on his skins. He's gentle
on the leather, popping sounds
from each corner. The drums bounce
around his lap like children.

When he snatched the eviction notice
from the door jamb's clutch and threw
as many clothes as he could carry
into his van, he saw the old note
from his ex. She claimed she had to sit
in the corner like a forgotten hobby
while he drummed and drummed, his hands
always moving too quickly to pin down,
even long enough to write a check
for the cash he borrowed, that kept their
bedroom floor covered in leather
for congas, looking like a crazy man's workshop.

Oklahoma on Four Dollars

Two days before my next payday, I shuffle
from bed to couch and tap my head,
expecting a plan to strike me, to take my shoulders
firmly and stop this. I have four dollar bills,

all wrinkled and bruised. I have two days
before I'll see any more money and I need
a plan on turning these bills into food.
I can drink tap water, I start. Money saved.

I strategize for an hour. My feet hurt from pacing.
I know the routine, including the worry.
The stress, the cursing, the lowered brow,
are mine. I bring them along, beloved friends.

SUSAN SHANNON

All Indian Clothes Are Ghost Dance Shirts

Fringe of my shawl
It swings
Rhythmically to the drum
We all sway together
We women
The men are on their own hunt around the drum
Straight Dancers
Dancing as they "look for tracks"
Of animals long since lost to a history
That still lives in the powwow
Fancy Dancers, Traditional Dancers
Grass Dancers
Are all looking for the best
Spot to dance, to track
They make their own
Space
As they twirl, jump and sneak up
Keeping time to the drum with their heads
Feathers rocking on
Rubber bands attached to spreaders
In the middle of their Roaches
Fastened just so…
Oh its lovely to be in the midst
Of a powwow
I believe this is the Ghost Dance
It morphed into the powwow
All Indian clothes are Ghost Dance shirts
We live again as we once were
We remember those that are gone
Maybe we are even wearing their Indian clothes
I smooth down my mother's shawl
She left it to my sister
But she can't dance anymore
The diabetes and arthritis have hobbled her (as it did my Mother)
I untangle the fringe

And throw it on in an electrical arc of fringed memory
And step into the living breathing circle that is
Powwow
Dancing to the song the fringe of my mother's shawl
Swaying
She is here

Native Sovereignty 2010

This slender web
Of legality
It shall become
Our only
Blanket
An ancient and strong weave
The many colors
Still bright
Though time is flying
We wear it into
The future
We are fearless
As we observe their
Constitution
So must they recognize
Our sovereignty
As modern as a force field
As ancient as our grandmothers
Tears
Frozen to their faces
I can still see the brightness in their eyes
Her eyes
Its the reflection of our
Triumphs
Is Sovereignty an art?
One generations work telling the next
What is was like
then
Is this their communication to us?
Then it is strong and clear
Stand

JUDY SING

Fever

The bed feels like it's
moving back and forth,
lifting and falling in smooth waves.
Fever bleaches moisture from my body.
Infection chills me beneath the woolen quilt
that scratches my chin.

Mother sits by the bed
Cooling my forehead with a wet cloth.
Knotted tonsils rip my throat
each time I swallow.
I lie there as the battle rages.

Above me on the wall at my feet
the Good Shepherd, painted by number
tacked up long ago,
gently holds a lamb in the curve of his arm.
Other sheep flock close around.
His dark eyes gaze serenely, tenderly.

His crimson robes leap out like flames—
lurid, crackling.
I speak of this to Mother.
She thinks I'm out of my head.
I want to refute her
but cannot speak.

My eyes rest on Jesus and the lambs,
till the fever draws me back
into a broiling sea of dreams.

A white ball arcs toward me from the far horizon
growing larger, ever larger, till it has become
larger than the world.
I spread my arms to catch it.
I do. It becomes me, passes through me.

I know I am alive.
I feel myself watching from far away
feel the blood pulse in
the machine my heart.
The sweat-soaked bed contains me.

The flames have died down.
From under the folded cloth on my forehead
my eyes open to Christ and the lambs
his orange robe quenched like the setting sun
in a calm tropical sea
and mother offering me water.

MICHAEL SNYDER

Beetles is Gone

Lazy Russ
Wake up
Reverse the hearse
First things first
Lazy Russ
Roll up roll up
Wake up Boo
Wake Boo Radley
Tell him we're waitin
Out in the alley
With Long Tall Sally
Lazy Russ
Please wake up
The Black Bus
Is calling us

Lazy John
Wake up
Wake up Boo
Wake Brian Epstein
Wake up Stu
And Brian Jones too
Lazy John
Get yr Chelsea boots on
Julian needs you
Come now John
Turn me on
Turn me on dead man
Wake me up
Dear Prudence
Come out to play
I have all day
And I want you John
I'd love to turn you on

I want to know why
Tell me why you cry
And why you lied
I'm crying
Julia your mother
Paul your brother
Yoko your mother
Sean your sun
Thinking man's beetle
Organic intellectual
Sharp and tart
Jealous and smart
Prudence plays
And prudence pays
You buried Paul
Cranberried Paul
You were the eggman
The walrus was Paul
From Sgt Pepper cover
L Carroll glances
Askance at it all

THEM is the anti-
Catchers in the Rye—
Their drive and their delight
Was to shove you over the side
I'm crying
Yoko let you down
Oh No never around
Tell me why you cry
lONElY HE DIE

9teen 80 clandestine
Nixon Reagan CIA spies
Plot your demise
Ronald Reagan 80s must
Avenge and vanquish 60s

John was seen again singing
Power to the People and protesting
As under Nixon
They were surveillin
Such activism is
Potentially threatenin
If you've seen one Redwood
You've seen them all

Mark David Chap Man
Eyre ht ni Rehctac
Associating with
Young Christian Men
Eyre ht ni Rehctac
Fondling young boys
Trained by Right-wing
Christian fundamentalists
Who conflate hate and joy
Who stoked beetle bonfires
When you got bigger than Him
(And when you said so
It got them pissed
Their sweet Lord dismissed)

Now I'm Changing my name to
Mark David Chapstick
It's sooo cold outside
NYC December 80
Dakota building
Rosemary's Baby
It's reeeeal…Chapstick weather
Changing my name to
Eyre ht ni Rehctac
Changing my name to
Suzy Chapstick
Changing my name to
Catfish Chapstick
Changing my name to

Catfish in the Rye
Changing my name to
Hunter in the Rye
Changing my name to
Holden Caul Field
Changing my name to
Jesus Christ
Changing my name to
John Lennon
(Double Fantasy)
Or Todd Rundgren
It really doesn't matter
Let me take you down
'Cause I'm going to
Cranberry sauce
Strawberry fields forever \
Lover of sleepy rivers
Matthew Mark Luke and John
Died with their Chelsea boots on
Ringo Paul George and John
Beetles…is gone

Jose J Perdomo
Dakota doorman CIA man
Anti-Castro Cuban
Maybe even the gunman
The deed done
Perdomo flips Mark's psych-trigger
Do you realize what you've just done?
Emotionless
I just shot John Lennon
Sits and calmly opens
A dogeared paperback
The Catcher in the Rye
Why don't you pass the time
By playing a little solitaire?
J David Salinger OSS pre-CIA

Mark the Man
The Man Can
The Man Candy Date
CIA M(ar)KULTRA
The Mani Candi
(Terry Southern looks askance
From Sgt Pepper cover
Calls R Condon)
Such an easy Mark
For Mind Kontrol
A weak hypocrite
A rubber soul
Soft lamblike mind
A pliable candyass
A vacuous sacrifice
I want to see him Krucified
lONElY HE DIE

Like M David Chap Man
J David Salinger
(Everybody's Favorite)
Was a pedophile
Seducing 12 year-old girls
In soft fuzzy sweaters
Epitomized his style
He sacrificed a series of virgins
On his small but angry rod
Solely out of vicious pride
Must have thought he was God
But he was just scribbling
A misanthropic recluse
Pop koans and mystic riddling
His later work abstruse
A pp drinking Zen dope
His silence stripped the
Silent Generation of hope
A sacred cow

Pretentious and middlebrow
To Jerry with love and squalor
But mostly squalor
Up your ass with
The Family Glass
In your eye
With fucking
Catcher in the Rye
Lean over on the bookcase
If you really want to get straight
Read James Purdy
Jerry's hands are dirty
I don't even
Want to know why
lONElY HE DIE

Lazy Paul
Wake up
Wake up Boo
Wake Boo Radley
Wake Brian Epstein too
Hey Saint Paul
Anoint us all
Lazy walrus
Wake up Paulrus
Dear Cute One
I want to suck your tusks
The Cute One
Muss your moptop
Melodic man
Lovable optimist
Caress your soft white chest
Give us a kiss
Want to kiss yr Chelsea boots
And lick them clean
Let's sit and talk awhile
Absorb your good humor

Dismiss your death
As hoax and rumor

But Paul is dead
He lost his head
Poor Jane Asher
Ashes to ashes
He blew his mind
Out in a car
He didn't notice
That the lights had changed
A crowd of people stood and stared
They'd seen his face before
Cranberry sauce
Oh untimely death
Paul is bloody
Bury my body
I'm fixing a hole
Father McCartney
Wiping the dirt from his hands as he walks from the grave
Beetles is saved

Magical mystery
Secret history
Bonzo Doo Dog Band
Death cab for cutie
These cars can kill
Death cab for cutie
Address unknown
No such number
No such phone
Nothing to do to save his life call
I want to go to Pepperland too
Find the number decode the clue
You know my name look up the number
And call today to start your secret journey
Be at Leso
Lazy walrus

Cranberry sauce us
Please wake up Paul
For Faul (faux Paul) will fail
Faul will fall
And just where will that leave us all?
Nothing is real
I YOU WAS
Abbey Road beetle
28IF he had lived
But Paul is dead man
He lost his head man
Miss him Miss him Miss him (3 beetles)
I'm so lonely
Wanna die
Yes I'm lonely
Wanna Die
If I ain't dead already
Girl you know the reason why
Poor Paul was
Erased replaced
Dopplegängered in (6)66
UK government
Were in on it
Beetles sehr gut für economy
My advice for those who die
Beware the pennies on your eyes
11/66 Faul sent to
Secret MI5 lab in Kenya
Facelifts Mind Kontrol
African Voodoo
Faul came to believe that he was Him
I am he as you are me
Maybe even bigger than Him
Mother Mary comes to me
Lady Madonna
Read the Record Mirror
Let it be
3 lonelyhearts

Bear in mind that
Death is a Drum
Beating forever
Sgt. Pepper's lonely
LONELY HEARTS
Read the Record Mirror
1ONEIXHEDIE
Death is a Drum
11/9 HE DIE
In US 9/11
1 2 3 4 5 6 7
All good children go to heaven
Nine eleven
The people who hide themselves
Behind a wall of illusion
Strike through the mask
Nine eleven code
CIA backed Chile coup
Allende annihilated
9/11 9teenseventy3
Paulisdead ha ha
Losthishead ha ha
The ghost in you
He will fade
So let it be

But Magick Crowley
From Pepper cover
Advises reverse—
Let it be \
He is dead
Number nine \
Turn me on dead man
Sgt. Pepper's lonely \
It was a fake moustache
Please don't be long \
Paul is bloody
Smacks of Crowley the Beast man

Paul would have never married
A groupie like Eastman
Nine eleven
Wall of illusion
Wake up lazy Paul
Wake up Boo
And Brian Wilson too
Tell me why you cry
And why they lied
lONElY HE DIE

And what of Billy Shears
The one you've known
for all these years
Wake up Lazyringo
Sad eyed Starr
Wake up Boo
And sad Brian too
Shears sang *You were in a car*
Crash and you lost your hair
You were nice to Yoko Oh No
(Ringo is Apple
In Japanese)
I wonder if they knew
That Starkey is a Jew
Laid back and regal
2nd best drummer in beetles
Ringo is dead man
Ringosoul is dead
We were talking about the love that's gone so cold
And the people who gain the world and lose their soul
Nowhere man
Wasteland man
No fan mail man peaceandlove
No beetle fan mail after 9/11
Peaceandlovepeacenandlove
Otiose melancholic

Morose and alcoholic
Rubbedout Soul
Billy Shears is dead
Hollow inside
Starr into the abyss
The abyss stares back
Play the game
Existence to the end
Of the beginning
Dark Starr crashing
Ringo died decades ago
I am the Nowhere Man
We are the Nowhere Men
We are the Hollow Men
Are you one of them?
Magick Crowley said
Every man and woman is a Starr
Starr had everything
The planet's banquet
Still life explains nothing
Après Faul
The deluge
Of Nothing
Après Faul
Everything means
Less than Zero
Cut off your hair your ear
No fan mail peaceandlovepeaceandlove
Return to sender
Address unknown
Destined for the
Dead letter office
All the lonely people
Bartleby is
Eleanor Rigby
Dead letters
Does it not sound like dead men?
All the lonely people

Ah, Bartleby! Ah, humanity!
I know why you cry
lONElY HE DIE

3 dead beetles
1 & 1 & 1 is 3
Ringo Paul and John
Beetles…is gone

Earth crawlers
Piles of filthy lucre
Dung beetles
Rolling in it
How many conquests
Rolling in it
Flesh and bone
How many bastard beetles

3 dead beetles
Returned to earth
Not 4 or 5 wizards
Beetles crawl in the dirt
They don't walk on water
(Except the ones that do)
Bigger than Jesus
But walking on water
Wasn't built in a day
As Lazy Jack
Kerouac would say
(Wake up Jack
Wake up Allen
Wake up Bill)
It was one small step for Man
But beetles…is gone
Beetles is done
Nothing is real
Nothing to get hung about

Nothing is true
Everything is permitted
Nothing is real
Nothing is true
Nothing is real
Nothing is real

Nothing Is

George is alive
He never died
A spirit living in the
Material world
Tnemneth gilne
Don't even try
To understand
We were talking about the space between us all
And the people who hide themselves behind a wall
Of illusion
Please don't try and
Don't try to not try
To understand
Life goes on
Within you and
Without you
All things must pass
With our love we could save the world
Nothing lasts &
Nothing gold can stay

(Oh by the way
John was gay
I am the eggman \
And I am a gay man
Paul his brother
Yoko his mother
Brian E his tender lover)

SANDRA SOLI

Don't Speak of Cold

> or this silver-
scissored weather that stabs the chest.
The empty nest, high in the shivering
pear tree, is a sign. Think of the ubiquitous
sparrow, the black-capped chickadee,
the tiny wren who slept in the pocket
of your patio apron last summer.

Where are they now, and their songs?

Witness to a Wreck
after Jane Hirshfield

An eye is not iris, retina, or corneal nerve,
nor nevus revealed by digital imaging,
> the hidden impairment.
An eye is no sudden flash from memory's
postcard, tucked within the brain.

The seen, the barely noticed, the shocked stare
combust in confusion among passersby.
Real or illusory, and which is which?
Each argument valid, the map
> cannot be refolded.

Always questions.

With sidelong glance, the peripheral perhaps,
an eye can be invitation, or envious green, the sly
mask of pleasure, the possible yes.

JONATHAN STALLING

Grotto Heaven

洞天 *Grotto Heaven*

一 。來到 Arriving

rust   riverbed roads   line with trees   of dried sunfish
-----------------------\   \-------------------------------------
eyeless fish   swim   down darkless   tunnels

a truck kicks red   dust up   against   the banks
--------------------\   \---------------------------------------
flowstone   smoothes down   to vein's origin

a farm houses   a man who   bends   space around   his children's   eyes
-------------------------\   \--
seeds drip   from stone straws and   grow in,   if not   a rhythm,   imagination

the spring   pools outside   perfectly   clear and cold
-----------------------\   \-------------------------------------
spleleathem-albras spill   from flowstone

eyes   claim space   as if from   origin
----------------------\   \---
pupils bloom   nocturnal to swallow   your eyes whole

Inner Exercises

内練習　　**Inner Exercises [from *Grotto Heaven*]**

一。

Now stand
sassafras root
spills down

through earth's
narrow absences
translucent stems
form from

curved
glass
cloud

Epilogue

Epilogue [for *Practical Chinese Reader*]

Foreign language
外国的语言

                         cannot be settled.
                         无法定居。

the darkness of its distance
                             is   its principle   measure.
        距离的黑暗   是   它唯一的尺度。

                         for
                         因为

Foreigness is not subject
        陌生的东西   to discovery
                     不能发现   cannot be dis-covered.
                                                 无法揭开。
Its cover   is not a language
        表面的语言
                  I can learn   or peal away.
                  我不能学会   无法剥离。

                     yet
                     然而

              Learning does not have to be a discovery
              学习不必成为发现

It is not after all a frontier
它毕竟不是征战
          Please let it not be a frontier.
          请不要让它成为征战。

LORI SUBLETT

Lolla

The sickly-sweet tar smell of cheap weed perfumes the humid air. My hair drips, the sweat running in uncomfortable rivulets down the length of my back. The bare skin exposed by my tank top and shorts feels dry and too tight, bypassing the normal redness that comes from Chicago in August, settling instead on a light, leathery brown. The plastic entrance bracelet sits loose on my wrist, scratchy and slick. I'll wash layers of grime, dirt, ash and exhaustion down the shower drain tonight but there will be a thick white band around my wrist where that bracelet has sat for two days already.

My sunglasses are thick and tinted dark, but they barely cut the glare as the sun bounces off the steel girders of the stage. I close my eyes to the late afternoon sun and listen to the quiet murmuring of a throng of people quivering in anticipation. My throat is raw, swallowing has become a chore I'm not accustomed to. The water bottle in my hand is empty, as are the other two I'd stashed in my backpack earlier. There's a water fountain about 20 feet to my left and a beer stand, that also serves the Sweet Leaf Tea with lemonade I've learned to crave, somewhere behind me. It doesn't matter. There's no way I'm getting to either place for the next few hours. There is no leaving, barely room to shift around. I am alone in the middle of a crowd of thousands.

I don't know if she's here yet, if she made it. I don't know if I really care.

Cage the Elephant is about to go on and they're one of the reasons we're here. This year's Lollapalooza has a heavy lineup with some amazing bands. We've seen *Cage* before, met them several times. It's become a thing with us, having Matt draw more and more pictures on a single t-shirt, creating a collage of random memories etched in permanent ink. I scan what I can see of the crowd, but I don't see the distinctive yellowy-orange hair of her dye-job gone wrong.

My cell phone is a heavy, pulling weight in my pocket, reminding me that I have a lifeline to my sister if I choose to use it. I pull it out and flip it open. The bright blue T-Mobile background stares at me. The screen goes dark, conserving energy; I've waited too long to do anything. I slide the outdated flip-phone she hates back in my pocket, right beside my blue plastic Metra Pass, the key to Chicago's Mass Transit.

I didn't really know what we were fighting about. I'm not sure she did either. Months of anticipation, weeks of excitement and days of forced togetherness had all blended into a maelstrom of emotions with nowhere to go but between us.

Our non-smoking hotel room had reeked of cigarette smoke and bleach. I sat on the scratchy red-striped bedspread and watched her tiny body vibrate with misplaced anger. One pale grey backpack strap slipped slowly down her arm. I watched it descend until it caught in the crook of her elbow, nowhere left to go. Her diminutive hands were clenched as tight as her jaw. She wanted to say them, the words she held on her tongue.

She just stood there, rigid and inflexible, outlined by the frame of the door. I didn't know what to say, I thought that we'd already screamed it all to each other. So, I said the only thing I could: "I don't want to fight with you."

I don't know what she was expecting from me. Clearly that wasn't it. She reached into the pocket of her shorts and withdrew two Metra Passes. She threw one at me, along with a muttered "Fuck you," lowered her bright green and blue framed sunglasses over her eyes and stormed out into the lobby. There was nowhere else for her to go. The shuttle from the hotel to the Metra station only came once an hour and there was still 20 minutes before 10 a.m.

Suddenly, I wanted to go home. I wanted to lay in my own bed, complete with the cat hair I'm sure my tabby had shed all over it in my absence. I wanted to go out and do something with someone I wasn't related to and hadn't been with every hour for the last several days. I just wanted a break. But Oklahoma City was more than 800 miles and 13 hours away. And she had the keys to the car.

I waited a bit before heading out to the lobby, trying to cool off. I might as well have waited an hour. When I got there, the shuttle had come and gone, taking my sister with it, more than ten minutes early. She hadn't said anything, stopped them, let me know. She'd left.

I wasn't going to stay in our dingy little hotel room, alone. I wasn't going to give her the satisfaction of knowing that she'd gotten to me. My body buzzed with an unleashed energy looking for an outlet. And I had just the ticket.

There was an entrance to the Metra that would have been within walking distance if it hadn't been surrounded by the entire O'Hare airport. I snagged a ride with a guy that barely spoke English, though he seemed nice enough. I hopped aboard the Rosemont entrance and rode the blue-line train down the middle of the freeway to the Jackson stop.

A couple of hours after she'd stormed off and I'm here, waiting for *Cage* to come on. The roadies are finished setting up. Lincoln and Brad have come on stage to tune their guitars. Jared and Daniel are stage left and everyone is waiting eagerly for Matt so the show can begin. When he finally emerges from the sidelines, his face is already red and his burgundy shirt has faded purple where sweat makes it cling to his body. It doesn't matter how hot it is, they've come here to play and we've come here to rock. The ground trembles with the first pulse of the bass, rolling in swells across the flattened grass. Suddenly, it's loud and raucous and there's no standing still in this undulating wave. There's an elbow digging into my side and the chick behind me is pulling my hair but it doesn't matter. Because there's a rhythm to the chaos, underlined by the hypnotic beat of the drum and the riffs of the double guitars, and we've found it, jumping, soaring, flying on the melody. The people around me have become my new best friends; we're sharing this experience, this closeness, this utter excitement, passing it back and forth like the weed that's still circulating.

I can't hear my phone beep, there's no way I feel the vibrations. But I sneak my hand in my pocket and pull it out. It's blinking. There's a text that wasn't there a minute ago. It's got her name on it. I open the message up and read it, not the easiest thing to do while moshing in the middle of a pit slightly smaller than the size of a football stadium.

Where R U? I'm @ Budweiser watching Kaiser Chiefs. I'm thirsty.

It was as much of an apology as I was going to get. My fingers were slick with sweat, sliding slippery on the keys as I texted her back.

I'm @ Citi Stage. I think there's a Pepsi vendor on this side.

It was as much of an apology as I was going to give.

Oh. Meet me here when ur done. Bring Pepsi.

I put my phone away and dug out my digital camera. I turned the video on to record the rest of the set. She may not be here, but I wouldn't let her miss out. I knew she'd be doing the same for me with the *Kaiser Chiefs*.

I'd meet her at the Budweiser stage, Pepsi in hand, as soon as *Cage* was done and I could make it to the North End of the park, three blocks away. Then we'd head to the F.Y.E. tent, complete with t-shirt and CD cases, to meet the bands and get autographs. Until then, I'd stay here, sweating in the middle of this pit, and listen to the music that surrounded us.

JANE VINCENT TAYLOR

Advice from the Runway Café
At the Wiley Post Airport: variations

Air

Try to stay in the middle of it.
Do not go near the edges of it.
The edges can easily be recognized by the appearance
of ground, buildings, sea, trees and interstellar space.

I.

Air, my dear, is what our love lives on.

Try to stay in the middle of it in spite of turbulence.

Do not go near the edges of it with flights of fancy or night-time arguments.

*The edges can be easily recognized by the appearance of ground, buildings,
    sea, trees, and interstellar space*, plus relatives and pricey rituals.

How long can we stay aloft? Until too much is said, and love runs out of air.

II.

Air—breathing in, breathing out.

Try to stay quiet in the middle of it.

Do not go, as Buddha said, *near the edges of it*, into form and its delusions.

The edges of the dharma, the heart and diamond sutra ,
   can not *be easily recognized*

by the appearance of a *ground*ed practice, or *building* up the ego,
  or making *trees* of habit to obscure the forest,
   or spacing out to *interstellar space.*

How long can we stay aloft? Don't, he said. Come down
and love the earth.

III.

Air comes from the antiseptic tube
   to help my baby breathe.

Try to stay calm and steady *in the middle of it.*

Do not go near the edges of It: fear—it will take us down.

The doctor *edges* toward the door. His air of nonchalance
   makes my mouth go dry. He *can easily recognize*
   I'm not on solid *ground*. Inside, I shake,
   a *sea* looking for a lifeboat. Without hope,
   I'm some kind of *tree* that never leaves.

I hold my daughter's hand to bring her back
from dreams and *interstellar space.*

How long can we stay aloft? Or can we land this thing
   in a meadow full of easy air?

SHEILA TIARKS

Still Life with Flowers

The coffins stood five abreast
the largest, the mother's, in the middle
their lids tightly closed
so as not to expose the congregation
to blue-black necks twisted unnaturally.

Instead there were flowers,
girly pink and lavender
blue for the lone son.

The pastor confessed to a lack of words,
and Bikers against Child Abuse
escorted the procession to the cemetery

while the accused, tattooed boyfriend
sat in his cell
massaging his massive hands.

HUGH TRIBBEY

Logolatry

I'm making my point
about patronizing the masses
to a mild mannered poet from Texas,
with Rothenberg's lore—
Klebnikov reading glossolalia for the first time
in a peasant Pentecostal newspaper in the Urals,
then Bernstein's Ren & Stimpy and the Pulitzer—
when the poet quotes St. Paul,
how one word of Gospel
is worth more than all
the gift of tongues.

His parry triggers,
parallel to our discussion,
a corner of my mind
grinding out mean blasphemies—
how often St. Paul was wrong
because he needed to get laid,
wrong not only about women
covering their heads and
their mouths in Church,
but wrong about how words of Gospel
become justification
for faith in strong opinions in Texas,
how demonic fascination
burns centuries of neurotic rage
for Corinthian teenagers
who find their Savior
in their orgasms,
drunk with the babble
of their pleasure.

But I shut up over debris of sub
sandwiches and Pepsi cans,
nodding and smiling like those pious women
centuries ago when the grim priests and bishops
were proclaiming what we should all believe,
like those women, keeping my own thoughts.
"Yes," I say. "Yes, I see."

BILL TURLEY

The Noble Savage Salutes Bob Dylan

The noble savage is walking down 4th Street,
going to a happening where they played
all Bob Dylan. All hippies
Ushered in this need for movement,
And the complete destruction of the past, old men,
standing together, speaking Greek or maybe Latin.
Then what of you, savage, a throw back from
Those later Lawrence novels where they run
naked through the hinterland fields, making love
to aristocratic women, actresses in the fall from grace.

I saw the best minds of a generation destroyed by madness
          Ginsberg

The noble savage remains,
chasing these longhair skinny chicks.
No doubt, these tribal dancers hear ancient drums,
As they whirl to jazz flute and bongos.
As each new dance soon becomes passé.

The Noble Savage retreats from all of this,
Once the cool has gone, once the money runs low.
"now you don't talk so loud, now you don't
feel so proud about having to scrounge for your next meal.
How does it feel?…"

The people on the streets are all poets;
they live their poems, as they forage for groceries,
or they go to the whiz-bang happening,
where they enter; a staged play, a poetry reading,
where pages are burned as they are read.

The crowd roars like Romans at their gladiators,
and another poet who is thinking that 15 minutes of fame is not
enough,

hangs on a street lamp till dawn.
"Now you don't talk so loud, now you don't feel so proud,
about having to scrounge for your next meal, how does it feel?"
How does it feel to watch atoms explode
 into some magically mysterious conga line?

Sometimes, a wistful jazz poem escapades,
the crowd is hushed; Now give me that line again,
that no rock slow bop turning things upside down line.
The noble savage is walking on the ceiling after that one,
bumping into light fixtures,

dancing with the uptown skinny girl;
here to defy her mom, missing her father.
The dance is some exquisite moment.
The savage is free, the chick is free, all
the lights are off except for the beating of hearts.

Then there is this wang-yankee scream,
And we all get into what Kerouac was getting at
between the lines. This no time like now American sludge,
with so much motion, you would have thought,
he could have pitched a perpetual groove, man. But no.

And maybe the noble savage is sold down the river by now.
Laos and Cambodia took what nobility he had,
and people were just not hanging out anymore.

Poets now live in letters home. "I am in shock,
but all right, sis". Where are my buddies, but dead
in some field. We are moving ahead now, and all that
living hell we are suppose to leave behind is still here,
and we struggle to hold fast the illusion of a painless war,
to shield our broken families.

How to mend the savage now,
When bullets become
"Masters of War", and the music

down the street is silenced
by some main street cool dude
Just Trying to be,
Just Trying to be.

Why I Cannot Say Anything

If you read wide enough and deep enough,
You will find those lines that speak for you.
Then you can return to your real life;
Buying groceries, folding towels,
Clearing the dinner table. Your heart
Can remain silent for a long time,
Even forever. How many unspoken lines
Can the earth hold before words just start
Bubbling up from the ground,
All that heat and pressure, burning down to the moment.
Then everyone is saying: Yes, That is what I meant,
then it is gone from the earth and our hearts.

All we have now is archival footage,
The sepia toned lives stuck together
into a tangle of old film.
We take what we are fed,
eating happily and hungrily

ALVIN O. TURNER

Calls From Home

Sabrina
is settling in
to career and relationships
miles and light years distant from
small town life and the ranch
from where Grandma still calls, asking
"When are you going to move
back home?"

Grandma thinks Sabrina just might
because she knows
there is more in calls from home
than an old woman's words.

Ranch Proprieties

She keeps a 22 rifle on her dining room table
loaded with bird shot
that she uses to
 "teach manners to the varmints"
who might hope to savor
her cats or chicks.

Others may conclude rightly,
hers is not the place to forget
one's raising, or how to act
in the presence of a lady.

RON WALLACE

The Whittler

He sat on a concrete edge of Oklahoma,
whittling the past
    in golden red shards of cedar root,
not giving any shape nor form,
but smoothing
        polishing
the natural curves and turns of wood.

The blades honed to razor thinness,
unfolded from
the bone yellow handles
    worn smooth
by rough, tanned hands
and decades of denim and khaki pockets.

He controlled the edge,
decided how much rough brown bark
to peel from twisting limbs
    how large a knot to cut as base.
carving time and space,
despite some East Indian doctor's ignorance
of a root's gnarled art.

Lifting up his one good eye
to a bright October sky
    the bluest one he'd ever seen,
he suspected spring might bring bluer still

…if he hung around till then

    then smiled at a still unfinished fall
and went back
to shaving curls from spiraled branches,
doubting that he could.

Time's a funny thing, he thought.
A man can't keep it
any longer than holding on to smoke

so he folded up his old three-bladed Schrade
        climbed inside the steel
and left the man he used to be
lying in the dark
    while he swam toward the stars.

MARK WALLING

Fingerprints

My fingertips looked like balloons
too small for the birthday party.
After the searing flame died

in my arm that night, and the five bubbles
throbbed, too tender for the brush of gauze,
they reminded me of Popeye's cheeks.

Then I looked at them.
The puffs of skin stretched the spyro-gyra
of lines so wide you could trace one

but see no pattern, a tiny bang
in the universe of each finger, casting
the compressed into a far-flung orbit.

If there are parallels, the stars will cool
and their cycling shrink, as did my flesh
and lines, rendering an original pattern.

But for ten days in a police station
my hand would have printed as no one,
wish-fulfillment of a long-dreamed desire.

I was mowing the block square strip of grass
around the parking lot of Mass Mutual's
downtown high-rise, employed by the City Green

Landscaping team, sweating, my only decision
to work up and down a side at a time
or navigate the entire square.

A year of college behind me, I was collecting
cast-off majors like keys on my belt,
changing three times already, a warm-up

for more uncertain selections. I walked
this block every Thursday morning,
and he was there, on his porch in a tank top

and wire rim glasses, his brown hair high
and thin but full to his shoulder, the glint
of a gold medallion below his neck, coffee cup

on the white disc of a table top but set beyond
reach, separated from him by a sheath of papers
that lifted, as did my peevish spirit, when

the breeze kicked them. I, reader of one novel,
The Exorcist, could not imagine an imagination,
nor the content of his work, nor the decorations

in his charcoal brick home, nor the relationship
he shared with the pony-tailed woman who appeared
before my rounds were done, a newspaper, book,

magazine, orange in her generous hands.
I was lost, a ball adrift around the tether
of this wide, packed, desolate, steaming, blinding lot,

deflating each night in my parents' home
with framed needlepoint on the walls
and Art Linkletter on the bookshelf.

I conjured ways to become their yard man.
I stopped the mower twice, but could not cross
the street. When they were gone, as on

the day the mower quit and wouldn't turn,
the string pull slack as a dead cat,
I wanted to break a windshield and run.

I could not see the yard or the street,
though they were in my field of vision.
I slumped, envying the ants beneath the curb

their purpose. I checked the gas tank and the oil,
which was low and smoking a little. And then I touched
this bulging rust-red cylinder, thinking it unscrewed.

The exhaust, my boss later called it, which I had never
been shown. My hand flew faster than my soul.
I was relieved for a moment, no pain.

I looked to the porch for help, when a flaming
voice sang the length of my arm, pushing the skin
at my fingertips, seeking escape,

an arm, enraged, that was not a part of me,
a voice that was.

Sirens

It's no wonder they lay awake at night,
listening for the sound of sirens or steel
bodies tumbling down, seeing us shake
their waits of concern, tires slinging
gravel like Sunday clothes aside.
What could we be doing under
the gym's low shadow, the water tower's
spectral rise, but bump on Main Street,
dispossessed of even the signs
girls could find in their blinking hearts.
Stop lights might brake but couldn't halt us,
and each brick building had windows
on the street but all they did was frame
the reflection of our passing.
The town's glow of lights we left behind
was mute and still, the highway a secret
pulsing jet stream that took us freely out
to the stars, to the open space,
to the bridge constructed to rail
our fury, designed, it appeared,
to launch us into sound.

THERESA-ANN "TRIXIE" WALTHER

Night Terrorist

My name is inmate # 318723.
I am anonymous,
processed, evaluated, certified
a danger to society. I remain
sealed inside my cell observed
accountable for saving my life, my daughter's too.

You do not know me.

I still dream

about him coming upon me
loving the quiet, the babies napping
lulled by rain music… a waterfall shirring the roof
like a living curtain.
I didn't notice him until he jerked my arm
pulling, upending chairs
wood chipping with the force of forward motion
it was the rain that took my attention that day.

I didn't cry
because the babies were asleep…
I stayed calm
but I felt the scream begin
low in my throat when I saw
the knife before me scoring a crimson path to
the place he wanted
and when he was done
tattooing me
drilling me
he took the rest of me.

I swear
he fell, the force, the knife, the blood
and I am still there and here
in my dreams
not because I forget what he looks like
but I can't remember how
the rain sounded right before

Faith

My fear killed him, coward I
cowered in the corner of the room
destroyed by rage at the baby
fussin' for his bottle
there was no milk
just Kool-Aid spiked with Wild Turkey
I remember though the one small lamp
left standing as if its light
could draw me out

His name is Thomas

Even though my arms rocked him
my tongue clicked
shushing him to drink enough to sleep
he just wouldn't stop
and anger grew up walls
like fire flicking heat
at the panic forced forward
through curses to *shut the damn baby down*
I couldn't hold on as he grabbed him and beat him
beat him to death while I did
nothing, nothing, nothing

We both got life ain't that a joke
and now all I got left is my faith
but I don't know how
much longer I can be good in here
without my man

ABOUT THE AUTHORS

DOROTHY ALEXANDER is a poet, a storyteller and co-owner, along with Devey Napier, of a micro poetry press, Village Books Press of Cheyenne, Oklahoma. She is the author of two poetry chapbooks, two full collections of poetry, and has edited two non-fiction story collections. She is currently cast in a role in a film directed by the poet, Diane Glancy, entitled *The Dome of Heaven*, based on Glancy's 1998 novel *Flutie*.

TINA BAKER is a recently retired public school speech and language therapist who is enjoying more time for her many interests, hobbies, and grandchildren. She lives in Chickasha with her husband, Dale.

DANITA BERG is an assistant professor of writing at Oklahoma City University, where she directs the new Red Earth Low-Residency MFA in Creative Writing. She has published or has upcoming creative works in journals such as *Redivider, Southern Women's Review, The Houston Literary Review, Quay: A Journal of the Arts* and *Florida English*, among others, as well as the anthology *Press Pause Moments: Essays about Life Transitions by Women Writers*.

PAUL BOWERS teaches writing and literature at Northern Oklahoma College—Enid. His short story collection, *Like Men Made Various*, was published by Lost Horse Press in 2006.

TIMOTHY BRADFORD's poetry has most recently appeared in *No Tell Motel, Upstairs at Duroc, ecopoetics* and *Drunken Boat*. His first book of poetry, *Nomads with Samsonite*, is forthcoming from BlazeVOX [books]. From 2007 to 2009, he was an associate foreign researcher with the Institut d'Histoire du Temps Présent in Paris while working on a novel. Currently, he is teaching English composition at the University of Central Oklahoma. He lives with his wife and two sons and an ever-changing menagerie just outside of Oklahoma City. "Concrete and Plums" as previously published in Individual Artists of Oklahoma's *Poets Bite the Bullet* in 1998.

MIRANDA BRADLEY is a poet enrolled in the MFA Program for Creative Writing at the University of Central Oklahoma where she teaches freshman composition with an assistantship and serves as poetry editor for the program's journal, *Arcadia*. Miranda's poetry is forthcoming in the *Tipton Poetry Journal*.

NATHAN BROWN is a poet, musician, and photographer from Norman, Oklahoma. He's published five books, the most recent of which, *Two Tables Over* won the 2009 Oklahoma Book Award. And just released in the fall 2009, a new album, *Gypsy Moon*, is his first musical project in over a decade. For more about Nathan, visit his web site: www.brownlines.com.

SHARON BURRIS's Language Arts Department teaching assignments for Murray State College (Tishomingo, Oklahoma) range from the required Comps to Native American Literature, from Brit Lit to Science Fiction Lit, and then she throws in some Creative Writing classes to spice things up. Besides writing during any free time she doesn't actually have, she also shows photographs in shows and exhibits, and is represented by a gallery in Ardmore, where she lives.

ALICE BYRD has been a carpenter, house painter and teacher. She has been published in *Blood and Thunder: Musings on the Art of Medicine*, and *Acapella*. Her passion is International Folk Dancing, reading, writing and spending time with her husband, son and his future wife. "Woody Sez" was previously published in *Travelin' Music: A Poetic Tribute to Woody Guthrie* edited by Dorothy Alexander (Village Books Press, 2010).

YVONNE CARPENTER has published in *Grain* (Canadian literary journal), *Concho River Review*, *Westview*, *Red Dirt Review*, *Blood and Thunder*, and *Terrain* (an ezine) as well as *Farm Journal* and the *West Wheat Producer*. She was an associate editor for the ezine, *Frostwriting*, and has published two volumes of poetry, *To Capture Fine Spirits* (Haystack Publishing), and *Barbed Wire and Paper Dolls* (Village Books Press). She and her husband farm in western Oklahoma.

K.L. CHAPMAN lives in Norman, Oklahoma, but that could change on a dime. She maintains the best poetry is written after wallowing in the mud naked, listening to others tell their naked mud stories. The meatier mud stories go well with fried okra. Others suspect Chapman is wreaking havoc within the space-time continuum during her off hours. The tracers are lingering for longer periods.

CHRISTOPHER W. CLARK lives in Ada, Oklahoma. His work has appeared in the online publications *Cabinet des Fees* and *Polyphony Online*. He finds it remarkably easy to believe in anything at least once.

DEZREA D'ALESSANDRO has been on a rollercoaster for 22 years. As a Senior in the School of Art at the University of Oklahoma, she joyously spends all her time in the printmaking studio. In 2009 she self-published a chapbook titled *Dandelion Seeds*, and now she is very honoured to be a part of this anthology. Next on her to do list: practice drawing dragons, write a poem about the handyman, and get more coffee.

DEIDRA D'AMICO was born on Mardi Gras day in New Orleans, heavily influenced by the jazz in the air, the scented trees, diverse people, and all the colors that don't match. "Whenever I start to think or write about my life-it comes out in the shape of a poem."

CHASE DEARINGER is currently finishing his MFA at the University of Central Oklahoma where he also teaches and is the managing editor of *Arcadia*, a literary journal. He loves to write about his native Oklahoma where he currently resides with his wife and two dogs. His fiction is forthcoming in *Cooweescoowee*.

DONNITA DEWEY lives in Moore, OK, where she works in a mostly male-dominated job for a gay-and-lesbian-friendly company that contracts with the not-so-gay-and-lesbian friendly US military. She writes for self-empowerment as a lesbian woman and to show other lesbians—especially those in rural and southern areas of the country—that they are not alone in their journey.

EMILY DIAL-DRIVER is professor of English at Rogers State University. Among her publication credits are textbooks, articles, television programs, poetry, plays, manuals, and short stories. Her latest work is as editor of and contributor to T*he Truth of Buffy: Essays on Fiction Illuminating Reality* (McFarland, 2008). She is currently copy editor and fiction editor for *Cooweescoowee: A Journal of Arts and Letters.*

JIM DRUMMOND is a criminal defense lawyer in Norman, Oklahoma. His work has been published or accepted in; *Crosstimbers, 8:30, Artists of a Different Caliber, Arts Journal,* and *OK Best,* an anthology of Oklahoma writing edited by Stewart O'Nan.

JEANNE DUNBAR-GREEN is an adjunct instructor of English at East Central University in Ada, OK. She resides in rural Sulphur , OK near the Arbuckle Mountains with her husband and two miniature schnauzers. She earned her MA in English Literature from Pittsburg State University and her MFA in creative writing, fiction from Wichita State University.

SALLY EMMONS is an associate professor of English in the Department of English and Humanities at Rogers State University. She has edited and contributed to two books, Voices from the Heartland, the book on which this essay is based, and *The Truth of Buffy* (McFarland, 2008). She is currently under contract to write a book about pedagogy. Sally also serves as Managing Editor of *Cooweescoowee,* Rogers State University's literary and artistic journal.

TERRY FORD is a native of Western Oklahoman. A former newspaper reporter, she is currently a Language Arts instructor at Southwestern Oklahoma State university in Sayre, where she is the faculty advisor for the student paper. Her writing has received Distinguished Honors from the Oklahoma Heritage Association; however, this is her first electronic submission.

JOSH GAINES recently separated from the Air Force and is currently traveling the U.S., living in his car, with his wife Anna and baby Ella. After earning his BA in Anthropology/Photography from Texas State University in 2003 he worked as a photographer, moving around the country, until he joined the military in 2005. In 2007 he relocated to Tinker AFB/Oklahoma City and started writing and performing poetry at local open mike readings. He went on to contribute to Oklahoma City's poetry scene as the Poetry Chair on the IAO Board of Directors during 2009-2010 and also co-founded the Oklahoma Red Dirt Poets, who have made their home in Oklahoma City's Paseo art district. Josh's book, *Cigarette Sonatas*, will be available soon from Village Books Press.

JOHN GIFFORD is a writer based in Edmond, OK, and a graduate of the MFA program in creative writing at the University of Central Oklahoma. In addition to writing fiction, Gifford is also a prolific nonfiction writer and has worked as a business, government, and sports reporter; newspaper columnist; outdoor and travel writer; technical writer; speech writer; and in corporate marketing and public relations. A passionate fly fisherman, Gifford is the author of *Oklahoma Sportfishing*, and he covers the outdoors and nature for the Oklahoma Department of Tourism and Recreation.

MARY B. GRAY recently graduated from the University of Oklahoma with a Bachelors of Arts in English Writing and a Bachelors of Journalism. Currently Mary is seeking her Masters in Public Administration with a concentration in Non-Profit Management. She hopes to someday start a non-profit organization while pursing a career as a writer. Her favorite writers include D. Nurkse, Wallace Stevens and Lucille Clifton.

KEN HADA has published critical articles in *The Philosophy of the Western* (Kentucky UP, 2010), *Southwestern American Literature, College Literature* and several others. He has two recent collections of poetry: *The Way of the Wind* (Village Books Press, 2008) and *Spare Parts* (Mongrel Empire Press, 2010). In October and November 2010, four of his poems were featured on Garrison Keillor's *The Writer's Almanac*. Ken directs the annual Scissortail Creative Writing Festival held the first weekend of April on the ECU campus in Ada, Oklahoma.

CAROL HAMILTON has publications upcoming in *South Carolina Review, Poet Lore, Atlanta Review, New York Quarterly, Southwest American Literature, Re:al, Karamu, Blue Unicorn, Sow's Ear Poetry Review; The Aurorean, California Quarterly, Hurricane Review, Xavier Review, Cold*

Mountain Review, Poem and others. Her most recent books are *Shots On, Contrapuntal,* and soon-to-be published *Master of the Theater: Peter the Great* from Finishing Line Press and *Umberto Eco Lost His Gun* from Pudding House Press. She has won numerous awards for children's novels and poetry. She is a former Poet Laureate of Oklahoma.

TRACY HAUGHT is a graduate of Cameron University, who majored in English Literature with a minor in creative writing. She is currently living in the Allentown, PA. area (Editor's note: Tracy was living in Oklahoma when her work was accepted). Her poetry has appeared in *Magnapoets, The Oklahoma Review, Poetry For The Masses, Polyphony* and *Sugar Mule.* Her book reviews have appeared in *The Oklahoma Review.* Tracy has written two novels, both works of literary fiction, and is currently at work on her first book of poetry.

LAURA ANNE HELLER is a photographer of sunsets and preserver of history living in Oklahoma City. She is the Electronic Archivist of the Dickinson Research Center at the National Cowboy & Western Heritage Museum because she values the preservation of historical photograph and manuscript collections. Her poetry blooms from Mississippi and Kentucky roots where the environment, culture, and people enrich her imagination. She has written two unpublished books of poetry, *Lexington Lives* and *Rise When the Rooster Crows.*

ARN HENDERSON is an architect and Professor Emeritus of Architecture at the University of Oklahoma. He has authored two books of poetry, *Document for an Anonymous Indian* and *The Surgeon General's Collection.* He also co-edited *The Point Riders Great Plains Poetry Anthology* and his work has appeared in several journals including *World Literature Today, Nimrod, Interstate, Southwestern American Literature, Renegade 10, Broomweed Journal,* and *Crosstimbers.*

MATT HOLLRAH is an Assistant Professor of English and Director of First-Year Composition at the University of Central Oklahoma. He lives in Edmond with his inspirations: his wife Julie, and their two children, Sadie and Simon.

MARIA RACHEL HOOLEY has been published in over eighty national literary magazines including *Kimera, The Hurricane Review*, and *Out Of Line*. She has written over twenty novels, including *New Life Incorporated, October Breezes*, and *On the Road With Ollie*. She lives in Oklahoma with her husband and three children.

LAYTON ISAACS is an educator, speaks three languages and writes poetry, travel memoirs, fiction and creative non-fiction. Layton has a background in journalism which she uses to write an online column about the Tulsa Literary Scene for www.examiner.com. She enjoys photography, reading, drawing, music, movies and travel.

RACHEL CONSTANCE JACKSON has lived in Oklahoma for her entire life: from birth until 18 years of age because she had no choice, from 18 to 25 years of age due mostly to familiarity and habit, and from 25 to 35 years of age out of principle. Currently living in Norman where she works hard and steadily toward a PhD. in English, Oklahoma's history, literature, culture, politics, economics, literature, and landscape get her fired up—especially the parts that don't get much attention otherwise. Her current side projects include Red Flag Press, the *Oklahoma Revelator*, and the Oklahoma Laborfest.

GRANT MATTHEW JENKINS is an Associate Professor of English and Director of the Writing Program at the University of Tulsa, where teaches contemporary literature and creative writing. He has published two books of poetry, *Joy of God and Other Series* (Blackbird, 2003) and the most recent in collaboration with Cheryl Pallant, *Morphs* (Cracked Slab, 2009). Recent poems appear in *Bird Dog, Cannibal, Syntax*, and *Big Bridge*. Other creative projects include work with digital flash poetry, image, and sound and can be found online at Turbulence.org, ToxicPoetry.com, and YouTube.

ROCKFORD JOHNSON lives and works in Chickasha, Oklahoma where he hosts a monthly poetry reading for the local arts council. He likes to take a different route to work quite often so that he can be surprised by what he sees. His poems have appeared in *Crosstimbers* and the *Red Dirt Book Festival Anthology*; his first book of poetry is *All Things Flow* (Village Books Press, 2009).

SUSAN KATES is an associate professor of English at the University of Oklahoma. "The Bird Watcher" is from a manuscript Kates is working on entitled *Plains Country Women*.

ABIGAIL KEEGAN is a Professor of English at Oklahoma City University where she teaches British and Women's Literature. She has published two books of poetry, *The Feast of the Assumptions* and *Oklahoma Journey* and a critical book on Byron's Oriental Tales, *Contextualizing the Homographic Signature: Byron's Othered Self and Voice*. In 2007 she received a merit award from *Byline Magazine's* Silver Anniversary Poetry chapbook competition. She is completing another book of poems, *Depending on the Weather*.

JENNIFER KIDNEY is a freelance scholar and award-winning poet. She is the author of five books of poetry, *Field Encounters, Endangered Species, Animal Magnetism, Women Who Sleep with the Dogs*, and *Life List*. She has twice been nominated for Oklahoma Poet Laureate. She has a B.A. with Highest Honors in English from Oberlin College and a M.Phil. and Ph.D. in English from Yale University. Kidney has more than twenty years of university level teaching experience, and has also worked as a technical writer, poet-in-the-schools, and arts administrator. For twenty-two years, she oversaw the statewide reading and discussion program, Let's Talk About It, Oklahoma, and has made hundreds of Let's Talk About It, Oklahoma, scholar presentations on almost as many books. In 2007, the Oklahoma Library Association presented her with a Special Project Award for Let's Talk About It, Oklahoma. Kidney has won awards for brownie baking as well as for writing, and lives in Norman with three cats and her dog Lizzie.

KELLEY LOGAN is a recalcitrant writer whose last publications were in *Westview* and various other small publications; many of which are now defunct. She lives in Weatherford, Oklahoma and professes to people who sometimes learn, grudgingly, to love their own language. She builds houses on the side and has recently switched from being a dog-person to being a cat-person and wonders how that shift will affect her life.

VERA LONG has been writing poetry for over sixty-five years, on country living, family life, and poetry to inspire and be enjoyed living in rural Oklahoma most of her life. Her poems have been published in various anthologies and on-line, and she was awarded the 2006 Anderbo Poetry Prize. She is a member of Poetry Society of Oklahoma and has been the area OPS Secretary of Stillwater for nine years.

J.C. MAHAN, known as Johnie Catfish to the poetry tribes of Oklahoma, has been reading and writing poetry for 12 years. Having been published in a few journals such as *Blood and Thunder*, won a few honorable mentions, and featured at some of the local poetry readings, he thinks that poetry is a habit best formed when young. J. C. is 58, married, father of 6 good kids (all want to be writers); he is also a painter and photographer. He has four self published chapbooks; *West Texas Gypsy*, *Tilling Native Soil*, *Entertaining Madness*, and *Conversing Art and Love*. Currently he owns JC's Funky Hair Ranch and is teaching pottery through the Edmond Parks and Recreation.

JULIA MCCONNELL lives in Oklahoma City with her partner and two dogs. She works at the downtown library and is finishing her Master's degree in library science at the University of Oklahoma. She likes to write with a sharpie and a cup of coffee early in the morning when the house is quiet and the sun is rising.

SUSAN MILLER is a writer and historian. She is from the Seminole Nation and lives in Lincoln, Nebraska, until she can figure out another scheme to get back to Oklahoma. Her selection, "Kickapoo Cane Women" is a passage from a mystery novel in progress; it is the scene in which the body is discovered. (Editors note: Susan was living in Oklahoma when her submission was accepted.)

BRYAN MITSCHELL's poetry has previously appeared in *The Lullwater Review, Mannequin Envy, Plainsongs, Poetry Midwest, The Portland Review, The Roanoke Review, Studio One, Soul Fountain, Tiger's Eye* and *Wavelength*. He holds an MM in Music Production and is currently a professor of music technology at the University of Central Oklahoma. Bryan is also a singer/songwriter and an active proponent to the open mic poetry and spoken word scene in the Oklahoma City area.

NANNETTE MOORE enjoys fishing the the lakes around Oklahoma with her husband and writing whenever and wherever the inspiration hits her. She credits her Grandmother and Mother for her love of poetry.

PHILLIP CARROLL MORGAN is the award-winning author of *The Fork-in-the-Road Indian Poetry Store* (Salt Publishing, 2006), co-author of *Reasoning Together: The Native Critics Collective* (University of Oklahoma Press, 2008), author of *Chickasaw Renaissance* (Chickasaw Press, 2010) and *Who Shall Gainsay Our Decision? Choctaw Literary Nationalism in the Nineteenth Century* (Chickasaw Press, forthcoming 2011). The father of three children, he collaborates professionally with Kate A. Morgan, his painter-sculptor wife of 30 years, and lives on his family's original allotment farm in the northwestern region of the Chickasaw Nation. He is a member of the Academy of American Poets and holds a Ph.D. in Native American literature from the University of Oklahoma.

JOHN GRAVES MORRIS, Professor of English at Cameron University, is the author of *Noise and Stories* (Plain View Press, 2008). His poems have appeared in such journals as *The Chariton Review, The Concho River Review, Jelly Bucket, The Flint Hills Literary Lantern, Westview, Crosstimbers, Blood and Thunder*, and others.

BENJAMIN MYERS recently published his first book of poems, Elegy for Trains (Village Books Press, 2010). His poems appear in the *New Plains Review, Chiron Review, The Mid-America Poetry Review, Ruminate* and many other journals and can be read online at *poetrybay.com*. His poetry was recently featured on the poetry podcast *Red Lion Square* (www.redlionsq.com). With a Ph.D. from Washington University, Myers teaches literature and writing at Oklahoma Baptist University. He lives in Chandler with his wife and three children.

JL MYERS is an Oklahoma indy film writer/actor/producer and literary fiction author whose gritty style of fiction has been read and appreciated by so few, for so long, that it's about damn time a wider audience got down and dirty with him. He's been published in the US, UK and BC and is finishing a new three volume novel titled *love in lowercase* while working on an MFA in Creative Writing at Oklahoma State University.

B. ADDIS NAYLOR is an Oklahoma physician, fly fisherman, photographer, genealogist, amateur musician, story teller and aspiring writer. This is his first published work of fiction.

JOE DALE NEVAQUAYA is a poet and visual artist residing in Norman, Oklahoma. Joe's written and visual works have been anthologized and collected nationally and internationally. He is tribally affiliated with the Yuchi and Comanche tribes of Oklahoma. His book of poetry, *Leaving Holes and Selected New Writing*, is scheduled for publication by Mongrel Empire Press in 2011.

JUDITH TATE O'BRIEN'S poetry has been widely published. Her latest poetry collection is *Everything That Is, Is Connected* (Village Books Press, 2007). She is somewhat housebound and says reading and writing poetry "saves my life." Her most recent book, *Crossing a Different Bridge: An Oklahoma Memoir*, was published by Mongrel Empire Press in April 2010. "Camp Women's Shoes" was included in *Crossing a Different Bridge.*

PATRICK OCAMPO is the author of *Surface Tension*, a collection of poetry and short stories published by Mongrel Empire Press (2009). Born in the Philippines and raised in Toronto, Canada, Patrick currently lives in northeastern Oklahoma with his wife Christine, their dog Lucky and a disturbingly increasing number of cats.

JASON POUDRIER is an Oregon native who has lived in Oklahoma since joining the military and being stationed at Fort Sill in 2001. In 2003, he was deployed to Iraq and wounded in action. He was invited to read from his manuscript of war poems titled "Baghdad International" at the 2008 and 2009 Scissortail Creative Writing Festivals and was the recipient of the John G. Morris Poetry Prize in 2008. His work has appeared or is forthcoming in the *New*

Mexico Poetry Review, Connecticut Review, and Cameron University's *Gold Mine*.

DAVID P. PRICE, born and reared in north Mississippi, has resided in Oklahoma City for the past ten years. He has a twenty-year old son named Nathaniel. In addition to poetry, he is currently writing a novel. Other poems have appeared in *Ole' Blue Press*, a free poetry journal in Oxford, Mississippi.

RANDY PRUS has three chapbooks of poetry: *Songs of the South and Slightly West, A New Time in a Very Old World*, and *ICE*. He is a professor of English and Humanities at Southeastern Oklahoma State University.

GREG RODGERS is a writer and Choctaw storyteller currently living in Oklahoma City. His first book, *The Ghost of Mingo Creek and other Spooky Oklahoma Legends* (Forty-sixth Star Press, 2008) is a collection of short-stories based on actual legends from around the Sooner State. As a storyteller and workshop presenter, he appears at schools, libraries, festivals, conferences, universities, and tribal events throughout the country and was recently added to the official list of Smithsonian Associates, the educational outreach program of the Smithsonian Institute.

AARON RUDOLPH lives and works in Lawton, Oklahoma. His poems have appeared in *Mid-American Review, South Dakota Review, Iron Horse Literary Review*, and the anthology *Two Southwests*, published by Visual Arts Collective, 2008. He also authored the collection *Sacred Things* (Bridge Burner's, 2002).

CARL SENNHENN, retired from Rose State College, after 50 years of teaching high school, college, and continuing education classes, is a former Oklahoma Poet Laureate, appointed by then Governor Frank Keating for a two-year term, 2001-2003. His collection *Travels Through Enchanted Woods* (Village Books Press, 2006), was awarded the 2007 Oklahoma Book Award for Poetry.

SUSAN SHANNON is Osage and the daughter of George and the late Mary Agnes Shannon. She is active in her tribe, and her adopted native community in Norman, OK. She has one daughter, Lauren, who recently married and Susan looks forward to being a grandmother. She hosts poetry readings, is an avid photographer, coordinates the University of Oklahoma Native Art Show and hosts/ produces KGOU's "Indian Times."

JUDY SING, who lives in Oklahoma City, holds a B.A. in English with a creative writing specialty from Creighton University; her writing has has been published in *Blood and Thunder* and a few other places. She was born and raised in south Pottawatomie County and attended a one-room school through 8th grade. Her maternal grandfather was a blacksmith whose family settled in the community of Brown, west of Tecumseh, in the second Land Run of 1891. A favorite of her late mother's many sayings is "Just try your best; that's all a mule can do.

BENJAMIN SMITH is a PhD student in Screen Studies at Oklahoma State University. Ben has presented at the Southwest/ Texas Popular and American Culture conference, the Oklahoma Film and Video Studies Society Conference, the UCO Liberal Arts Symposium, and was an Invited Lecturer for the Oklahoma City Metro Library. He has written a chapter on comic book films in the anthology *The Theme of Cultural Adaptation in American History, Literature and Film: Cases When the Discourse Changed.*

MICHAEL SNYDER has lived in Norman since 2004 and earned his PhD in English at the University of Oklahoma. His peer-reviewed articles, criticism, and creative writing have appeared in the journals *Windmill, Critique: Studies in Contemporary Fiction, Studies in American Indian Literatures, American Indian Culture and Research Journal,* and *Huxley Annual,* plus two books—*Across Cultures/Across Borders: Canadian Aboriginal and Native American Literatures* and *Gerald Vizenor: Texts and Contexts.* An article on the crossblood Osage author John Joseph Mathews, a subject of continued research, is forthcoming in *Chronicles of Oklahoma.* Snyder is currently a Professor of English and Humanities at Oklahoma City Community College.

SANDRA SOLI, recipient of a 2008 Oklahoma Book Award, served in Oklahoma's artist-in-residence program for a decade, followed by nine years as columnist and poetry editor for *ByLine* magazine. Her writing has appeared widely, with work featured on NPR and two nominations for the Pushcart Prize. Sandy enjoys collaborative projects with artists in other disciplines and photography.

KATHRYN SPURGEON, a prolific poet, has over 4,000 poems, although she claims only one percent are worth publishing! Her poems have appeared in *Candle Flames, Poetry of Today, Voices in Time, Hearts of Hope,* and *Treasure from the Heart.* She has won many poetry contests, among them those sponsored by *Byline, Reflection Pond, Oklahoma Writer's Federation, Illinois Poetry Contest,* and *Poetry Society of Texas.* She has published a book of poetry, Anna Lee's Diary.

JIM SPURR resides in Shawnee, OK with his wife, Aline. He has a B.A. from O.B.U.; he is a retired Insurance Adjuster and an honorably discharged veteran. His book of poems, *Open Mike/ Thursday Night* was a finalist in 2008 Oklahoma Book Awards. Jim's writing has been nationally published.

JONATHAN STALLING lives in Norman, Oklahoma with his family and teaches poetry and East-West literature at the University of Oklahoma. He is the author of *Grotto Heaven* (Chax Press) and *Poetics of Emptiness* (Fordham University Press), and is the Deputy Editor-in-Chief of Chinese Literature Today magazine.

LORI SUBLETT first knew that she would be a writer in 3rd grade, when she was assigned a 3 paragraph essay on Christopher Columbus and ended up writing 23 pages. Lori holds a Bachelor's in Creative Writing and is currently working on attaining her Master's in Creative Writing. She was born and raised in Oklahoma and, while she loves to travel, she has no plans to leave.

JANE VINCENT TAYLOR has a Master's in Creative Writing from University of Central Oklahoma. She is a Virginia Center for Creative Arts Fellow and teaches poetry at Ghost Ranch in New

Mexico. Her most recent book is *What Can Be Saved* (Finishing Line Press, 2008). Link to other poems and talk with her at janevincenttaylor.blogspot.com.

SHEILA TIARKS is a social worker who turned to poetry when she retired recently. Although born in Ireland, she has lived in Oklahoma for 36 years and has learned to love the land and its people.

HUGH TRIBBEY's poetry has most recently appeared or is forthcoming in *Otoliths, Peter Ganick's Archive Project, Spaltung, We, Moria, Apocryphal Text, Crash-Test, 5-Trope, Aught, xStream, Lost and Found Times*, and *Eratio*. He is the author of four collections of poetry: *Finish Your Sentence, Juvjula Detours, Asteroid*, and *Waitinale Glasses*. Hugh holds a Ph.D. in Poetics and Contemporary Literature from Oklahoma State University and teaches literature and creative writing at East Central University in Ada, Oklahoma.

BILL TURLEY is a graduate of Oklahoma State University with a degree in English and Creative Writing and he has worked for the Oklahoma Arts Council Artists in the Schools program. He first began publishing in small magazines in the late 70's; in 1991, Turley's book length poetry manuscript," Something As Reckless as Wind," won a Tulsa Literary Arts Grant. Turley's writing has also been published in *The Blue Collar Review* and *Breath and Shadow*.

ALVIN O. TURNER is emeritus dean of humanities and social science and professor of history at East Central U. He remains active in research, writing history and poetry and pastoring a small Presbyterian church. His most recent book, a biography of progressive preacher L. W. Marks, was published by Mongrel Empire Press in December 2009.

RON WALLACE is the author of three volumes of poetry, all published by TJMF Publishing: *Native Son: American Poems from the Heart of Oklahoma*, a finalist in the 2007 Oklahoma Book Awards, *Smoke and Stone: The Voices of Gettysburg*, and *I Come from Cowboys… and Indians*, the winner of the 2009 Oklahoma Writer's Federation Best Book of Poetry Award. He is a native born Oklahoman whose Scots/

Irish roots are woven securely into his Choctaw, Cherokee, Osage lineage; Ron is currently an adjunct faculty member of Southeastern Oklahoma State University in Durant, Oklahoma.

MARK WALLING is Professor of English at East Central University in Ada. He has fiction and poetry in recent issues of *New Plains Review*, *Louisiana Literature*, and *South Dakota Review*.

PAMELA T. WASHINGTON is an Oklahoma native and part-time poet and writer. She is currently Dean of the College of Liberal Arts at the University of Central Oklahoma and teaches English whenever she can. She has previously been published in Mid-*America Poetry Review*.

THERESA-ANN "TRIXIE" WALTHER grew up in the idyllic little town of Kilbride, Newfoundland, Canada until she moved to Oklahoma City when she was seventeen-years-old. Her poems often concentrate on the darker side of human nature, most particularly illustrated by the stories of women who are incarcerated. As a professor of English at Rose State College, she teaches a Composition 1 course in several prisons across the state, and it is through these interactions that she finds the subjects for much of her poetry.

PAMELA WASHINGTON is an Oklahoma native and part-time poet and writer. She is currently Dean of the College of Liberal Arts at the University of Central Oklahoma and teaches English whenever she can. She has previously been published in *Mid-America Poetry Review*.

L. MICHAEL WEST studied history and communication at East Central University. After 10 years of professional speaking, he now tells his stories through the written word, usually on his blog at www.pastoralurbanite.com. He lives in Ada, Oklahoma with his dog, Bella.

Editor Jeanetta Calhoun Mish is a poet, writer and literary scholar; in 2009, she earned her Ph.D. in American Studies from the University of Oklahoma. Her first book, *Tongue Tied Woman*, won the Edda Poetry Chapbook Competition for Women in 2002. Her second poetry collection, *Work Is Love Made Visible* (West End Press, 2009), won the 2010 Oklahoma Book Award for Poetry, the 2010 Western Heritage Award for Poetry from the National Cowboy and Western Heritage Museum and the 2010 WILLA Award for Poetry from Women Writing the West. She was was also awarded a 2010 residency at the Anderson Center for Interdisciplinary Arts. Dr. Mish was previously Poet-Scholar in Residence with *World Literature Today* and is currently a member of the faculty of the Red Earth Creative Writing MFA program at Oklahoma City University.

Mish has published poetry in *LABOR: Studies in Working Class History of the Americas, Oklahoma Today, Poetry Bay, Sugar Mule*, and in "Walt's Corner" of the *The Long-Islander*. Mish's creative non-fiction essay, "This Oklahoma We Call Home," appeared in the Fall/Winter 2008 issue of *Crosstimbers*. Anthology publications include poems in *Returning the Gift* and *The Colour of Resistance*. She is also the editor of Mongrel Empire Press (www.mongrelempire.org), and web administrator for the Oklahoma Poetry Portal and the PoetryArtsOK email list.

For more information, visit www.tonguetiedwoman.com.

www.ingramcontent.com/pod-product-compliance
Lightning Source LLC
Chambersburg PA
CBHW072020020726
47501CB00006B/1885